The R.E.M. Companion

The
R.E.M.
Companion

Edited by

JOHN PLATT

Schirmer Books
An Imprint of Simon & Schuster Macmillan
New York

Prentice Hall International
London Mexico City New Delhi Singapore Sydney Toronto

Schirmer Books
An Imprint of Simon & Schuster Macmillan
1633 Broadway
New York, New York 10019

Library of Congress Catalog Number: 98-29178

Printed in the United States of America

Printing number
10 9 8 7 6 5 4 3 2 1

Library of Congress Cataloging-in-Publication Data

REM companion / edited by John Platt.
    p. cm.
  Includes discography, videography, bibliographical references (p.), and index.
  ISBN 0-02-864935-4
  1. R.E.M. (Musical group) 2. Rock musicians—United States—Biography.
I. Platt, John.
ML421.R46R46   1998
782.42166'092'2—dc21   98-29178
                                                          CIP
                                                          MN

Contents

Acknowledgments

Without the assistance of R.E.M. scholar and archivist Tim Abbott, I would have had a lot less material to select from. For his invaluable help I extend my gratitude. Many thanks, Tim; I couldn't have done it without you. Thanks are also due to the effervescent Richard Carlin at Schirmer Books, Bill Forsyth at Minus Zero Records in London, and Jon Storey, longtime editor of *Bucketfull of Brains*. Lastly, thanks as always to my wife, Marylou Capes, still the love of my life and a great editor to boot.

Buck, Mills, Berry, Stipe, 1982. *Photo © Sandra-Lee Phipps.*

Introduction

Sometime around the end of 1982, I received a letter from my friend Peter Holsapple, then a member of the wonderful dBs. Aside from news of his band and his continued inability to come to grips with New York winters was a mention of a new band that had really taken his fancy: R.E.M.

That Holsapple should have been aware of them was not that extraordinary; both the dBs and R.E.M. were operating in a similar musical territory (melodic post-punk, guitar-based rock and roll), both worked in the so-called indie area, and—for whatever it was worth—both bands were from the South: the dBs from Winston-Salem, North Carolina (although they had moved to NYC some years previously), and R.E.M. from Athens, Georgia.

In retrospect, it was perhaps more surprising that *I* hadn't heard of them. I was, after all, a rock journalist and publisher of a music magazine. My tastes may have run primarily to '60s music, but there was enough common ground between several of the punk and post-punk bands and my real musical passions to keep my interest in contemporary music alive. Being English I could be forgiven for missing the fact that R.E.M.'s first record ("Radio Free Europe") had been voted single of the year in the *Village Voice,* but somehow I'd even overlooked the small but glowing reviews that had appeared in the British press. In fact, Richard Grabel's review in the *NME* of their second release, the *Chronic Town* EP (reprinted here), must have come out around the time of Holsapple's letter. I missed that, too.

In any event it was nearly eight months before I paid serious attention to the band. The change came simply because I obtained a copy of their first album, *Murmur,* which I played over and over again—something I had rarely done with a new album since the '60s. I was taken not only with the obvious things—the tunes, the playing, and the energy—but also with the air of wonder, an aspect of rock that had all but vanished in the previous ten years, especially during the punk days, with that genre's fondness for dour realism.

My plan, such as it was, was to pen an extensive review of the album in *Comstock Lode* (my oddly named magazine) and leave it at that. Fate, however, had something else in store. Just before Christmas 1983, I was invited to appear on *The Tube,* a networked and widely respected British rock show. I was there to promote my new book, but, much to my delight, also on the show were R.E.M., making their first appearance in Europe. I met the band, we got on well, and I arranged to interview them a couple of days later. In the event, it was only guitarist Peter Buck, with singer Michael Stipe showing up about halfway through. I was nonetheless pleased with the results and figured to have the magazine out . . . soon. For various reasons *Comstock Lode* was on its last legs, and I was unaware that I had already published the last issue.

Weeks went by, and, before I knew it, it was April '84 and the band were back in London. Making the excuse that I needed to speak to bassist Mike Mills and drummer Bill Berry for a fuller picture, a further interview was arranged, and (I still believed) the new issue of the magazine was mere weeks away. It didn't happen. By the end of the year I had admitted defeat, and the article was finally published in *Bucketfull of Brains,* edited by Jon Storey. It was to be the start of a long and successful association between that magazine and R.E.M. (my somewhat unfavorable review of *Fables of the Reconstruction,* notwithstanding).

Partly out of vanity (of course) I'm reprinting most of my original piece herein. More important, I think it's as good a summation of their early days and the band's musical approach as any of the articles from that period and, mainly because I was able to write to whatever length I wanted, it is probably the most extensive.

Even if I had published my article as soon as I had interviewed Buck and Stipe at the end of '83, it would by no means have been the first article about the band. One of the best early pieces was J. D. Considine's "R.E.M.: Subverting Small Town Boredom," written for *Musician,* in which the old question "How do you escape your small-town surroundings?" is posed. The answer: Form a band. As Mike Mills says in the article, in regard to Athens: "There aren't any out-of-town acts that come through, except for the one or two major acts the university will bring in. So when you get bored with listening to records, you get up and do it yourself."

At the same time, there was a converse attempt, with some justification, to portray Athens as a center of alternative arts, with the local bands, R.E.M. included, as only the tip of the iceberg. The culmination of this approach was not a written piece, but a 1986 documentary film, *Athens, Ga.—Inside Out.* By that time, R.E.M. had become not just the focal point of a burgeoning local scene but also had acquired a considerable national and international reputation.

Early articles, not unnaturally, dealt with the band members' biographies and obvious musical influences, but in due course (certainly by the time of their third album, 1985's *Fables of the Reconstruction*) the press began finding that there was more to the band than four Southern boys from a small town. To maintain momentum, every band needs publicity, and there comes a point where the press needs more than the standard biographical details in order to write about them. If it transpires that the band in question turns out to be articulate and with interests beyond the narrow confines of rock, so much the better.

Such was the case with R.E.M., and particularly with Michael Stipe, whose enigmatic pronouncements (e.g., that R.E.M. sounded like "two oranges nailed together") made for great copy. To be fair, there was a considerable intellect at work behind the mutterings, and any journalist who took the trouble to get beyond his slow delivery found that Stipe was well read and had a deep interest in the arts and the mythology of the United States, particularly the South. A good example is the piece on Stipe entitled "The Black Mountain" (*Melody Maker,* April 27, 1985), in which he demonstrates a knowledge of the pre-beat, alternative literary college of the article's title as well as a fondness for the novels of Lawrence Durrell, and—more to the point—for the tradition of storytelling in Southern culture. Although he is at pains to point out that "I've never been fond of songs with a storyline," he is grateful that people recognize the "homespun feeling" that he tries to bring to his lyrics.

Despite the critics' frequent attempts to elevate R.E.M. to "art band" status, the band have always played down their arty image. As Peter Buck said in a 1985 *NME* piece, "We're not artists, we're just working very hard to do the best we can do. Art doesn't come into it. No matter how hard we twist it or mutilate it, or tear it apart, we're still a rock 'n' roll band."

Certainly, Peter, but a rock band with opinions. The *Document* album (1987) is rife with political statements, and, in print, Stipe and Buck both derided the presidency of Ronald Reagan, with Buck going so far as to describe him, with charming accuracy, as "a complete moron" (*Melody Maker,* September 12, 1987).

At the same time as they became the darlings of the literary rock press, the band were also building up a considerable cult following. Quite why a band becomes the center of a cult is largely imponderable. An air of mystery and enigma always helps, and R.E.M. had that in spades. Likewise, there was (and still is) R.E.M.'s predilection for issuing nonalbum singles in different configurations in different parts of the world, virtually guaranteeing them a following among serious collectors. Finally, there was R.E.M.'s known tendency to vary the set list at every gig and to include a whole raft of bizarre covers, garnering them a Grateful Dead–like fan base who tried to see as many gigs as possible, or at least to acquire tapes of them.

The cult aspect of the band's following was made powerfully manifest in the number of fanzine/collector magazine articles on them. Two examples are included here. The first is from *The Bob* (a U.S. magazine not to be confused with the English *Bucketfull of Brains*, which is sometimes abbreviated to *BoB*) from early '86. It's an excellent, well-written piece, but the authors are in the presence of their heroes, and it is palpable. The collector mentality is also evident—the authors provide set lists for all the shows they attended while compiling the piece, and several of their questions to the band concern obscure songs and outtakes.

The second example, "R.E.M.: Live Adventures in Hi-Fi," is far more recent, from August 1997. It was originally published (in a slightly different form) in the English magazine *Record Collector,* a periodical noted for its authoritative articles. In it, author and R.E.M. scholar Tim Abbott concentrates on the history of R.E.M. as a live band, a subject touched on, but never thoroughly explored, by other writers. The second part of the article details the best (unofficial) live recordings of the band, providing an excellent resource for interested parties.

The publication of Abbott's article and others like it attest to the band's continued cult status. And, in truth, they remain a cult—a remarkable situation since they are one of the biggest acts in the world. As a rule, cult bands rarely draw fans from outside the cult and rarely play outside the indie circuit. Remarkably, R.E.M. have had it both ways. They should have lost cult status at least as far back as 1988 with the release of *Green,* which contained, as one writer put it, "Stadium-friendly anthems." Not only could they fill stadiums by 1988, but their act also began to reflect the larger surroundings with the addition of big production values. In a January '88 *Musician* piece, Stipe comments, "I realized last year that people were paying $16.50 to see something." By contrast, in the same article, Buck plays down their newfound prestige and declares that the band have more in common with Woody Allen or Neil Young, both being examples of artists who are well known without being superstars.

Perhaps that's it. You are what you declare yourself to be. In spite of the year-long "Monster" world tour in the mid-'90s, which had most of the attendant trappings of a Stones' tour, and a succession of mega-selling albums, they are—or would like to be seen as—"just plain folks": Buck, the hard-working journeyman musician and family man, Stipe the self-effacing intellectual, Berry the (now full-time) gentleman farmer, and Mills the successful businessman who prefers to spend his time on the golf course. It's a hard act to pull off, but they seem to have done it.

What's really remarkable is that the rock press—both "serious" and fanzine—and the mainstream press still love them. In the eighteen years of their existence, there has been nothing remotely like a critical backlash. In the course of going through hundreds of articles on the band for this book, I could count the number of negative pieces on the fingers of one hand, and these were reviews of specific albums or gigs, not a general condemnation of the band or their music. The easy answer is, perhaps, that they have never made a bad record. While that may be true, it's never stopped the press from writing off other acts. The question remains then, What's so special about R.E.M.? To that, I regret, I have no answer. Perhaps you, the reader, will find it in these pages, containing, as they do, the very best writing on one of the world's finest bands.

John Platt

Part One

MURMURS

WILLIAM BARNES

"UNDERDOG" R.E.M. UPSTAGES THE BRAINS (extract) (1980)

The Red and Black, *May 7, 1980*

Tuesday night, however, really belonged to R.E.M., short for Rapid Eye Movement. From the first, jangly, British Invasion chords of Pete Buck's guitar, there was strong evidence something very impressive was about to happen. It did.

The Athens foursome, which also included Mike Mills (bass), Bill Berry (drums), and Michael Stipe (vocals), exploded with energy in only their third public appearance. Tyrone's may have been cramped and hot, but it hardly mattered when R.E.M. pulled out Johnny Kidd and the Pirates' rhythm and blues workhorse, "Shakin' All Over." This was dance music impossible to resist.

A crackshot "Secret Agent Man" dedicated to "Athens' finest" showcased Buck's guitar talent. He looked like a hired gun, peeling off ancient riffs that sounded as fresh as if they'd just been learned last week. And they could have been.

R.E.M.'s original material was even more amazing than their excellent cover choices. They switched tracks from funky R&B to pulsating reggae with an ease and speed that belied their short history. Picture James Brown fronting the Dave Clark Five and you only begin to get a handle on the excitement this band causes.

R.E.M. encored with the Monkees' "(I'm Not Your) Steppin' Stone." The Brains may have years of clubbing and a record contract under their belt, but R.E.M. won the hearts and feet of the crowd at Tyrone's.

RICHARD GRABEL

NIGHTMARE TOWN (1982)

New Musical Express, *December 11, 1982*

A town is chronic because we are fated to revisit it time and time again. A chronic town might also be a carny town, jammed full of colour, with incomprehensible barkers and terrible secrets stowed away behind the tents.

This chronic music revisits us, reminds us of the wonderfully, excitingly familiar but of nothing in particular. There are of course precedents, influences if you like. Ringing and chiming '60s guitars are a part of it. Voices and harmonies that are distinctly American, not by being any kind of nostalgic throwback but inherently, deeply, are a part of it; as is a modern English pop sensibility, an openness to the possibilities of what pop music can carry or suggest.

Chronic Town is five songs that spring to life full of immediacy and action and healthy impatience. Songs that won't be denied.

Mystery is a thing that is lacking in run of the mill pop product. Michael Stipe's voice comes close, gets right up next to you, but his mumblings seem to contain secrets. Intimacy and distance. The voice tells of knowledge but doesn't give too much away. The songs have mystery but are in no way fuzzy. No, they have a cinematic vividness, they paint pictures.

Sometimes the pictures are clear and particular, but shaded and shadowed by the singer's mumblings. Sometimes the pictures are made of sharply seen fragments whose composition is a puzzle. This is the way Stipe scrambles language, plays with it like a dyslexic poet, scatters loaded words around like leaves in the wind.

Pete Buck's chords ring memory bells, push buttons of good feelings. Stipe's voice vibrates with wonder, too. It's a voice that is guarded at times, astonished at others. Voices and chords and melodies form rhymes with each other.

"I Could Live a Million Years." Stipe makes such outrageous promises. And makes us believe them.

The construction of these songs is classic. There are bridges and balances, put to original use. The logic of these songs makes me smile, makes me want to sing along.

You can read all sorts of things into these songs. Like the thematic balance in "Wolves" between outside and inside, which are also suspicion and relaxation, danger and safety. The verse tells us what's creeping in the garden: "wilder lower wolves." And the chorus invites us in, with a group harmony that is airy and open, to a "house in order," a-a-a-a.

"Carnival" makes us imagine a movie, its entire plot outlined and its scenery suggested in seven short lines. "Diminished carnival . . . stranger to these parts . . . boxcars pulling out of town." Perfect economy of expression, a perfect puzzle, perfect enchantment.

Well, not perfect, of course. I suspect these songs could have been mixed better, the guitar given even more of that clearly pitched sound, the voice given more presence, some extra force.

But R.E.M. ring true, and it's great to hear something as unforced and as cunning as this.

JIM SULLIVAN

MUSIC DREAMTIME WITH R.E.M. (1983)

Boston Globe, *April 26, 1983*

R.E.M. stands for rapid eye movement, the scientific term for the deepest, most vivid stage of dreaming. Singer Michael Stipe, guitarist Peter Buck, bassist Michael Mills and drummer Bill Berry, ex-college students from Athens, Ga., appropriated the term for their rock 'n' roll band when they formed it in 1980. Talk about descriptive acuity: The music of R.E.M., who opened for the English Beat at the soldout Walter Brown Arena Friday night, has an explicit dreamlike quality. Dreams wander and drift, they can be clear or disjointed, familiar or frightening. Or all of those qualities can become tangled. In the course of their 13-song set Friday, R.E.M. wound their way down those convoluted paths—and anchored them with a crackling dance beat.

In an obvious sense, R.E.M. states a case for obliqueness as an art form. The band favors musical shadowplay—melodies that are slightly skewed, guitar textures that swirl, and murky lyrics that seem like mere fragments of thought. Friday night they were often lit indirectly by blue stage lights. But obliqueness is only part of R.E.M 's sonic appeal. There's another strong, distinctly different, pull. Buck, who is always charging this way or that on stage, weaves a rich guitar tapestry—his chiming, jangling lines soothe and then sting subtly, recalling the bittersweet melodicism of the Byrds or Love. His sound lends R.E.M. a familiar ring that is warm and reassuring.

But with that reassurance comes challenge, an edge that hints at danger, disappointment or indecision. Part of that comes through the charging rhythms. Much of it comes through Stipe's lyrical snippets—vague thoughts that make sense in R.E.M.'s dreamlike context. Friday night the band had the crowd swaying to the pleasant melodic tides of "Gardening at Night." (A rock 'n' roll song about gardening at night?!) In the gorgeous "Wolves, Lower," Stipe posed danger—"wolves at the door"—and then pulled back to safety—a soft refrain of "House in order, ah-ah-ah-ah."

As mysterious moods mingle with spirited melodies, R.E.M. is positively addictive. And with catchy, uplifting songs such as "Catapult" and "Radio Free Europe" (on their debut LP, *Murmur*), R.E.M. has the potential to break into the mainstream—with music that is creative and on terms that remain uncompromising.

JOE SASFY

RECKONING WITH R.E.M. (1984)

Washington Post, *May 10, 1984*

When the annual critics polls were tallied for 1983, lots of people were surprised to find R.E.M.'s debut album, *Murmur,* topping records by vastly more popular and equally creative acts like the Police, U2, Talking Heads and David Bowie. *Murmur* won the *Rolling Stone* Poll for best album and ran a close second in the *Village Voice* to the most successful album in pop history, Michael Jackson's *Thriller.* There was no doubt that R.E.M.'s evocative instrumental fabric and atmospheric moodiness had captured the critics' imaginations and those of the more adventurous portions of the rock audience.

Much of what was written about this quartet from Athens, Ga., focused on the organic impenetrability of its sound and, even more, on lead singer Michael Stipe's knack for rendering his lyrics indecipherable. Of course, Stipe occasionally dangled an intelligible phrase, which could be taken either as a provocative clue to the band's collective unconscious or as a meaningless snippet for the critics to mull over.

Some even concluded that R.E.M.'s music was an aurally rich but empty intrigue—a murky pool of jangly guitars, Stipe's mumbling and surging rhythms succeeded precisely because you could dive into them again and again and always come up empty-handed. It was suggested that the band's appeal was built on not conveying anything but sound itself, albeit an extremely attractive, rippling synthesis of post-'60s guitar pop.

R.E.M.'s second album, *Reckoning,* proves that both Stipe's lyrical obfuscation and the band's textural haze, both of which are cleaned up here, are irrelevant to this band's wondrous music or its meaning. Producers Mitch Easter and Don Dixon are back again, but this time they have cut back the undergrowth of overdubs and let some light in. The music rings clearer, Stipe's vocals are at least as intelligible as Mick Jagger's (i.e., the choruses can all be understood), and the band's 10 originals trump even *Murmur*'s outstanding songwriting.

Best of all, *Reckoning* retains the band's wholly original sound and the emotionally disquieting feel of all of its previous work. Song after song conjures a mood of cultural estrangement and weariness that can become surprisingly uplifting, as the music climbs out of the solemnity of the verses into a gorgeous, hook-laden chorus.

If Stipe is still largely unconcerned with his words, it's probably because he has fashioned a more emotionally fluent language from the sound of his voice. A little burry and slightly nasal, Stipe's singing conveys a feeling of both lassitude and perceptiveness, not unlike that of early Bob Dylan. The missed connections of "Letter Never Sent" are conveyed by Stipe in painful, syllable-stretching moans and groans, while the ominous desolation of "So. Central Rain" is underscored in a despairing crescendo of cries. The stirring choruses of "Pretty Persuasion" and "Harborcoat" become almost spooky as voices float to the surface like specters.

What can be made from the few words and richly emotional sound R.E.M. offers is a sense of personal unease and cultural dislocation that can find neither answers nor a place to rest. The romantic remembrances of "Letter Never Sent" and "Camera" are consumed by a tragic air of estrangement and loneliness. In "So. Central Rain," Stipe cheerlessly mumbles, "the cities wash away," before crying out the chorus, "Sorry . . . sorry." In this sense, R.E.M. is a wholly American rock 'n' roll band, not unlike X or Green on Red or even T-Bone Burnett, all acts that convey a sense of America lost, unmoored from its past and with no vision of its future.

If much of what Stipes conveys is disconsolate, even depressing, R.E.M. remains a resplendent rock 'n' roll band, one that basks in the shimmering textures of Peter Buck's guitar and its irresistible minor-key melodies. In "Time after Time," Buck's droning guitar figure casts an exotic psychedelic aura, while "7 Chinese Bros." takes on a childishly innocent air thanks to Buck's delicate and ornate guitar work. The rhythm section of Mike Mills and Bill Berry swells and subsides in such faultless sympathy with each song's emotional structure that the band sound is rendered indivisible.

The musical triumph of *Reckoning* comes to a grand, if unsettling, conclusion on the album's last two numbers. The band indulges in a few seconds of inept funk (perhaps a satiric comment on rock bands who insist on copping fashionable black rhythms) before breaking into a rolling country-western tune, "Don't Go Back to Rockville." Stipe pleads for a woman's return, before knowingly confessing, "If you were here I'd only bleed you." Then comes "Little America," a rousing, propulsive rocker about life on the road that finds Stipe matter-of-factly stating to the band's manager, "Jefferson, I think we're lost." Lost or not, there isn't an American rock band more worth following than R.E.M.

JOHN PLATT

R.E.M. (1984)

Bucketfull of Brains, *December 1984*

Part I: "Little America"

"WE'RE NOT FROM ATLANTA, WE'RE FROM ATHENS."

—*Michael Stipe on* The Tube, *November 1983*

Driving through America you can go practically anywhere in the world— London, Cairo, Paris, Rome and . . . Athens. Which as Michael Stipe has just reminded us is where R.E.M. come from, or to be exact where they live, as only one member actually grew up there, but more of that in a moment.

Athens is a college town. The University of Georgia is where your parents send you if you're middle class in order, as Peter Buck puts it, "to drink it up for four years, get girls pregnant and get in car wrecks. It's not a serious school." There does, however, seem to be a thriving community of artists, film makers and the like (not to mention aspiring musicians) most of whom seem to be drop-outs from the college.

There have been bands in the city for at least 25 years. In the early sixties there was a band called The Jesters who, according to Peter, were "a really cool band, did James Brown covers, had crew cuts and wore alligator shirts. They actually put out records, too." Mid-sixties Athens produced a small but significant number of kaftan-bedecked groups and of course the last five or six years has produced a whole new crop of good bands like the B-52s, the now defunct Pylon, an instrumental group called Tractor, the Method Actors and last, but by no means least, R.E.M.

Peter Buck is the only real native of the area and although he never played a musical instrument before joining R.E.M., he's been a rock 'n' roll fan virtually as long as he can remember. "When I was about five or six I got a little radio that I listened to under the pillow and tuned to whatever AM station I could find. I had no real knowledge at all. I liked the Supremes and along with every kid in the world I loved the Beatles." Slightly later he thought that the Monkees were the hippest thing on earth. By 1970, prompted by reading the more astute rock critics of the day, he had started to buy albums—the Kinks, the Move and the Stones and then, perhaps not surprisingly glam-rock in the shape of T. Rex and Slade. All by mail order: "I didn't like going out of the house."

Then one day fate took a hand, Peter found a Velvets album in a garage sale. They became his favorite band. In short order he discovered the Stooges and again by accident, the New York Dolls. "The Dolls opened for Mott the Hoople. I was about 14 at the time. Mott were horrible and the Dolls were by any definition wretched, but I thought they were wonderful." It wasn't until late '76 that things really started to knock Peter out on a large scale when he started buying virtually any punk single from England that he could get hold of. "Yeah, I bought anything on the basis that it had to be interesting at the very least. Sham 69, who are they? I'll try it. Chelsea *Right to Work,* all that stuff, I bought the lot. It just thrilled me no end that there was something with energy and excitement coming out."

Most of the interesting bands were from England or New York but eventually Peter discovered one semi-local band worth investigating. "There was an Atlanta band at the time called the Fans, who never made a record as good as they were live. They had 60 or 70 original numbers and the band sounded as though John Cale had joined Roxy Music—really cool stuff. They'd play these cowboy bars where the locals would threaten to beat them up. Them and their ten fans."

At the end of the seventies Peter found himself working in a "fairly hip little used record store" in Athens. Among his regular customers was a guy who seemed to have pretty good taste. They got to know each other, and Peter started setting aside records for him. His name was Michael Stipe.

To anyone even vaguely aware of R.E.M. and their music it will not come as a surprise that Michael is the most enigmatic member of the group. It has been suggested in certain quarters that this is a purely deliberate creation, part of the group's "image." This seems most unlikely to me. I can hardly claim to know the man well but what little I do know confirms his own description of himself (in an article I can't lay my hands on) which went something like, "I'm basically a shy person by nature who's trying to be open and friendly." To be sure, he is far less gregarious than the others (particularly Peter—the amiable chipmunk, etc.) and conversations with him can frequently become serious and pretty intense, nonetheless he comes across a genuinely friendly and intelligent person and, like the others, he is incredibly polite to strangers and friends alike. Mind you, when I walked into the Whistle Test dressing room the others were on the far side of the room drinking beer and generally having a good time, whilst Michael was sitting in an alcove reading a book which was upside down.

The point of all this is that very little is known of Michael's background—a subject he prefers not to discuss in any detail. "That's all in the past" he will tell you. The little that is known is still quite interesting. It seems that Michael is from a military family (his father is an army officer) and grew up in all kinds of places, including Germany.

Prior to living in Athens, Michael lived in Illinois where he fronted a garage/punk band around '76/'77. He claims it was no great shakes, but the people he was hanging out with at the time had a large influence on him, particularly in terms of music. They introduced him to the Velvets and the Stooges, which added to his taste for Patti Smith and Television amounted to pretty much his entire musical interests. Prior to that he'd taken little interest in music, beyond his parents' tastes which ran to Gershwin and a little gospel. In '78 he moved to Athens to go to college and in due course started hanging around the record store.

Although the Illinois band had been no big deal, Michael must have caught the bug, because soon after meeting Peter he started proposing the idea of a new group that would involve Peter. Oddly, Peter had always resisted the idea of playing. "I thought it would be an arrogant thing for me to do, sort of, so I never did."

In the space of 6 months Michael convinced Peter otherwise, and they started looking for other musicians. By luck or otherwise they met two guys at a party who were friends of friends who fit the bill (if you pardon the pun).

Bill Berry and Mike Mills both grew up in Macon, Georgia, and both went to the same high school and have known each other all that time. They weren't always friends, as Bill relates: "We were arch enemies until the 10th grade (about 15) when a mutual acquaintance organized a Southern Boogie–style jam session. It turned out to be in the basement of the bass player's parents' house. In walks the bass player and of course it's Mike, but it worked out real well and we've been friends ever since. Right through the remainder of high school we were in bands together. Usually top-40 cover bands playing school sock hops. Making good money, too. For a while we were called Shadowfax, and later we were known as the Back Door Band. We played mainly originals plus a few Freddie King numbers and a couple of Meters songs. Never went anywhere or did anything but it was OK."

According to Peter, the Shadowfax/Back Door Band's biggest moment was playing the South Eastern Music Hall— "a hippie hang-out where the top local bands played." Apparently a tape exists (which may or may not be this gig) comprising various covers plus "one horrible original their guitar player wrote, in 6/8 time. The worst thing you've ever heard."

Mike and Bill also found time for other, quite unrelated musical activities. Bill, for example, played percussion in the local theater orchestra two years running, performing in such extravaganzas as *Fiddler on the Roof* and *Guys and Dolls*. Plus, at various times, Mike and Bill were in "a lounge trio" led by their music teacher. Bill: "We'd dress up in suits and ties and play country clubs, weddings and the like. Hell, that was good money, too. I was 17 years old and making 60 bucks a night. That's when I became addicted to playing."

Their highlight, without question (!) was playing in the high school marching band. Both dressed up in those silly double-breasted military jackets now worn by Michael Jackson. However, Mike ultimately switched instruments and, consequently, outfits. "I started out on sousaphone but switched to electric bass, which is how I came to play one at all. The switch also meant I had to wear this awful leisure suit. The change of instruments came about because it became the rage in the three big Macon high schools to have an electric bass. Whenever we had a football game against a rival school it became a contest as to who could turn up their amp the loudest. Oh yeah, and for some reason we used Led Zeppelin's

'Whole Lotta Love' as our marching song. So it was Da Da Da Da Dum Dum—'Go Go Go.' And for the half-time parade we had to get guys to carry the enormous [speaker] cabinet across the field." Apparently their team was so awful that all the band did was have cross-stadium battles with the opposing rival band. On one occasion they were having the shit kicked out of them by the team that went on to be National High School champions. So Mike's band, in desperation, struck up War's "Why Can't We Be Friends."

After graduating from high school, Bill, at least, got fed up with playing in top-40 bands and/or Capricorn Southern–style boogie bands and sold his drum kit. Bill: "I went to work for the Paragon Booking Agency who booked all those Capricorn bands plus they had a great R 'n' B roster. I was just the gopher but after about 6 months Ian Copeland started working there, and he brought in all these great new British bands like the Police, Gang of Four, Chelsea and the Motels. It was great because you never heard those bands in Macon. One guy in the whole town liked Bowie. Everyone else listened to the Allman Brothers and Marshall Tucker. Really stagnant."

After about a year, Mike and Bill decided it was time to go back to college. So they headed off to Athens where they enrolled and, in short order, found themselves at the party.

Just prior to this fortuitous encounter Peter had moved out of a "hideous concrete place" and had taken the lease on a converted church—a now legendary dump that will go down in history as the birthplace of R.E.M. Peter: "The guy I was working for said I could lease it, so me and about 18 other people moved in. It was really cheap for that reason, about $30 each per month, that was at the end of '79."

It was indeed an old church, but an enterprising developer had stuck a rectangular box inside, with two stories, so that for the most part you didn't know you were in an old church. However, if you went through the false wall at the rear, there was plenty of space behind it, big enough to throw parties and, should you so desire, rehearse a band.

The whole place was, of course, a real slum but needless to say a slum with romantic, bohemian overtones. Peter: "At one time or another we all lived there. Mike didn't pay rent, he just slept on the couch. It was a great place to rehearse, which we did, a great deal. We used to set up on the stage, get real drunk and play. We had so many parties the place was finally condemned after we moved out. The law still wants me because my name was on the lease!" Just to keep the chronology straight, they were in fact only there for a few months—the band formed around March 1980, and they moved out during the summer—but legends aren't overly concerned with exact time-periods.

They were, of course, still (in theory at any rate) students. Peter, although working in the day was (more often wasn't) at night school. Bill—whose grade point average had dropped alarmingly after moving into the church—was about to be asked to leave college, and Mike was undeclared as to his major, which meant he would have dropped out sooner or later. According to Peter, Michael is the only one who would have graduated had he been left to his own devices. He wasn't.

Almost immediately people started offering them money to play, which they thought was pretty miraculous—$200, hell, yes we'll do it! For whatever reason they were popular right from the start, drawing really big crowds. Having fun was (as it still is) of primary importance. Peter: "It was really loose, we'd get drunk, I'd fall off the stage, but people liked it. We started doing weekend dates in the Athens clubs, which was quite prestigious. Places like Tyrone's which is basically a large bar. Anyway we thought, well, if we can do it here we can do it somewhere else."

It seems that "punk" had never caught on in the South but suddenly, in 1980, all these places that had steadfastly refused to book punk bands started having "new wave night." Peter: "We were always the first band to play these places. We did that in almost 200 bars, most of which closed immediately afterwards. Really strange places some of them; usually biker bars or pizza parlors, all over North and South Carolina. Some places we did go back to and it was OK even if the first time half the audience had hated us and threatened to kill us!"

They did that for about 8 months, begging bar owners to let them play—usually to three people and a dog. But they enjoyed it all, sleeping on the floor of the bar or in the homes of people who they'd just met. Peter: "Usually these 'tours' lasted three days and we thought, 'Let's enjoy ourselves' which meant we generally didn't bother to sleep at all."

These trips, and their lifestyle, obviously placed a strain on their "other" lives. Mike and Bill quit college straight away (too soon really, according to Peter) but Michael and Peter continued to work and/or study right up to the end of '81, when they all became full-time musicians.

Success for R.E.M. has come, relatively speaking, gradually and was not something they ever courted. In true sixties fashion they slogged around the States, gradually getting better and better reviews. Sensibly, they postponed playing New York until quite late on, waiting until they thought they were ready. Playing live is what they enjoy most and, basically, that's what they've done for the last $3^{1}/_{2}$ years—playing to more people in more places. That time has not, of course, been without its significant moments. I could fill the next four pages with anecdotes about life on the road but such anecdotes could apply to any band. Instead I'll recount just two which will stand for all.

Michael: "We once played in Nashville, in this big circus tent. There was no real stage, we had to stand on tables. They had these amazing psychedelic lights that they must have dug out from someone's basement. It was really fine. Looked like something out of the Exploding Plastic Inevitable."

Peter: "That was the time I smashed my guitar. Everytime I turned round something broke off my guitar. So I finally stomped on it, and it made this great sound; I then threw it into the audience."

Michael: "That was also the gig where the girl stood in front of you wearing a see-through plastic shirt. This is in Nashville, mind you. It was very hard to concentrate on music."

The other story concerns Alex Chilton, who by a circuitous route (Mitch Easter and the dB's) can be said to have connections with R.E.M.

Peter: "At one point we were in Memphis and I said to some locals, 'Will Chilton come and see us?' and they said, 'What hotel are you staying at?' I told them and they said, 'Oh you'll see him' and I said 'Why, does he hang out at the hotel?' and they said, 'No he drives a cab and will probably be dropping by to pick up fares.' So I spent the whole evening looking for weird cab drivers."

Well that just about wraps up this section except to say that for the foreseeable future the band have no intention of leaving Athens. None of them would feel comfortable living in a large city and, really, it's a case of either New York (which they like, but only for brief periods) and L.A. (which they loathe).

It's now time to look at the band's musical history, so roll on Part 2.

Part 2: "Carnival of Sorts"

Despite their predilection for doing strange cover versions, none of the band had wanted R.E.M. to be, essentially, a cover band. For Bill and Mike it was simply that they'd been all through that, but for Peter the reasons were altogether different. "When the band started no one was really sure what instrument I was going to play. Mike could play guitar better than me, and I knew I wasn't going to play the drums. It was suggested that I play bass, but I could never work it out, so in the end I became a guitar player.

"I couldn't learn the simplest songs: 'Gloria' was about all I could manage—three chords and a cloud of dust. So we just started writing our own. Some were OK, most were horrible. We wrote about three a week, a load of songs that, thank God, the world will never hear. There's probably about 60 floating around on tape which we'll never play again, which makes me happy. There's about three songs from our early demo tape from that period that we still do from time to time. They may end up as B sides or something. I'll throw one in the set occasionally, and we won't remember how to play it. We'll be looking at each other wondering what comes next."

The band's method of writing hasn't changed much since their inception, so it's worth mentioning at this juncture. Basically, they all play instruments to some degree and they all come up with ideas; anything from two notes to a whole song.

Not surprisingly, Michael writes most of the lyrics, although the band often give him ideas, which he then works on. Michael had this to say about his writing: "I'd never written before R.E.M. was formed. The first song we wrote was outside the church at about 6 A.M. after a party.

"The early songs were all really skeletal and the lyrics were like simple pictures but after about a year I got really bored with that. So I started experimenting with lyrics that didn't make exact linear sense, and it's just gone from there. However, more recently I've been doing things like writing love songs using the first person, which I wouldn't have done a year ago. I guess I made up my own rules which I'm now breaking. The new songs, although not strictly less abstract, are more pared down. I use less words, but I don't think I've ever made a concise statement in my life. Unlike Peter, who is the king of the concise statement."

This is also the time to discuss Michael's influences (although he denies any direct ones). At times they seem obtuse to the point of randomness and full of odd juxtapositions and, consequently, various people have brought up the William Burroughs/Brian Gysin cut-up method. This involves cutting up bits of existing text and fitting the pieces together in a random fashion. Michael is certainly aware of Burroughs and had this to say about the technique: "I think that it's a really interesting method of writing, but I don't do it at all. I think that it takes a much more brilliant person than I am to do it properly. Also it leaves it all to chance, and if you've only got four minutes to get an idea across you can't really use chance that much. So my lyrics aren't stream of consciousness or cut-up at all." I should mention that another member of the band, unprompted, suggested something quite different—that when stumped for ideas, Michael writes phrases onto bits of paper and throws them into a hat, then pulls them out at random and fits them together just as they come.

Michael does, however, admit to using the Lou Reed method of writing, whereby you write down things people say and use them more or less verbatim in a song. A good example is "We Walk" from *Murmur*. Michael: "I used to know a girl who lived on the second floor of this house and every time she walked up the stairs she would say, 'Up the stairs, into the hall." She didn't get a credit, but I did say thank you."

Actually I've always thought that "We Walk" had a distinctly nursery rhyme quality to it (more specifically A. A. Milne). There's a great danger, however, of turning into a Weberman over Michael's lyrics, especially as there is a good chance that you've got them wrong anyway. It's not quite the same thing, but on one occasion Michael mentioned, in an interview, that he likes the Inkspots. The writer then wrote the whole piece on the basis that R.E.M. in general and Michael in particular were incredibly influenced by the Inkspots. He even described the band as "an Inkspots, for the nineties."

Whilst we're on the subject, one major criticism of the band is that most of the time, even on record, you can't work out the lyrics. Michael's only comment is. "It's just the way I sing. If I tried to control it, it would be pretty false."

I did venture one question about a particular lyric, although I'm not much wiser even with the answer. The song in question was "Laughing" (from *Murmur*). Michael: "The first line is about Laöcoon, a Greek mythological figure who had two sons, all three devoured by serpents. It was a popular theme in Renaissance painting. It's also like the photo you see of the women in Nazi Germany. You know, the woman with the shaved head clutching her baby, running from all these people who are laughing at her. But that's a real expansive definition of the song. There's also John Barth's novel *End of the Road* where a statue of Laöcoon features heavily. Oh! I did change the gender in the song from a man to a woman."

Well, that's really a help Michael. I checked out Laöcoon, both the myth and in the Barth novel—which was fine, but I still couldn't work out what any of it had to do with the song.

So much for lyrics, but what about the music? At this point you're probably expecting me to start going on about sixties' influences: the jangle of the Byrds, the Velvets' textures and lyrics, etc., etc., and, indeed, whether the band admit it or not, they are there. In the end, though, R.E.M. has so much else going for it that those things, while not irrelevant, are only part of something I find totally contemporary. If anything they've struck a perfect middle ground between the linear melodic qualities of sixties' music and the more abstract and angular qualities of the avant garde '76 bands, for whom melody was not of primary importance. Michael summed it up thus: "One part of the band will be doing this very rhythmic or melodic type of thing, and then someone else will come in and do something that's the exact opposite. The bass may be carrying the melody, and then the vocal might come in and do something without any resonance or melody at all. I'm really pleased with that!"

According to Peter the band all have floating parts: Mike changes his bass lines, Bill can alter his drum parts if he feels like it, Michael constantly alters lyrics on stage. Oddly Peter himself is the most stable.

I've always been very reluctant to discuss musicianship since the danger is always to think in terms of form rather than content—i.e., the great God Technical Expertise—but I must say I can't fault R.E.M. in any department. The interplay between the instruments is extraordinary: Mike and Bill form the best new rhythm section I've heard in years, and for someone to play the guitar as well as Peter with so little experience is uncanny. He is not, as someone suggested, "the best guitarist in the world," but he's probably unique.

To return to the notorious sixties' influences, there is the whole question of the 40 or so cover versions they perform, about which Peter had this to say: "Some of them are horrible. Most we haven't sat down and actually listened to the record, so the lyrics are wrong, and we don't know the bridge. We're too lazy to sit down and learn them. A lot of the songs we really like; some we do because they are silly and fun. We did 'In the Year 2525' about six times. Not one of the world's great songs but not a bad version. We do several Velvets songs, Them songs, a Troggs song, even an Abba song, 'Does Your Mother Know.' A really cool song."

I had prepared a list of all the covers that R.E.M. have been known to do, but listing them now seems a somewhat fatuous exercise. I will, however, say this: Personally I like the fact that R.E.M. aren't really conversant with said material for two reasons. Firstly it is, in a way, more authentic. If asked, most of us could not recite the lyrics of songs we have heard thousands of times. What you get with R.E.M., therefore, is an aural representation of those songs as you actually remember them, thus putting the band totally outside the "human jukebox" style of revivalism. Secondly, the fragmentary nature of the covers fits more easily with the more fragmentary nature of their own songs. Does that make sense? I'm buggered if I know.

I think it's now time to look at the band's recordings to date and some of the stories behind them.

Their earliest "real" recording was done in an 8-track studio in Atlanta in late 1980. The songs were as follows: "Dangerous Times"; "I Don't Want You Anymore"; "A Different Girl" (narrator, Jacques Cousteau); "Just a Touch"; "Baby I"; "Mystery to Me"; and "Permanent Vacation." Peter had this to say about the recording: "We did the songs in two hours, we didn't know what we were doing. Inept, but on reflection not that bad."

The most obvious thing about these songs is that they sound very much like '64/'65 garage band songs. Sort of naive but punky. They played all of them live for well over a year and, as Peter said earlier, one or two still crop up. Basically, none of them are a patch on their later material.

Around this time they acquired the services of an old friend, the affable Jefferson Holt, as a manager. He didn't like the tape at all and contacted Peter Holsapple of the dB's (an old friend from Chapel Hill) to suggest a sympathetic studio and producer. He mentioned Mitch Easter, who had played in various bands with Chris Stamey and had just opened a studio. Peter recalls, "We made the original 'Radio Free Europe' single with Mitch which ended up getting mis-mastered and sounds really crummy! The single came out on the Hib-Tone label and, to everyone's surprise, was a critical if not commercial success." It does sound a little weird—Peter actually went so far as to ceremonially break it and tape it to his wall. After the single came out they figured they'd form their own label. They (a) wanted no truck with a major and (b) it was doubtful that a major would be interested in their sort of band. So they went back to Mitch's in October 1981 and recorded a bunch of songs with the idea of releasing a record themselves. This time they recorded "1,000,000"; "Ages of You"; "Gardening at Night"; "Carnival of Sorts"; "Stumble"; "Shaking Through"; and "White Tornado." The other intention was to learn how to use a studio. Peter: "That's why it's so over the top. Every trick we'd ever heard of we wanted to try. Backwards guitar? Sure, why not. 'Let's tape some crickets and synch them in time with the music.' We even used kitchen utensils as percussion instruments. We recorded it, mixed it, mastered it and were going to release it on—I can't remember—something like 'So what' records. However, we'd just been approached by I.R.S., probably the only company we'd have signed with, the biggest anyway."

As it happened I.R.S. weren't wild about the tape but the band didn't want to wait another year without a record, so the deal was signed and the tape, minus three tracks, came out as the *Chronic Town* 12". Of the remaining three, "Shaking Through" was used on *Murmur*, "White Tornado" is the surf-style instrumental that they still perform (they did it at the Lyceum in December '84), and third is "Ages of You," an excellent song that has nearly been on both the albums. Some of the band would like to see it out, but for various reasons they no longer perform it and for the same reasons it probably won't be released. But you never know. There was another track recorded at about the same time that is generally not regarded as part of the same tape. Peter: "It's a 10-minute noise tape which we did just for fun when we were drunk one night.

"Partially, it's me making guitar feedback onto which we synched a drum tape and overdubbed some Hawaiian chanting. Plus there is Michael reading from a *Playboy* article from 1957, about the jazz scene. So you can hear all these Bohemian phrases over the top. It's really terrible, and I challenge anyone to listen to the whole thing."

It wasn't my intention to go into detail about the meanings of too many of R.E.M.'s songs, but Peter told me this about "Gardening at Night": "It's basically a metaphor for the uselessness of everything, but if you didn't get that I'm not surprised. It's kind of a confused song. Actually there was an old guy in my neighborhood who would be out gardening at 2 A.M. in his suit and tie. I'd see him when I was out trying to get beer at the Magic Market or somewhere. I told Michael about the guy, and he wrote the song." Confused or not it's a wonderful song, although to be fair it is probably their most Byrds-influenced piece. Overall the EP is incredibly strong, especially when compared with the earlier tape, recorded less than a year before. They toured on the strength of the record, and to I.R.S.'s surprise sold about ten times what they had expected.

But I.R.S. wanted them to record an album and, being sensible chaps, the band had already written six or seven of the *Murmur* songs before the EP came out. As Peter says, "So often bands make one good record and then, for the second, write all the songs in like six days—just before recording them. We figured we wouldn't have anymore time off between that time and recording, so we sat down and wrote a bunch of songs that we could work up on the road."

At the risk of repeating myself I consider the album some kind of masterpiece. I have no intention of describing it in detail as I suspect that you all own a copy. (You do; don't you?) One thing that is of interest is that the cello part on "Talking about the Passion" was not played by a band member. Peter: "We hired this lady from the symphony orchestra, and we paid her $25. We told her roughly what we wanted and she was dumbfounded that we weren't going to give her a score. But she was great in the end."

Overall the album is in some ways a continuation of the EP in that the production, outwardly simple, is actually very complex, full of overdubs and strange effects.

Although virtually all the tracks have been performed live at one time or another (including "Perfect Circle") *Murmur* is very much a "studio" album and it was generally decided that the follow-up should be much sparser and nearer (in terms of the sound and general feel) to the live act. Bill says: "*Reckoning* is much more straightforward. We wanted to record as far as possible with all of us, including Michael, playing and singing at the same time. There are overdubs, but mostly they are the same parts doubled or tripled. It's not such a dark album as the first."

One of the things I really liked about the EP and *Murmur* was the air of mystery and enigma—a facet of rock that I felt had been absent for too long. I was, therefore, taken aback by the simplicity of *Reckoning*. I realized after a few plays that the enigmatic quality was still there but it was more subtle. Added to which, of course, the songs are all gems. Not all of them are new, incidentally. "Pretty Persuasion" dates back to '81, as does "Rockville," about which Bill had this to say: "We used to play it as an uptempo rock thing. Our lawyer liked the song so much that one night in the studio we decided that we would record it just for him—not release it at all. We thought, let's give it a real country twang, and it came out really good. So we added a few parts to it, like the piano and the screeching tremelo guitar. We thought it was good, but even then we almost didn't put it on the album as we thought it wasn't really representative of us. But then we thought, 'What the hell,' so we did; Rockville is in Maryland by the way, a real factory town. Not anywhere you'd want to visit."

To date, then, R.E.M. have made two albums as good as, if not better, than any new band since the sixties. And if that's not a biased opinion I don't know what is. And on the basis of the new songs they've been doing, the next album should be great as well. In the end though, they are, like most of my favorite bands, primarily a live act and despite the melodic

On the porch of the Barber Street house where Berry and Mills lived, 1982. *Photo © Sandra-Lee Phipps.*

quality of most of their numbers, a suprisingly dynamic live band. Indeed they have to be the strongest live act I've seen in years. On that point, and as an indication of how healthy their attitude to life is, I'll leave you with a comment from Bill Berry: "We're not based on commercial success. It would be foolish to think that it will last forever and get progressively better. You can't count on it. We all get along still, we keep sane. We are playing the game to a certain extent—as soon as you sign a record contract you're playing it, even with the likes of I.R.S. We're not about to sell out but signing with I.R.S. was a move in that direction. Essentially, we make records to get gigs, which is still what we enjoy most."

J. D. CONSIDINE

R.E.M: SUBVERTING SMALL TOWN BOREDOM (1983)

Musician, *August 1983*

Almost everybody else at the Athens, Georgia Holiday Inn was there for some convention being held at the University of Georgia—seminars in bovine prosthetics or some such. I was there to interview the members of R.E.M. on their home turf and in the process soak up local color. After all, given Athens' ability to churn out interesting and unusual rock bands, ranging from nationally known acts like R.E.M. and the B-52's to such stalwarts of Independent America as Pylon, the Method Actors, Love Tractor and the Swimming Pool Q's, the local scene here must be some sort of new music nirvana. Imagine the insights to be gained, the sounds to be savored.

Imagine the 40-Watt Club, the hub of the Athens club scene since Tyrone's, the only other venue willing to book untried talent, burned down. Standing outside the club, a discreet distance from the door, is R.E.M.'s Michael Stipe, an accordion strapped to his chest. Along with two friends, one on xylophone, the other on snare drum, Stipe is faking his way through Nino Rota–style Italian Cafe music. On the sidewalk in front of the trip is Stipe's accordion case, propped open with a few dollars inside to give passers-by the right idea. They play for about an hour, get harassed by a drunken Atlanta club owner, and make about four dollars.

This is the Athens new music scene?

"There's not much else to do, unless you just want to sit and drink in a bar," says R.E.M.'s bassist Mike Mills the next day. Although Mills was not party to Stipe's bit of busking, he's no stranger to the sort of boredom that sparks such adventures. "There aren't any out-of-town acts that come through, except for the one or two major acts the university will bring in. So when you get bored with listening to records, you get up and do it yourself."

Which is essentially what R.E.M. did, although with uncommon success. Within a year after the band's formation in February 1980, R.E.M. was touring the southeast. A single, "Radio Free Europe," was released in 1981 and astonished the band by topping the singles category in the *Village Voice* critics' poll. Nor were the critics alone in their ardor. According to Mills, I.R.S. was "as surprised as we were" by how well

Chronic Town sold; *Murmur,* the band's album debut, leaped up the charts at an even more surprising rate and looks likely to catapult a redone "Radio Free Europe" onto the singles chart.

All of which should make the band extremely happy. "Success beyond their wildest dreams," and all that. But at a point where other bands would be waiting with bated breath for the next week's charts and spending their spare time at the local Porsche dealer, R.E.M. is unusually wary of success and its trappings.

"We're kind of unassumingly ambitious, in that we never do anything expecting any kind of feedback," explains guitarist Peter Buck. "We just do things to please ourselves—we write to please ourselves, do the cover, hand in the record and we think, 'Hmmm, I wonder how this is going to do?' And we still wonder—we still talk about how many records we want to sell. 'Okay, no more than this many, because more than that and it starts getting kinda bullshit.'

"I don't know," he shrugs. "The record just took a big jump today, thirty places or something and I'm really pleased. I'm really happy. It's nice to be appreciated. I just don't know when it would start affecting us adversely."

If worrying about the adverse effects of success when your first album makes the prodigious leap from #130 to #97 on the *Billboard* charts seems a bit, uh, premature, singer Michael Stipe puts things into perspective. "I was shopping the other day," he says, "and this guy walked up to me and said, 'You're Michael Stipe, and you're going to make a lot of money.' He went on to explain how he was going to start a production company in Athens and use the Athens calling card to sell unheard-of-songwriters, get them published around the country.

"I was going, 'Great. . . .'" He shakes his head in amazement. "It was a real gregarious kind of thing for this guy, while I was trying to plan my menu for the week."

No wonder the band is tired of hearing about the wonderfully unique Athens Sound. This theory, which came into play after the B-52's emerged from a Georgia town that none of the New York critics had ever heard of, takes the argument that if more than one band worth listening to can come out of a town nobody has ever heard of, all the bands must belong to a school founded by the first group to make it big. After all, how many ideas can there be in a town that gets the *Village Voice* a month late?

"It's just a mistake to lump all the bands together," complains Mills. "In the first place, we don't sound like anybody else, and if you listen, they don't really sound that much like each other, either. What it really comes down to is the same thing that's happening in a lot of other places—there's just a real good atmosphere here, and club owners who will let you play when you're small and unknown. It's a very low-pressure area, in that you can play, play a lot, and improve yourself. Because everybody is horrible when they start out. We certainly were."

As drummer Bill Berry puts it, R.E.M. got started as "nothing more than something to do, maybe annihilate a little of the boredom that you get around here." The quartet first met at a party through a mutual friend. Berry and Mills had come up to the University of Georgia together from Macon, where they had played in an assortment of high school ensembles as well as a few southern-style top forty bands. ("We did a few originals that I would be afraid to even think about," confesses Berry.) Stipe, whose previous experience included "a real bad punk band in St. Louis," was living in a dilapidated church in Athens with Buck, the only one in the group who was not a day-only student at the university—he studied at night, while selling records during the day.

"When we first got together, it was just, 'What song does everybody know?'" recalls Stipe. "We played old '60's, like 'Stepping Stone,' Troggs' songs, stuff like that. Then Kathleen, the woman who lived there with us, had this grand idea to have a birthday party in three weeks, and she said, 'Why don't you guys play?' So we sat down and wrote a bunch of songs which probably took as long to play as they did to write. I guess we had fifteen songs and bunch of covers: we ended up doing three sets that night. It was a real hootenanny."

Despite R.E.M.'s garage band—or, given their rehearsal hall, abandoned church band–origins—the sound they emerged with was a far cry from the usual Gospel According to *Nuggets*. Buck's guitar figures tend towards lean, graceful arpeggios instead of jagged power chords, while Mills' bass lines emerge more as a form of counter-melody than anything else. Strap on Stipe's dark, nasal vocals and power the whole thing with Berry's practical, melodic drumming, and you've got a package that's irresistible to almost any rock fan.

But try to work out historical antecedents, and you're fishing in an empty pond. Because of the group's twangy guitars and resolute tunefulness, any number of listeners have likened R.E.M.'s best to "Eight Miles High" or "Turn! Turn! Turn!" But as far as the band is concerned, such comparisons are for the Byrds.

"It's just coincidental to the way Peter picks guitar," shrugs Mills.

"None of us really listened to the Byrds until after we started getting all these comparisons. So I went out and brought a couple of Byrds albums to see what everybody was talking about, and a lot of it is in the picking style."

"I use a pick, but also these two fingers," says Buck, holding up his hand and waggling his second and third fingers. "What I'm trying to do now is to teach myself the Chet Atkins style without learning what Chet Aktins really sounds like." He laughs. "I'm really limited. I certainly like the way I play, but I'm more style than anything else. I can't sit down and play anything but what we play. And I can play a little country and western, because I've always liked the kind of stuff, but that's really about all."

Noble new wave sentiments, to be sure, but Buck has other reasons for shying away from solos. Earlier in the day, Michael Stipe and I had been out on the porch of the house where Buck and R.E.M.'s manager, Jefferson Holt, live, discussing the relative merits of Blue Oyster Cult's "Don't Fear the Reaper" (one of Stipe's favorites). I mentioned that it would be a great tune for R.E.M. to cover, provided they left the guitar solo out, and Stipe replied, "That's okay. Pete only knows one guitar solo anyway, and he did it on *Murmur*."

"Yeah," Buck agrees later, "and Mike (Mills) taught it to me. One 'Talk about the Passion,' that little thing. That was something Mike just taught me. I probably could have figured it out myself, because I come up with things that are pretty much similar, but I thought it was really funny—my one little guitar solo, and the bass player came up with it."

Mills, in fact, turns out to be R.E.M's real utility player. In addition to the bass, he also provided the keyboard parts for *Murmur*. Given R.E.M.'s straightforward stage sound, the amount of detail on the album—multitracked acoustic guitars, piano doubling the bass line, even a bit of cello on "Talk about the Passion," vibraphone on "Pilgrimage"— may come as a surprise to fans of the band's energetic live shows, but as Mills puts it, "Well, there's no way that we're going to be able to come into the studio and reproduce the live sound, and why should we? We figured we'd go into the studio and approach each song separately, both separate from our live performances and separate from the other songs, and see what we could do with them. As long as you're in the studio, you might as well use what you can, as long as you're avoiding the tinkering syndrome, of using everything you can put your hands on."

One thing you won't hear on an R.E.M. record, at least not all that clearly, is lyrics. Between Stipe's swallowed enunciation and producer

Mitch Easter's intentionally murky mix, the listener is lucky if he or she can make out two words in six. Which is fine with R.E.M. "If there is a philosophy to the band," says Stipe, "it's that every individual person who hears or has anything to do with the band has their own idea of what it's about and what's going on. What they get out of it is what they put into it, kinda. It's great—with the EP, people would send in their idea of what the lyrics were, and often I would like what they sent better than what they originally were."

Nonetheless, Stipe has been toying with the idea of making up an official response to requests for lyrics. "He was just going to mimeograph a sheet and say, okay, these are the lyrics—they're not necessarily in order, some of them are missing and some of them are extra things," explains Buck, "but this is a vague idea of what we're doing."

An even vaguer idea of what the band is up to can be gleaned from the video to "Radio Free Europe," which shows neither Europe nor free radios. Instead, it has the band wandering around a church in Summerville, Georgia, and other seemingly unrelated terrains. Perhaps R.E.M. has some secret mania for old churches, sparked by their early days in Athens; perhaps not. When Peter Buck took me by the band's first Athens home, he was surprised to see that it was no longer condemned. "It's a real dump," he said, "but it's a such a cool idea, living in this old church, that every year there are kids from the university who move in. I think we lasted the longest—we were in there for almost a year." The Summerville church, on the other hand, is the home of Howard Finster, a renowned folk artist and self-taught preacher who, among other things, receives the word of God in visions of Elvis Presley, and who, in an attempt to save the world, is fashioning a sort of Garden of Eden out of other people's junk.

What's the point? "I think there's a particularly southern sensibility to it," offers Buck (who, by the way, was born in Indiana but has lived the bulk of his life in Georgia). "When we were making the album, it struck me as having a real southern sensibility, real Flannery O'Connor. That was one of the things we wanted to do on this album, affirm that we're a southern band without pandering to the Lynyrd Skynyrd–type mentality. I don't know if that came across, though," he adds, laughing. "The cover's probably more southern than the record is."

But if R.E.M. doesn't quite come across as the rock 'n' roll equivalent of "Go Down Moses," they certainly shape up as a band with an immense potential. Although Berry admits that, "we're still basically an untight garage band," R.E.M. is very together when it comes to managing its career and putting its "untight" musical ability to good use. It all comes down to working within certain limitations, and R.E.M. seems no more likely to hit the coliseum circuit than to hire the London Symphony Orchestra for its next album. So far in its brief career, the band has turned down opening spots with the Clash, U2 and the Go-Go's—moves that have left the band's agents scratching their heads in bewilderment.

But, as Mills explains, passing up such opportunities makes far more sense than accepting them. "The thing with U2—what they were saying was that touring with U2 would be a shortcut to getting bigger. But that's not our goal. We didn't start this whole thing to get a record contract and to be big. We started it in order to play live and have a good time. And it's so much truer to the spirit of being a live band to play where everybody can see you. You can't really communicate with people more than a hundred feet away; you lose an incredible amount of intimacy when the closest people to you are ten feet below you and twenty feet out.

"We would much rather set up in any bar in the country and just play."

ADAM SWEETING

HOT NIGHTS IN GEORGIA (1984)

Melody Maker, *May 5, 1984*

The Carioca, Worthing [England]

Earlier in the day, R.E.M. had arrived at this tiny South Coast disco, switched on their PA and promptly blown every fuse in the house. Bassist Mike Mills thought the place they'd played in Hamburg the other day had been smaller, though.

But no matter. Though Jefferson (the manager) thought he was lost, and Mills' bass perversely decided to take the first number off, the itinerant Georgia rockers swiftly hit their stride. Somewhat to their surprise, the front of the stage was besieged by a small but zealous knot of R.E.M. fanatics, who sang and pogoed all night.

The band served notice of intent with a fiery "Second Guessing," Peter Buck's Rickenbacker ringing eagerly over nimble bass and drums. As they ploughed into the affecting "Letter Never Sent," they made a few fine-tuning adjustments, with Michael Stipe's soft moaning voice meshing into overlapping layers with the more direct tones of Mills and drummer Bill Berry.

R.E.M. onstage can handle all the things they do on record and tonight, in a place as small as this, they benefited greatly from intense eyeball contact with the pressing crowd. The front-row aficionados were close enough to Stipe to hold conversations with him between songs, and before very long they'd persuaded him to have a go at "Femme Fatale." "Okay," Stipe warned them, "but you'll have to help me out on the second verse." The entire house took care of choruses.

Much the same occurred in "Talk about the Passion," plainly an R.E.M. staple down in Sussex, while a strong, eerie "Pilgrimage" was greeted with roars of recognition.

Here in close-up, it was apparent that there's a little more to making that distinctive R.E.M. sound than you might guess from hearing the records. Buck somehow manages to cover an incredible amount of ground on guitar, switching from those rich singing chords to smartly tuned melodic fills with amazing nonchalance. Mills' bass, meanwhile, fills in harmonies as well as performing the usual anchorman function. Finally, the tireless Berry rivets the whole shifting structure together with casual displays of careful timing.

All this would make R.E.M. an outfit to remember in any case, but add the mysterious Stipe to the equation and you're looking at a unit in a million. Stipe, hair tumbling in ringlets around his bemused-Botticelli features, doesn't sing so much as squeeze notes out of the air around him, clinging fast to his microphone like a medium waiting for the message. He is thus ideally suited to parable-like "Seven Chinese Brothers" or to the enigmatic whirl of "Harborcoat."

Indeed only in "(Don't Go Back to) Rockville" did the spell look like unraveling, since they seemed to have kicked off on the wrong foot and the thing plodded embarrassingly, despite some expert vocal harmonies. Fortunately "So. Central Rain," "Radio Free Europe," and an overdriven "Pretty Persuasion" blotted this from memory, and the only complaint from your correspondent (among others) was that they'd failed to play the heroic "Shaking Through." Maybe another night, eh?

Halfway through this unforgettable performance, somebody behind me turned to his friend and said, "That guitarist looks really sixties, doesn't 'e? Like somebody out of the Lovin' Spoonful or summink."

Or to put it another way, R.E.M. possesses the gift of making time stand still. Somewhere in those plangent melodies and rich and strange voices there's a little bit of magic. We should make the most of them while we have the chance.

HELEN FITZGERALD

TALES FROM THE BLACK MOUNTAIN (1985)

Melody Maker, *April 27, 1985*

Last time I saw Michael Stipe he was lurching and skipping around a Dublin stage with his long hair tied up with a sludge-green legwarmer. Today the man before me has a shaven skullcap on his crown. He looks like a Pennsylvania Amish farmer, someone close to the ploughed soil. A long denim jacket and scrub beard make him seem like a weird figure from a sepia photograph. A hillbilly.

"I just got a haircut," he drawls. "I guess I enjoy being contrary, y'know?" His contrariness and his introverted, ornery humor have deepened the mystique of the Stipe persona. He doesn't like to do interviews and when he does it's often hard to make sense of it. He talks very slowly with a languid Southern burr. He speaks in gentle sarcasms—he enjoys being oblique. "I think in general you could say I'm being a little tongue in cheek," he smiles. A radio interviewer recently asked him what the new R.E.M. record sounded like. He told her it sounded like two oranges nailed together. "For the moment there I really thought she took me seriously," he grins.

Michael Stipe is quite a funny guy. Last time they played in Dublin he grabbed girls onto the stage with him, jiving bodies, sweaty palms. Just for once he couldn't resist rocking out.

R.E.M. have formed part of the vanguard for the new American bands—particularly the Southern ones. Bands like Pylon, the Bongoes, the dBs and Sneakers had been playing since their high-school days and before that Big Star had ploughed a similar course. R.E.M.'s success has helped to make people focus on more of America's lesser-known regional bands.

"I think there's a lot of real good bands getting attention now who never would have before," he mumbles quietly, staring at the tape recorder. "Some of the better ones have given up though, like Mission of Burma from Boston. They were a great band, and Pylon, one of the best bands I have ever seen. I think that there are a lot of better bands in America than Britain. It's just that you're discovering them now."

To understand R.E.M. or any of Stipe's strange recorded meanderings you first have to appreciate the character of Southern State Americans. Michael's parents live close by. He wasn't brought up in

Michael Stipe, 1982. *Photo © Laura Levine.*

Athens. His father was stationed in Germany and Michael spent a lot of his childhood traveling.

Now his parents have a farm. "With a trampoline and a lake and they look after my dog for me. She's very old. She's going to die soon. There's turtles in the lake. There's a cow pasture and if you go and dig in the cow patties you can get all kinds of psychedelic mushrooms. My father's real interested in horticulture and he knows all different mushrooms."

Michael lives in a house with his pet rats. "I'm terrified of them. I have redbirds that come and sit on the mulberry tree behind my house. I look at them a lot. I ride my bicycle around. It's green."

R.E.M. were in London recording a new album with Joe Boyd when we met. Why did they choose him?

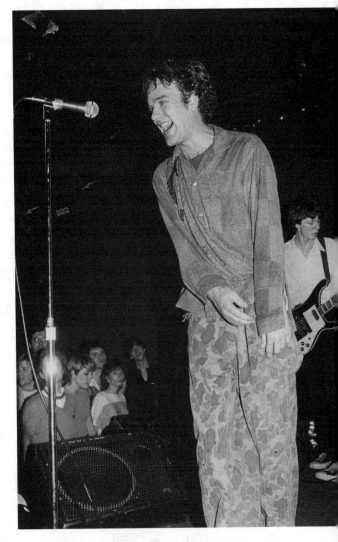

"I liked his name," Michael chuckles. "It was short and concise."

Routine, practical questions are fielded with oblique politeness. But ask Michael Stipe which way the wind blows or how to catch caterpillars on a sunny day and he'll ramble on as long as you let him.

"I hate interviews." Why do this one? "Because I felt like it."

His great grand-mother was a Cherokee Indian from Black Mountain, North Carolina. He feels a strong blood-bond with the area.

"My great-grandfa-ther and his wife lived on Black Mountain. He was out chopping wood one day and he fell on his axe. But before he died he walked back to the cabin, looked out over the mountain, turned to my great-grandmother and said 'it's all right.' My grandmother was the middle one of three children. Her mother was able to carry on with the farm but my grandmother was taken away when she was four years old.

"She didn't meet her mother again until 1957—50 years after they'd been separated. I go up to Black Mountain every now and then. It makes me feel really good. There was a college there some years ago, it's now a summer camp. All the people who went to that college were the forerun-ners of the beatniks.

"When Hitler took over Germany a lot of people from the Bauhaus movement came to America and settled in Black Mountain working for the college. The place was a breeding ground for the forerunners to Ginsberg and Kerouac. There's been a book about it called *Black Mountain* by Martin Duberman, on Doubleday Books. It's kind of amazing to me that first the Indians were attracted to the place. Then all these artists and poets arrived. And later the Bauhaus people settled, probably the most inspired group of architects and artists. They all wound up there. I don't think it's gonna be too long before something else happens there."

It's obviously been a great influence on Michael.

"There's a group up there called the Jargon Society who publish poetry. They put on this folk art exhibit as well and I went up there for a week. We visited this man who has a tobacco farm. He builds these tiny buildings, about four feet high. He builds Indian villages and elephants and bumble bees that you put on sticks that go round and round in your garden.

"He has a green hat that he wears all the time that comes down a little below the eyes. There's a lock of red hair that sticks out over his eye. He's about 60 years old."

The Southern redneck attitudes are still alive and well and thriving in Georgia but Michael, like a lot of white Southerners, wearily accepts the fact.

"It can be very scary. There's this kind of weirdness in the South, where something like ingrained prejudice can be somewhat accepted. Whereas in the North people are much more subtle about their bigotry yet it's much nastier in a lot of ways."

The uncanny hysteria that Southern revivalist/born again religion promotes is a recurring theme in R.E.M. songs. It's like Stipe has a fixation with Hicksville, U.S.A., for the kind of bluegrass, hillbilly existence of his ancestors and that is still to be found in parts of rural America. R.E.M. seems to lament times past without being out of place in times present. Storytelling, the magic of the spoken word, is Stipe's obsession. Folklore and legend.

"There's a very wonderful old tradition of storytelling, I think it comes with every culture, but in the South it's kind of been built up into a wonderful thing. In a way I think I am carrying on the tradition. Although I'm not really telling stories because I've never been very fond of songs with a storyline."

R.E.M. go far beyond a mere country-chic revival, they go back to the Appalachian Mountains and bluegrass Sundays where the whole family

Stipe and Buck on stage, 1984. *Photo © Ebet Roberts.*

would gather round for a hoedown with their neighbors. They go back to the days when everyone in a town knew everyone else's Christian name and used it. Back to the kind of America that the Pilgrims helped to form with their simple-minded zeal.

"America is so big and there are so many different parts of it that it could never be described by one sentiment. But yeah, I do like that kind of homespun feeling and I'm glad it shows. I'm proud of it."

His luxury is solitude. "I spent three weeks alone in Greece after the Little America tour," he sighs, "and it was really great not to have to talk to anyone. I read. Lawrence Durrell mostly. And a book by Bruno Schultze called *Street of Crocodiles.*"

You get the feeling that Michael could very easily adapt to living as a hermit in a log cabin in the woods.

"No, I need people a lot," he laughs. "No man is an island, no woman is safe!"

He likes taking photographs, especially of faces.

"I take lots of them and then sit at home and look at them. And as for politics, well R.E.M. aren't an overtly political band but their sentiment is an elegy for the simple man.

"I think what America is doing in Central America is nothing short of genocide," he whispers. "What they're doing to the Indians is disgusting. It's always the most peaceful people who suffer in the end."

Stipe has a low tolerance for hypocrisy.

"I admire Bruce Springsteen because he carries his beliefs through. He's been involved in trade union actions, repealing laws, it's quite covert but that's the way he likes to keep it. What I do hate are all the people who bought the Ethiopia record to salve their conscience. That whole 'I gave at the office' mentality. It's good that people are being fed but it doesn't change attitudes."

What is Michael Stipe frightened of? "Horses, rats and heights. I climb trees a lot because I quite like to feel frightened sometimes. I don't like computers and I don't like large farms. I think that by losing small holdings we're gradually losing a lot of America's identity. The backbone, if you like.

"There are families who have been on the land for years, struggled through the Depression, who are being forced to quit the land. What happened to the Indians in the 1890s is happening to the small farmer now. It's ruining communities and decimating the population. Young people have nothing to stay for now."

R.E.M.'s America is a green land, a land of simple people and family loyalty, of old ways and traditions, a slow and friendly place. The days of singing guitar and a bluegrass verse.

Stipe is a man so hooked on his own imagination that even in company, his pleasures are reserved and solitary. He traveled around with his parents as a child and didn't ever get to make permanent relationships.

"I had a lot of friends but you learn how to make and break friendships really easily, you have to for your own sake. It makes relationships difficult sometimes."

He carries a permanent aura of detachment. "I speak very slowly," he drawls, "so most people don't normally have the patience to wait to hear what I say. So I usually don't bother." And at last a heartfelt laugh.

As for the new album, Michael's giving nothing away. "It's real different," is as far as he'll go. "I'm real pleased with it."

Any free time from the recording schedule was spent in galleries and bookshops, which is where Michael feels most at home. On his own. His favorite stories are "Uncle Remus," "Aesop's Fables," and *The Wind in the Willows*. He's also a fan of surrealism and of a Czech photographer named Kudelko.

He wears a suit with a "live bear" tag that he stole from the black bear cage in the tourist village in Cherokee. *Bury my Heart at Wounded Knee* is one of his favorite books, and he carries that kind of nobility around inside him. He also knows a fine recipe for hushpuppies which in his neck of the woods seem to be eaten with almost everything.

"Take a cup of corn meal and mix it with water into a paste. Add a little bit of salt and form it into a dough. Pull off pieces, form them into balls and drop them into hot oil."

Michael Stipe will probably become a writer when all this is over. There's something in there dying to come out.

"I'm pretty happy right now" he blushes, and as you're reading this he's probably at home, gone fishing or walking the dog through the 'baccy fields. Happy? He's in clover.

Berry, Stipe, Buck, Mills, 1984. *Photo © Laura Levine.*

Part Two

SOUTHERN ACCENTS

JOHN PLATT

R.E.M.:"FABLES OF THE RECONSTRUCTION" (1985)

Bucketfull of Brains, *June 1985*

Rock History suggests that few bands have made three consecutive flawless albums; even fewer have made three such albums in their whole careers. It would please me no end to report that R.E.M. had managed that feat and, bearing in mind my known predilection for their music, I would be prepared to overlook the odd fault when viewing the album as a whole. Unfortunately I can't do that—quite. But the good news is that at least five of the tracks are as good, if not better, than anything that the band have recorded to date.

The album opens with "Feeling Gravity's Pull," an odd first track, as it has a jarring and unnerving quality that almost distances the listener from the music, rather than drawing him or her into it. It builds up a tense edgy quality that is only released when the key changes and Mike Mills's harmony comes in and it suddenly sounds more like what one expects from the band. Curious but ultimately compelling. Next up is "Maps and Legends," and despite repeated playing I can only see this as minor league R.E.M.—pleasant, melodic and probably lyrically interesting (difficult to tell as usual) but by no means gripping. That's followed by "Driver 8," one of the best of the new numbers they were performing here on the last tour and it sounds great—no ifs or buts—simply classic stuff. Not so, "Life and How to Live It" which sounds as though it was written five minutes before it was recorded (probably wasn't of course) and has all the hallmarks of filler. In fact I can't even recall the tune as I write this, an indictment if ever there was one.

Last on side one is "Old Man Kensey" which, again, dates from the last tour (and before) and one of the numbers they did on the Whistle Test. It's a number oddly devoid of the dynamics associated with the band (even on their ballads) and in consequence I've never quite been able to decide how I feel about it. Whatever, it is an excellent and evocative song.

Side two opens with "Can't Get There from Here," the big horn extravaganza number. Personally I think the brass was a mistake, but others (including the band) would no doubt beg to differ. I think they bury what was probably a good melody. Also the fact that Michael sings in his

39

bogus Southern drawl (usually reserved for those bits of between-track banter) doesn't help—I can't tell if he's taking it seriously. With "Green Grow the Rushes" we are back on course again—a terrific song full of mystery and blessed with one of their finest melodies. We move up a gear for "Kahoutek" and it's another killer, suggesting that it has to be one of their best live numbers. "Auctioneer" is also high drama territory but like "Gravity's Pull" is slightly unnerving, revealing hints of an as yet unexplored darker side to the band's music. "Good Advices" which follows, may just be my favorite R.E.M. number to date. It's a vague stylistic relative of "Camera" on *Reckoning* but less stark and with more melody. A beautiful song, what more can I say?

"Wendell Gee," the last number is an oddity. If it wasn't for Michael's vaguely surreal lyrics, I would say that it bordered on the sentimental—an effect heightened by the plunking banjo and the wistful chorus. Not vintage stuff but quite likeable.

Taken overall it's hard to point to anything on this album different from the predecessor (despite the strings and the horns)—hardly the radical experiment some observers would have us believe. No, it's a progres-

At Walter's Barbeque, Athens, Ga., 1984. *Photo © Laura Levine.*

sion along existing lines and with such a high proportion of good songs, that's fine with me. There is, however, a serious problem with the album which has little to do with the music. I think the production (or more often the mix) is really weak. Is this down to producer Joe Boyd? I'm not sure. Either way it sounds really flat in comparison with *Murmur* and *Reckoning;* almost no bottom end at all. Also a lot of the overdubbed instruments (acoustic guitars and the like) are frequently buried completely. All in all it's a really empty mix (!!). Oddly a couple of tracks sound much beefier (though still not up to the previous Mitch Easter stuff) notably "Driver 8." Bearing in mind that "Driver 8" would make just about the only single on the album, this begs several interesting questions. What goes on guys?

FRED MILLS AND TODD GOSS

R.E.M. '86—DOGGED PERSEVERANCE (1986)

The Bob, *June 1986*

Monday December 2, 1985: I roll into Raleigh from Charlotte, call Todd in Durham and tell him to get his butt over here. I drop off a stack of *Bob*'s at Schoolkid's Records, then zip down Hillsborough Street to the World's Coolest Record Store, the Record Hole, and find two promo copies of *So. Central Rain.* Good omen. Then I head over to the Civic Center where R.E.M. is playing that night. Aiming to set up an interview for the *Bob,* I bear a gift in the form of an Air Jordan basketball to soften 'em up. I hang around a bit, waiting for the rock gods to show. Uh-oh, nature calls, so I locate the closest W.C. The band apparently arrives while I am in conference. I'm not sure what Bill Berry thinks of the guy who burst out of the stall clutching a red-and-black b-ball stuttering "HihowyadoingBill"? but I wisely let the drummer wash his face in peace. Heck I'll get my "Wendell Gee" pic-sleeve signed later.

Post soundcheck. I blabber at Buck a bit and thrust a coupla *Bob*'s his way, dropping the bomb that yes, I wanna try my hand at an R.E.M. piece. In the dressing room are a few plates of fruits, veggies, cheese and crackers; a coupla tubs of ice housing Buds 'n' Heinekens 'n' fruit juices. What decadence. Speaking of which, Mike Mills and Bill Berry are engaging in various time-honored forms of life-on-the-road madness: Mills (no relation, although he once confessed he aspired to be) is placing Ritz Crackers on the floor of the dressing room, then bouncing the ball on them, causing miniature crumb explosions to reverberate wickedly throughout the room. A similar exercise with a strawberry proves to be somewhat less spectacular. Bill Berry shoots the shit with members of the crew, occasionally throwing pennies against the wall. Nervous guy, I think to myself. Buck sits quietly reading and I resist the urge to ask him about his favorite French bands. Michael Stipe, he of the currently-blond and shorn locks, is rumored to be sitting on the bus. Tour manager Geoff Trump and band manager Jefferson Holt come and go, taking care of Band Bizness. Trump hands out bills from a metal briefcase, but I don't press my luck. I content myself with a warm greeting from Jefferson, he of the currently-blond and shoulder-length hair. Hey—there's Mike Watt, he of the regulation-green jump-suit and vaguely communist beard, over in the corner with his bass! I remind him we'd met in Columbia at the Beat Club a year previous and he seems pleased to renew the acquaintance. I hear a basketball thumping somewhere.

Showtime arrives. Even though I'm about to drop from all the excitement, I manage to drag myself upstairs to a prime spot in the rear balcony. No chairs on the floor. I locate Todd and give him his after-show pass.

As the lights go down, the Minutemen anxiously take the stage. They open their set of punk-metal-funk-jazz-core with "Anxious Mo-Flo," which leads into "Toadies." The bemused crowd does not know what to think of the Minutemen and become restless for R.E.M. The M-men don't let up for a second, playing a powerful set. Before beginning the song "What Is It," bassist Mike Watt announces that D. Boon will be "dancing to rival Michael Stipe," and during the break of the song Boon begins to leap high in the air like a lightweight. Yet, instead of letting the audience's reaction weaken their set, the Minutemen seem to thrive on it. Sadly, this was to be one of their final performances.

Break, then lights dim and the unmistakable sound of a locomotive rattling down the tracks, lonesome horn a-blowin', comes over the P.A. An eerie intro creaks out from Buck's side of the stage and "Feeling Gravity's Pull" commences. Set list for the evening: Gravity, Harborcoat, Maps and Legends, Pilgrimage, Driver 8, Letter Never Sent, Hyena, Green Grow the Rushes, Moral Kiosk, So. Central Rain, Swans, West of the Fields, Can't Get There from Here, Auctioneer, Old Man Kensey, Pretty Persuasion, Life and How to Live It, (encores) White Tornado, Pills, Rockville, See No Evil, Two Steps Onward, Toys in the Attic, Second Guessing, Little America.

At the Rat, Boston, 1984. *Photo © Laura Levine.*

Little America

It's a loose and fun show. The crowd is packed tightly. Dancing in the rear, please. Green and purple lighting. An airborne roll of toilet paper prompts Stipe to quip, "Keep asswipe in the audience where it belongs!" Holy Cushytush! There is sparse, moving vocal/guitar duet between Michael and Peter on "So. Central Rain"; followed by a still-young but rapturously hypnotic "Swans." "Toys in the Attic" is candidate for Best Unrecorded Cover. "Born to Run" is candidate for Worst. Surf Instrumental "White Tornado" is dedicated to Mitch and Con. Michael gives his patented knobby-knee'd shimmies during the video-perfect "Can't Get There." Peter leaps, dips and spins. Let's not forget Mike's nimble fretwork and perfect harmonies; and Bill's relentless propulsion of the whole machine.

Impressions Two: Norfolk

Wednesday Dec. 4: We roll into Norfolk from Raleigh fueled on caffeine, Sonic Youth and Television. Thanks to directions from the folks at Electric

Smiles Records in Virginia Beach we locate Chrysler Theatre. By sheer coincidence an elevator from the parking garage deposits us smack dab in the lobby of the place, and we wind up at the soundboard. The sound-check consists of "Catapult," "Driver 8," "Green Grow the Rushes" and "Ages of You"—the latter being a nice surprise, another good omen. Mr. Trump scrutinizes the two intruders carefully, decides we're relatively harmless, and hands us a pair of the coveted orange passes.

Well the Minutemen were not pretty, not pretty at all. They were aggressive, political, harsh, powerful, yet still accessible and enjoyable to those who'd bothered to listen. As before, some booed. Rude Neanderthals. If you don't want to see the opening band, stay in the fuck-ing lobby! How could anyone not be charmed by D. Boon's dancing show-manship and fluid guitar playing? Yeah, we'll miss him. Todd found a napkin Boon had been scribbling on before soundcheck, a cryptic sketch of a man who's head was turning into a flowerpot. Ashes to ashes. . . .

R.E.M. set list: Gravity, Harborcoat, Letter Never Sent, Hyena, Maps and Legends, Pilgrimage, Driver 8, Fall on Me, Bandwagon, Sitting Still, Good Advices, So. Central Rain, Swans, Can't Get There from Here, Seven Chinese Brothers, Ghost Riders in the Sky, Auctioneer, Old Man Kensey, , Pretty Persuasion, Life and How to Live it, (encores) See No Evil, Dream, Rockville, Toys in the Attic, Second Guessing, Talk about the Passion, Little America.

Well, this was a hot one, and both sets of balconies visibly shook from the dancing. From row three we saw it all: Michael's stylish paperbag hat, aggressive shadowboxing with the mic-stand during "7 Chinese Bros.," and storytelling talents utilizing dramatic pauses, funny gestures and smooth punchline delivery. The imperfect yet still lovely har-monies in the Everly's "Dream." The acid rainshower of "Fall on Me," a new song that showcased Mike's counterpart lead vocal. The spellbinding "Swans," with still-new lyrics affixed to a music stand, acoustic guitar duet gentle on our minds and the subtle urgency of the percussion. "This is a request. Someone's been asking for two nights—we never play this one!" Then "Bandwagon," a real surprise. Ditto for "Ghost Riders" and the honest-to-gosh two full verses of "Born to Run." The band troops back onstage for the "See No Evil" encore. Mike Watt plugs in a guitar too! Stipe comes out with a towel wrapped around his head from nose up: trips, falls, and Berry hits a vaudeville drumroll, announcing with talk-show glee, "Mr. Michael Stipe!" The closing song is "Little America": bombs whistle overhead, the singer recites the Pledge of Allegiance and blurts out, "I think I'm Rambo!"

Post-gig: Usual hospitality room scenes for guests and local media types (there had been a film crew lurking around earlier). Congrats 'n' shakes 'n' album sleeves are thrust forward. Peter and Fred escape upstairs for a quick int, *Bob* style.

Interview One: Norfolk at Midnight

The Bob: The Peter Buck Interview, Part One!

Peter Buck: Have a drink. [leans toward mike] What you hear now folks: No, it's not Miller Beer, It's another beer. It's not brewed the American way. [sound of beer tab popping] Aaah! [gulps]

The Bob: The sound of Bud. . . . Oh, I gave it away. . . .

Peter Buck, 1986. *Photo © Ebet Roberts.*

Peter Buck: I wasn't gonna tell ya! Don't want be misconstrued as giving credence to rumors that we drink a lot.

The Bob: So how long has R.E.M. had this drinking problem?

Peter Buck: I don't have a drinking problem! I can drink as much as I want to!

The Bob: Whew . . . Okay, you got your couch there, I'll be Sigmund Freud. Instead of "Peter Buck Talks about American Bands."

Peter Buck: How about my favorite French bands. Les Variations, remember that record, "Moroccan Roll," where they had the old Tunisian guy playing violin?

The Bob: What about Telephone?

Peter Buck: Yeah, well, they're naked on the cover of their record! Yeah, boy, I got that one! We played with a French rock 'n' roll band that was like, umm, equal parts Dr. Feelgood and, ohh, well actually, Dr. Feelgood and Dr. Feelgood. They were called The Fixed Up. They were pretty fixed up! I liked 'em. Rouen, or Lyon, one of those places that ends in "on." That was a while back. . . .

The Bob: Hey about fanzines, how'd you get hooked into Bucketfull of Brains's flexidisc?

Peter Buck: They've always just been real good to us, and I like them, and they said "Would you do it?" And I said, yeah, absolutely. I'm real nice, and I always say yeah about things that I think would be nice. And so it took us about a year and a half to convince I.R.S. to let us do it.

The Bob: Well, I've been corresponding with Jon [Storey, editor of B.O.B.] for ages . . .

Peter Buck: Yeah, he's pretty cool!

The Bob: . . . and when he first told me about that I said, "God, this is great!" Going back, you know, to just the pure fanzine ethic of Do It Yourself and everything.

Peter Buck: See, we'd do it as much as we could, but I.R.S. isn't real happy about any kind of material coming out—they won't let us do a fanzine single. Which I can understand. When our contract is up, well, our new contract will be different. It will be—we'll have a lot more latitude as far as doing fanzine things and doing outside projects.

The Bob: What about that threatened compilation of tracks in the can? I heard ya'll mention doing a mail-order-only thing.

Peter Buck: Well see, I would love to do that, but I.R.S. right now just isn't in a situation where they can do something like that by mail. And they won't let us do anything like that by ourselves.

The Bob: Well, the Grateful Dead does it. . . .

Peter Buck: You know, the thing is, next time that we sign a contract, we'll be able to get away with doing that. It won't be a big deal. When we signed our contract the first time we didn't have enough power.

The Bob: How long did you sign the contract for?

Peter Buck: It's five albums, so we got two more to go. And I.R.S. is a perfectly fine company! I'm just saying that when we sign with them again, or whatever, there will be different things in the contract.

The Bob: Are you going to do a live album?

Peter Buck: I don't like live albums; I always hated 'em.

The Bob: Well, Reflection [Studios] recorded those shows in Charlotte and Durham. . . . [Sept. 23, 25, 26, '84] What's gonna happen with that?

Peter Buck: We recorded eight shows. We wanted to have them because we knew it was the last tour that we'd do a lot of those songs; we wanted to have tapes of 'em. Unluckily enough, out of the eight shows they recorded, about four of them were pretty mediocre.

The Bob: Someone told me that something fucked up the first night [25th] in Durham.

Peter Buck: Yeah, the first night really sucked. . . .

The Bob: Yet that was one of the most incredible shows I have ever seen.

Peter Buck: Really? I remember it as not being real great.

The Bob: Well, I gotta admit, I'm a fan of the loose, sloppy shows.

Peter Buck: See that's it—It was loose and sloppy!

The Bob: Yeah, at the end you got into this stuff where you're just riffing away in—what do you call it? "Skank" or "Tusk," "Skank-Tusk" . . . I call it "Marble Table."

Peter Buck: Yeah, whatever, we don't really have a name for it. It's whatever it happens to be that night.

The Bob: Umm, you've got a bunch of songs that I've heard in one capacity or another. Like, uhh, "Walter's."

Peter Buck: Yeah, that was just a joke. We kinda came up with a little riff and then we decided we'd do a commercial for Walter's Barbecue. Every time we tried to cut it we were really drunk, so it always came out real raggedy.

The Bob: Well, you tagged it onto the beginning of "King of the Road."

Peter Buck: Well, we were really drunk, and that's just what came out.

The Bob: What about "Cushy Tush"? (Doesn't your family deserve the best asswipe?)

Peter Buck: [laughs] Yeah! We just sit around, and it just seemed like one of those things to do.

The Bob: Undoubtedly one of my favorite non-LP songs.

Peter Buck: Ohh, well . . . I just had that little riff to do, and I went, "This sounds exactly like a toilet paper commercial." And Bill just went "Cushy Tush"! We've got like two or three versions of that recorded that are just hilarious!

The Bob: How did ya'll decide to put out "Burning Down" and "Ages of You"? I remember "Burning Down" was also on that Seattle Source broadcast.

Peter Buck:: Well, they were around, and we kept thinking we'd put 'em on an album. But as time goes by, the older they get the less likely it is that we'll put 'em out. So we decided that rather than not have them out at all, we'd put them on a single.

The Bob: You did "Ages of You" at the soundcheck today.

Peter Buck: Yeah, we always try to do something that we're not going to do at the show just so we don't get tired of playing the same stuff over and over.

The Bob: Do y'all ever play "Burning Down" live anymore?

Peter Buck: Hmm . . . I'm not saying no, but we don't do it a lot. We've done it maybe once this tour, maybe twice.

The Bob: What about all that ancient stuff, like "Narrator"? Do you ever fuck around with those songs anymore?

Peter Buck: "Narrator" [laughs]—It's safe to say we haven't fucked around with that in a long time. Although it'll be out on the Hindu Love Gods single, y'know in February.

The Bob: The fan club said to write I.R.S. and demand it. They're finally gonna put it out?

Peter Buck: Yeah, you know, they were just kind of slow. But obviously it's not like a huge money-maker, so it's not as if they're gonna rush it right out to compete with The Alarm or General Public or anything. It's not going to make anyone's fortune! But it's a fun little thing, and it was meant to be fun. You know, you'll buy it for $1.79 "at better record stores everywhere."

The Bob: Correct me if these new song titles are wrong: "Fall on Me," "Theme from Two Steps Onward" . . .

Peter Buck: Actually it didn't really have a good title; Michael just called it that. "Two Steps Onward" is right.

The Bob: *And then the other one; someone just called it "Johnny Reb" the other night . . . [title: "Swans"].*

Peter Buck: Yeah, we don't have a title for that one either, yet. We wrote that on the bus about $2\frac{1}{2}$ weeks ago, about three in the morning when we were all really drunk.

The Bob: *I noticed Michael still had the music stand for the lyrics.*

Peter Buck: Yeah, Michael had some words and we had this stuff, and we were driving in the bus and we were drunk, and I just started playing it. And he said, "Yeah! I've got words that will fit that!" We worked it out in about 20 minutes.

The Bob: *That's a really "southern" sounding song.*

Peter Buck: Irish, too—fake Irish. I mean, that's where the southern stuff comes from, you know, the Child ballads, the Appalachian songs and stuff.

The Bob: *Are y'all getting deeper and deeper into "the southern mystique"?*

Peter Buck: Nah, we're getting deeper and deeper into debt! [laughs] No, not really. I mean, all this stuff was always in my listening tastes; but especially when you start out as a bar band, some of those things don't come to the fore. As you have more time to experiment and play around, you come up with more, uhh, diverse stuff, more stuff that's out of the norm.

The Bob: *Do y'all listen to a lot of traditional stuff? I know Bill listens to country.*

Peter Buck: Yeah . . . We listen to lots of stuff, but it's not as if I'm real knowledgeable. The only thing I really know is rock 'n' roll, but I listen to a whole lot of everything.

The Bob: *I've started checking out a few Irish groups lately.*

Peter Buck: Oh, Planxty, and all them?

The Bob: Yeah. And there's some rock 'n' roll bands, actually. There's In Tua Nua, which kinda sounds like early Jefferson Airplane.

Peter Buck: Yeah, I know those guys.

The Bob: Hey, Steve Wickham [Tua Nua violinist, now with the Waterboys] played onstage with you guys one time didn't he?

Peter Buck: Well, funnily enough, I went to junior high school and high school with his wife!

The Bob: Small world.

Peter Buck: Yeah! We show up in Dublin—never been to Ireland, I think it was maybe the second time we'd been to England—walk into the lobby of this hotel, and this Irish guy comes up to me and says, "Excuse me, I think you know my wife." I went, "Never laid a hand on her!" "No, you went to high school with her." "No, I didn't lay a hand on her then, either!" But she was someone I knew, knew very well, when I was a teenager. Steve was really nice, we hung around, had a few drinks, and then he played with us when we played Dublin.

The Bob: He played on the Long Ryders B-side of "Lewis and Clark," uhh, "If I were a Bramble and You Were a Rose." Lessee, there was a guy—when U2 played Atlanta—they pulled out of the audience to play "Knockin' on Heaven's Door." The guy turned out to have lived in the same flat with Steve Wickham when he was over in Dublin.

Peter Buck: I know that guy! He's friends with the Nightporters. Everyone laughed at him when he went over to Ireland because he brought like five cases of Pop Tarts with him 'cos he didn't think they'd have 'em and that's what he liked to eat!

The Bob: Small world. Hey, looks like everybody's leaving, we better get going. Oh yeah, something specific to you: Producing Dreams So Real, working with Keith Streng, the Dream Academy. Any comments on those three?

Peter Buck: Umm, Dreams So Real? They just asked me and I said yes; first time I'd ever done something like that. It came out good, mostly because they're a good band. Keith Streng, that was more of a thing we did together. We were just talking about how he was going to do a solo record, and I said, "Well fuck, come on down to Georgia and you can stay at my place. There's an 8-track right around the corner and you can make a record for nothing there. And, you know, we'll do pretty well." And it did. It turned out pretty good, I think. It's out now, on Coyote. It cost like $300 to make, a three song EP. That's pretty good. And Dream Academy: I was just at this party, I was just standing around. And this guy goes up to me, and we talked for awhile. He seemed like a really nice guy. He said, "You're Peter Buck, right?" I went, "Yeah." "You're my second favorite guitar player in the world!" "Well, thank you—who's your first?" He goes, "Johnny Marr." I went, "Well . . . okay."

The Bob: HA HA HA HA HA!!!

Peter Buck: You know, I don't laugh! Johnny Marr's fine, I guess. I don't know much about him or anything. He goes, "Well, Johnny's busy this weekend, and I'm making a record. Would you come do it?" "Well, I'm kind of busy myself." "We're recording at David Gilmour's house, and I'll give you a hundred pounds!" I went, "I'll be there! Sure, great!"

The Bob: Had you met Gilmour before?

Peter Buck: No, never had. So I basically wanted to meet David Gilmour; the money didn't really mean that much. Although money's nice! So I took a train out there and got to meet David, hung around and talked and had a few beers. It was just real simple stuff, he was wanting me to play some ringing guitar stuff. I was real nervous because David Gilmour is standing there, so I blew it about twenty times. It was fun.

The Bob: What's the name of the song, "The Party"?

Peter Buck: I don't know. Didn't have words to it when I did it. I played electric twelve-string. And then, like, Telecaster with a Leslie, but I don't know if that made the record.

The Bob: There are three bootlegs that just came out, I've been told. One is called "We're Blinking as Fast as We Can" and it's just a boot of the Seattle show, the Source show.

Peter Buck: Really? I'd like to hear that. Is that good quality?

The Bob: I dunno, I've ordered it. Gosh, I mean, I paid sixty-five bucks for an original copy of the Source discs, and it's already going for $120. . . .

Peter Buck: Oh, you've got a real copy of that? I don't even have one of those! That's kind of a pisser because when we said we'd do it, it's in our contract that we get like 15 copies. They said, "Fine! We always get them returned, we've got hundreds of 'em." Of all the hundreds they said, they only got five back! "It just never happened before, everyone kept 'em." "Wait a minute, I'm in the band! I should get one of the records!" But I couldn't get one. . . .

The Bob: Radio shows are real hot in the record collecting circles.

Peter Buck: I know, I know, I've got a couple myself. But I'm not going go pay a million dollars for 'em. I mean, I wanted one with *me* on it.

The Bob: Did you know that the "Radio Free Europe" remix is on a bootleg called "Smoking in the Boy's Room"?

Peter Buck: Yeah, I've got that one, It's a dub, that's what it is.

The Bob: That's cool! Awful packaging, though, looks like a real cheap. . . .

Peter Buck: I kinda liked that. . . .

The Bob: Time to go. Say hello to all your fans, Peter.

Peter Buck: Hello to all my fans, Peter.

Impressions Three: Winston-Salem

Sunday December 8: I roll into Winston-Salem from Charlotte. I had missed the Richmond show on the 5th and Lexington on the 6th (which was an unusual one—the show was overcrowded and marked by lots of pushing, so the band sat down and did a four-song acoustic set to try to calm things a bit). Upon locating Reynolds Auditorium at Reynolds High School I discover Peggy Leisure and Caryn Rose in the parking lot busily defacing a purloined orange "End of Construction" road sign. This sign, it will turn out, is to reappear onstage at the last show reading "End of

Reconstruction." I head in for the soundcheck. It makes me feel a little fanish asking the band to sign my "Wendell Gee" sleeve, but heck, that's what I *am,* so why worry. Michael seems to scrutinize the sleeve closely and responds to my question that yes, he designs all the R.E.M. sleeves. I come upon D. Boon in one of the dressing rooms as he's working on a detailed sketch of a trucker in the cab of his semi. We chat briefly and I get my "Tour-Spiel" EP signed.

The soundcheck consists of "Driver 8," "Green Grow the Rushes" and "Catapult" (instrumental). Then they retire to the incredibly tiny/cramped dressing rooms. Michael eats rice cakes with peanut butter, and shows off some of his Polaroids. Bill occupies himself with his acoustic guitar, its dulcet tones echoing pleasantly throughout the backstage area. Peter heads up to the lobby in search of a pay phone (a scene I observed numerous times). Mike disappears. The band is visibly weary, Peter especially, and I feel guilty for asking him to come outside for a photo session. Peter says he fell asleep at 9 last night and woke up around 10:30, then couldn't get back to sleep. The man is a gentleman, though, and follows us outside to a grassy hill for sunset photos. As we head back inside for the rest of the interview, several fans run up with pens in hand. Peter again demonstrates that he is indeed "a nice guy" and signs their tickets and pieces of paper.

Interview Two: Winston-Salem at Six P.M.

The Bob: Part two, same sounds as last time. [sound of Buds opening]

Peter Buck: Mine's already open.

The Bob: What'd ya think of the Record interview that just came out? [Record, Jan./Feb. 1986]

Peter Buck: Yeah, I read it; It's fine. Pretty much what I said, I guess.

The Bob: Do you ever find yourself horribly misquoted?

Peter Buck: It's hard to tell; you say so much bullshit. I don't think I've ever seen anything that I know I wouldn't say. No one's ever put words in my mouth. Sometimes it's taken a little bit out of context, but I've never seen it done out of harm. Maybe I meant one thing and I wasn't quite clear enough, and that's *my* fault. I don't really have any complaints. . . .

The Bob: I just wondered if you actually enjoy the interview process. Do you feel self-conscious after it comes out, or anything weird like that?

Peter Buck: Well, I enjoy them when they're good, when they're interesting questions that you can mess around with 'em and enjoy yourself. But I feel stupid when I read one and I think I've come off badly if I've said something I really didn't mean. But usually I try not to put my foot in my mouth. I try not to slag off people that I don't like. Every once in awhile people ask you a question like, "What do you think of this band?" And you say, "Well, I think they really suck," or "I think they're stupid." You know, and that's just what I say to friends. And I like a lot more than I dislike, but it so happens that usually I get asked about things I don't like. And that's what they'll always use: that's the "important" thing, it's controversial or it's different.

The Bob: Your Jackson Browne quote is legendary.

Peter Buck: [laughing] Yeah, I was talking to Warren Zevon; he saw it and he thought it was pretty funny too.

The Bob: Zevon played onstage a couple times with you this tour, didn't he?

Peter Buck: Once in L.A. Then we played with him a couple of times. . . . We did his stuff. When he played with us we did one of his and one of ours. Sometimes we do "Gloria" or something like that.

The Bob: Is anyone interested in signing him yet?

Peter Buck: I dunno, I think he's gotten close . . . He is going for a major deal, big cash or whatever and all that. He's real normal. I mean, he's calmed down. He's 38 or whatever and not nearly as wild as he used to be. And he doesn't drink anymore, or take drugs or anything.

The Bob: How old are you now?

Peter Buck: I just turned 29.

The Bob: You gonna get depressed when you turn 30?

Peter Buck: No, it's just another birthday. I would get depressed if I weren't aging! Can't think of anything worse than living 70 years and being the same. That's why it's good, as life goes on, you feel different things. You become an adolescent, then you get older, then you get decrepit, and bald, and weird, and you start saving string. . . . Yeah, I wouldn't want to be the same. I'm not dying to leap right into senescence or whatever, but it's a natural thing and I don't really mind. That's why I hope there isn't any kind of thing like Heaven, or anything where they stick you for about a million years.

The Bob: Do you like to look back at old photos of yourself, jog some memories?

Peter Buck: Well, from about the age of about 12 onwards there aren't many pictures of me until I'm 20, 'cos I just didn't like having my picture taken. There's a couple of high school pictures, and I guess an arrest record picture or two. But naah, I never look at 'em.

The Bob: [laughing] What arrest records?

Peter Buck: Ahh, just teenage stuff, nothing serious. Just the kind of stuff that they laugh at when you go into court. I don't think I've been around in this business long enough to have old photos; it's only been five years now. So I look back at the photos of five years ago—as a matter of fact I just looked at a picture someone gave me, of the very first time we ever played in public—and we all look *exactly* the same. Michael's hair is a bit different, and Mike Mills's is a bit longer. I've got the same haircut and I've even got the same jacket—I still wear it sometimes.

The Bob: The back of that first picture sleeve ["Radio Free Europe" b/w "Sitting Bull" on Hib-Tone]: I had no idea who was who.

Peter Buck: We just wanted something kind of different. Everyone at that time seemed to be putting out records with those Sex Pistols graphics, you know, the cut up letters. We were trying to combine different aspects of rock 'n' roll, so there's this kind of weird arty front cover—even though the reproduction wasn't done all that well. And a kind of moody back cover photo, whereas a pop group. . . .

The Bob: What is the cover? Is it anything?

Peter Buck: It's just a smear. I think Michael took a picture of something when he was sneezing.

The Bob: When it came out I thought it might be a picture of something like a close-up of a dinosaur's rear end. . . .

Peter Buck: Nothing symbolic. I think it was just a picture Michael took that didn't turn out, but he liked the way it did.

The Bob: I was going to ask about the designing of your early fliers and stuff. I remember seeing this little tiny booklet that Michael handed out. Do you remember that?

Peter Buck: Yeah, we used to make those at home. We designed all that stuff; it was always kind of fun. I mean, when we sent out our tapes we made all these weird Xerox baseball cards that we colored in. We sat around and did that for days. I remember stuffing those things in the tapes. And everyone had to make their own posters. Especially in Athens. Everyone would try to outdo one another. Us, and Pylon, and Love Tractor, and the Method Actors, and the Tonetones. You'd Xerox 'em and stick 'em up around town.

The Bob: Do you remember those real early gigs at The Station and The Pier [in Raleigh]? I didn't know what to think back then!

Peter Buck: Yeah! I didn't either! [laughs] We'd never done the road. We just decided if you go on the road that what you were supposed to do is stay up all the time and drink 24 hours a day. So, the first time we played the Station, and then Raleigh, we'd never left Athens to play. Never even played Atlanta. So I think we'd left on a Thursday after noon and didn't sleep until we got back Tuesday. We were just drunk the whole time.

The Bob: Now, one thing I wanted to ask, because I haven't seen that much coverage of the tour in Europe and England: How'd it go over there and how'd people react to you? Not necessarily the crowds, but also the press. You got a couple of negative album reviews in the British press.

Peter Buck: The first two albums and the first four tours, we got the "This is the only band in the world worth listening to!" reviews, that kind of thing. Which is going too far the other way. This time around we got, well, I think *Melody Maker* and *NME* gave it really rave reviews like, "It's a great record and a great tour." *Sounds* didn't. The guy who reviewed it really hated it, said it was a bunch of bullshit. Which is his prerogative! We're still batting .700 as far as rave reviews! It was just our turn. Things happen there in a cyclical manner and they decided that it was time that all this American stuff be put a stop to. I can understand that! A lot of our bands, I don't think were all that great—I'm not gonna name names—like on the cover of magazines and stuff. Or if not on the cover they're just like, "Wow, these guys are really wonderful!" And maybe they'd just popped over and done one date. 'Course, some really worthy bands were discovered then, too. . . . You know, it's good to see Chilton getting appreciated, . . .

The Bob: How is it that this mystique builds up—how do we, meaning the folks who sit here and interview you, turn you into gods anyway?

Peter Buck: Well, in a way it's a natural thing not to be godlike. But when you're going to write about someone, you write about the most definable characteristics, and so that tends to turn you into a character. And by the time you've had 50 things written about you, no one will *dare* write the opposite. "Well, I don't think he's really interesting and charming; he's a real asshole." That doesn't happen. And so you tend to become the sum of your most obvious characteristics. And nothing more, nothing less.

The Bob: When an interviewer is asking for the millionth time, "Now you started in a little church in Athens, . . ." do you ever feel like putting him on or being a real jerk?

Peter Buck: The thing is, you always want to, but you can't; I can't look someone in the eye and lie to them like that. As much as it would be funny, I can only do that if they *know* that I'm pulling their leg, and then it's always amusing. . . . Usually I just give short shrift: "I started in a church five years ago, blah blah blah. . . ." And then that's the history. At this point in time we don't really need to be rehashing how the band started. We do get that in foreign countries. In Belgium, where we only played twice, they wanted to know it all. But then, sometimes we do get some guy from a major newspaper in, ohh, Hohumsburgh, Ohio, and he's kind of, uhh, it's for the people that are in Hohumsburg, and he has to tell everything about you. It happens to everyone.

The Bob: What you should do is carry around your best article-reviews, and when they start asking questions say . . .

Peter Buck: "Here!" We send out this really comprehensive bio—the record company does—[leans over to the microphone, speaks loudly] and here's a tip for you journalists: Don't *ever* quote someone's bio and then ask them to comment on that! 'Cos all you can say is, "Yes" or "I have changed my mind."

The Bob: Let me throw some things out at you. . . . You did some TV shows in Europe this time?

Peter Buck: Yeah, yeah, we did some the time before that too. The funniest one was called "Music Caravan" It's outdoors all the time, even in the dead of winter, an outdoor show. They change the location at different times, so we were at this little swimming pool place. They said they'd had films of 'em doing it in the snow and stuff, it was us, the Ramones and OMD; all lip synching! Except that we didn't lip synch, we had real vocals.

The Bob: Y'all refuse to lip-synch, don't you?

Peter Buck: Yeah. I don't really care; I'll fake playing my guitar, because all I have to do is turn on my guitar and play anyway. But the whole thing with Michael is that he really doesn't like to lip-synch, and so, we just cut a new track without vocals. We all play; we just don't play very loud, and then he sings. So we played, all those bands played. And the Ramones were just Big Stars! Live TV show, do three songs, then do an interview with the guy who does the show. $3/4$ of the way through the third song the Ramones just threw down their instruments and walked off with the music still playing, the audience going berserk. And there was five minutes left! It was great! You could see the announcer running after them trying to catch them. [laughs] And it stopped, and he had three minutes to fill up. Totally dead air. He and his friend were talking. I could hear them, it was like, "Der rock musikun der America!" Good for the Ramones! They looked so miserable, though.

The Bob: That's great. Who approaches you? How do you decide to do something like that?

Peter Buck: Our record company lines them up, but we've told them we'll do basically any TV show as long as we can play on it. . . . I mean, the worst we've done—twice now, we've done those things where we fake a backing track and we have Michael do vocals. But every other show we've done, we do live.

The Bob: I saw you on Solid Gold Hits.

Peter Buck: That was the same thing, where they cut a new track and then there's no vocals, which is really weird. It takes all the pressure off me because I don't have to play. I do lead guitar stuff. It's really great when you're filming it, 'cos I'm doing all these sliding-downs. On Solid Gold, for about half of it, if you take a look at it, I purposely played half a step up [on "So. Central Rain"]. So I'm doing this C chord that wouldn't make any sense, so that if people look at it: "He must use a really strange tuning."

The Bob: "What an innovator!" What about radio shows? We talked about the Source thing last time. The first few tours I think there were more radio shows than I have heard recently.

Peter Buck: We found, in this year especially, that anything that we don't have complete control over is screwed up. We have a real good organization. We have a good P.A. We have people taking care of everything. We spent a lot of money to make sure things were right. When we put it in someone else's hands it's *always* horrible! You know, whether it be the CMJ thing and the P.A. was falling apart and no one gave a shit. Or, umm, like radio shows where, well, like the first one we did in Boston [7/12/83, at the Paradise], we did a three hour soundcheck so it'd be fine for the radio. And the P.A. column blew up in the third song! So it was like, "scritzy, scratchy" for everyone that was in the hall.

The Bob: That reminds me—wasn't that the one that was filmed for a video?

Peter Buck: Uhh, no. There's some announcement on the tape that they were filming it, but I think there were just people taking pictures. I don't *think* it was filmed.

The Bob: I've heard that the last Pier show in Raleigh was filmed [5/3/83]. That was the one when Michael had the audience laying down. Really strange.

Peter Buck: Yeah! I've seen it; we've got the tapes of that one. I don't sit and watch all of them. What we do is, every year we have a little party in February. We retain the rights to all these things that we've done on TV; so, we have them send 'em to us. Then Michael and these people who work with us that do films, edit together a two-hour "R.E.M.: This Was The Year That Was on Television." It's usually like the ludicrous things from interviews, hand held cameras. We'll put 'em all together and watch that. I've seen the Pier tape. Some of it's pretty funny. . . . You want another? I'm gonna get another one.

The Bob: Nah, I'm fine. Videos: "Can't Get There from Here" was a lot of fun, stayed on MTV a little while. "Driver 8" disappeared completely!

Peter Buck: Yeah, it's not very commercial, that's for sure. I mean, we don't really do it for commercial purposes—well, we *do,* we wouldn't do 'em if it did not help—we just try to do things that are entertaining to us. "Can't Get There" was a silly song, figured we'd have to be real silly: "Let's do it at a drive-in, use all the cool cars we own." So we did that.

The Bob: You climb out of the trunk. Is that a steal from Repo Man?

Peter Buck: I've never seen *Repo Man!* [laughs] I did get that from some-where, I can't remember what. . . . I think it was from some zombie movie or something like that.

The Bob: Are videos kind of a drag to make, take a long time?

Peter Buck: Yeah . . . Michael kind of enjoys it because he knows some of the technical stuff and he'll be helping with the editing and stuff. But for me it's just, y'know, I'd rather be fishing. And I hate fishing!

The Bob: Lessee, Michael designs stage lighting, is that true?

Peter Buck: Yeah. Well, he doesn't weld it together or anything. [laughs] He and Chas, our lighting director, get together and kind of map out what they want.

The Bob: Do you have any interest in that side of a stage show?

Peter Buck: Only in that I want it to be good. I pretty much trust Michael's judgment. He'll show me the ideas that he has and I'll see the technical drawings. And when it comes time, when we start doing the warm-up for the tour, I'll suggest things like moving lights different places so this is more clear, or whatever. By and large Michael usually gets it right.

The Bob: Does he pick the backdrop shots that are projected?

Peter Buck: I think a lot of those are his photos. It's just little things, nothing real symbolic or anything.

The Bob: I heard you played with Robyn Hitchcock in London. [Dingwalls, 3/15/85]. Was that for an entire gig or just guesting on a couple of songs?

Peter Buck: Let me see. One night I played most of the gig, but it was a short one. I played like eight songs out of 14 or something. Another time I just leaped onstage and did three with him. I know him real well and I've done some taping with him. I'd like to make a record; get to it someday. He just kind of said, "Well, you wanna get up and play? There's a guitar here." "Fine, why not?"

The Bob: You jump onstage a lot of places. I've got a tape of Green on Red [6/27/85, Warwick University, England] and you played with them, even "Sympathy for the Devil." Do you like to get up onstage with bands, do they just say, "Hey, Pete Buck's in the audience! C'mon up, Pete!"

Peter Buck: [laughs] No one's ever called me when I didn't want to go. I get up because I like to play. I like to play with people, and it's fun to see if you can sit in with someone that you don't really know the material all that well. The first time I sat in with Green on Red, I knew them, but I didn't know them really great. It was in England, they were supposed to go on after us, and they'd gotten there over two hours late. They'd already done a gig that day and Dan was so drunk he could barely stand up. After about the third song he just threw his guitar down, so I just leaped onstage and grabbed it. "You're okay, let's play!" And yeah, I knew some of the songs—some of 'em were real new, but I just figured that's okay, 'cos they're all kinda like that Neil Young, D-E minor G thing. So I said, "Tell me the key and plan it when I'm supposed to solo and I'll go for it."

The Bob: You also played with Mojo Nixon. What's he like? Is he strange? Uhh, that's not fair, I guess what I meant was . . .

Peter Buck: Well, depends on what you mean by strange. If you brought him over to your parents' house they would think he was strange. But if he came over to my house I wouldn't think he was strange at all. I first met him out in San Diego. He was opening for the Beat Farmers. I walked in to see them, I'd never seen them, and he was playing. After the show I grabbed him and kissed him, "Man, you're a genius!" He was like, "Who the fuck are you?" Somebody said, "Oh, that guy's in R.E.M.!" He goes, "Oh yeah, you guys, man mushroom mania, man. You guys are really great!" So we were talking and we just liked each other.

The Bob: I've heard y'all often enough to hear some pretty bizarre covers. Do you just start playing something, or do you look at each other and say, "We're gonna do this . . . ?" Or does someone just holler out a number from the audience?

Peter Buck: Well, all those sometimes. I mean, a lot of covers, we don't know how to play. "Toys in the Attic," obviously, we learned that one. Sat down and figured that one out. Some of the other ones we just start doing 'em one day. A lot of things that we do, they're not like Yes songs where they're really very complicated. They're rock 'n' roll and everyone has a pretty vague idea of how they go. And after you do it once then you just kind of have this rough arrangement. Like, we've done "Paint It Black" probably ten times, and we've never played it the same way twice. Sometimes it has guitar solos, sometimes it just goes verse-chorus, verse-chorus. It just depends.

The Bob: You attempted "My Generation" one night.

Peter Buck: Well Michael just started singing it. We were all pretty drunk. I fell down and hurt my knee as soon as we started playing it. We didn't really know how to do it or anything. That one, I don't have a clue to.

The Bob: What's the worst cover song you ever did?

Peter Buck: You mean played worst, or worst song?

The Bob: Played worst.

Peter Buck: "Born to Run" has to rank right up there! [laughs] But that, we didn't know we were gonna do then. See, when you start just *doing* those songs that are real complicated that no one knows how to play, it's going to be disastrous. We're actually at the point now, we've played it 1 $\frac{1}{2}$ times, we can actually get through "Born to Run." It's kinda scary. . . .

The Bob: Tell ya what, when I'm talking about a band it's often real hard to resist saying something like "Post-R.E.M. Band." Do you ever read reviews and just cringe when they say that?

Peter Buck: Yeah, I always say, "Gee, those poor guys, they probably hate it as much as I hated getting compared to Roger McGuinn!"

The Bob: Yeah, well, you talk to some folks and they say, "If I hear one more fucking band that sounds like R.E.M. I'm gonna puke!" But, y'know, in a way it's a sincere compliment to you.

Peter Buck: I'm not so sure all those bands are imitating us. I hear bands that are compared to us that don't sound like us, so. . . .

The Bob: Lessee, nothing else incredible to ask you. Hey, put my mind at ease; I heard that you guys are taking nine months off, and I also heard that you're going back to Europe.

Peter Buck: Well, it's not like it's gonna be nine months off. What's gonna happen is that we're gonna get home, take about a week and a half off, rehearse for about a month and a half. There's a possibility we might go to Australia in March. Record the album probably in April: April until middle of May. And then we'll probably have a couple of weeks off in

May. Then June we'll be doing videos, interviews, press, all kinds of stuff like that. . . .

The Bob: Never stops, does it?

Peter Buck: No!

The Bob: [standing up, preparing to close up shop] Uhh, are y'all gonna play "Crazy"?

Peter Buck: I don't know. [laughs]

The Bob: Say goodbye to all your fans, Peter.

Peter Buck: Goodbye to all my fans, Peter.

Impressions Four: Winston-Salem, continued

The place is packed with kids and veteran fans. Lots of local band members are in attendance. The crowd responds well to the Minutemen who play their best set yet. Watt pummels his bass mercilessly and snaps a string. We get a kick out of Boon's lengthy solo while the bass is restrung. He dances, as usual. Hurley is a blond blur behind the drum kit.

R.E.M. setlist: "Gravity," "Harborcoat," "Crazy," "Maps and Legends," "Hyena," "Shaking Through," "Driver 8," "Good Advices," "Sitting Still," "So. Central Rain," "Swans," "Can't Get There," "7 Chinese Bros.," "Auctioneer," "Kensey," "Pretty Persuasion," "Life and How," (encores) "Gardening at Night," "9–9," "Wind Out" (a cappella unknown), "Second Guessing," "Rockville," "Little America," "See No Evil."

R.E.M. is tired and rushes through several numbers. Some *Fables* tracks are a bit ragged, but they make up for this by resurrecting stellar versions of older tunes. "Sitting Still": Bill and Mike add "woo-ooh" backing harmonies as Michael points at them; he intro's it as "another happy song." "Gardening at Night": a chestnut surprise, enhanced by stage manager Curtis Goodman who uses the music stand to "shovel" while silhouetted behind the backdrop. "Wind Out": sheer primal punk energy. "Crazy": yup, they played it. Even though this is not the best show of the tour it is marked by some of the finest singing yet. The harmonies are absolutely chilling and mesh perfectly with Stipe's uncanny sense of melody and rhythm. There are nice a cappella interludes, too. At the end, Mike Mills unstraps his bass and exits as the vocalist keeps going. "Act of God or act of man? Seventy Six." Watt has strapped on a guitar, so Mills returns and once again it's a travel back to CBGBs with "See No Evil." "Good Night—drive safely."

Post-gig: A lot of fans hang out near the stage, as there is no hospitality room available. Just as well, for this is like a low-key party with rapping and laughing and renewing of old acquaintances; none of the friends-of-the-promoter type schmoozing. Todd and D. Boon debate the relative merits of the Meat Puppets. Me, I just enjoy the camaraderie.

The Review: Charlotte

Whether they know it or not, Charlotte concert-goers got one of the year's more unique shows on Friday, December 13, at the Park Center. Not only was it the closing date of R.E.M.'s grueling tour that began back in April (as "Preconstruction"), covering the entire U.S. as well as U.K. and Europe ("Reconstruction"); there were also a number of surprises, trimmings and chestnuts that befitted the holiday season and demonstrated the band's commitment to their fans—and to rock 'n' roll.

Perhaps all present did sense, as the concert progressed, that they were witnessing something special; for the capacity audience was both reverently appreciative during the quieter moments and wildly responsive during the rowdier ones. This tour has drawn fans from R.E.M.'s college legions, of course; but high school MTV freaks seemed to form the bulk of the pulsating floor-standers, oblivious to the crush and intent on the party at hand. More than just the usual groomed and plumed concert fashion parade, this show contained a tangible spark of youth that added to the basic rock 'n' roll excitement. The beer on sale at the stands no doubt fueled a few fires as well.

Opening act the Minutemen, playing one of their final gigs as it would later turn out, went straight for the jugular and did the confrontational bit. Blasts of noise and sheer cacophony alternately baffled and angered much of the crowd. Some of us understood, however.

R.E.M. setlist: "Gravity," "Harborcoat," "Pills," "Maps and Legends," "Sitting Still," "Fall on Me," "Green Grow the Rushes," "Hyena," "So. Central Rain," "Swans," "Ghost Riders," "Can't Get There," "Seven Chinese Bros.," "Dream," "Auctioneer," "Kensey," "Gardening at Night," "9–9," "Pretty Persuasion," "Little America," (encores) "Second Guessing," "Time after Time," "See No Evil," "Just a Touch," "Driver 8," "Life and How to Live It."

From opening P.A. tape "Ballad of Jed Clampett" (replacing the customary sound of an approaching diesel train), to the closing whistles of "The Andy Griffith Theme," R.E.M. presented a show that reaffirmed and reveled in their uniqueness. Michael Stipe's between-song homespun tales of woodcarvers, drunks and dreamers cemented and celebrated the regional, oral traditions. And his good-natured onstage persona tended to recall that permanent fixture of small towns everywhere, the Town Character. Dressed in an odd array of ill-fitting layers and a homemade paper hat, Stipe danced/whirled/flailed as if suffering from too potent a batch of moonshine, all the while moaning/crooning/slurring his obtuse yet powerfully evocative lyrics. Fellow kinfolk Peter Buck, Mike Mills and Bill Berry similarly filled the stage with more movement than a cloggin' showdown, more sound than a hollerin' contest. It was a rich and delicious as one of Aunt Bea's pies and as intimate and joyous as a Founder's Day Parade.

Yet, an R.E.M. show is no '80s version of Goose Creek Symphony. It is a thoroughly modern carnival (of sorts) of the true spirit of rock 'n' roll, the indefinable beast that certainly claims its roots as Southern (from the plantation slaves through Robert Johnson through Chuck Berry and Jerry Lee Lewis and Elvis and . . .) but ultimately transcends regions, cultures and decades to encompass everything that is both real and mythical. At an R.E.M. concert, a music fan can experience the joys of love and the concomitant heartaches; the innocent dreams of childhood and the darker nightmares of later years; the vibrant erotica that infuses rock and the delicious decadence that surrounds it as well.

The highlights were many and memorable.

Fables of the Reconstruction was ably represented. Naturally, "Can't Get There from Here" drew the loudest cheers of recognition; it's a fun song to goof with and said goofing ensued, Stipe doing his video knees-akimbo chicken dance as imitations were spawned throughout the hall. "Gravity" has grown from an LP experiment to an ominous, surreal show-opener that informs the novice concertgoer, "This will be a different kind of show." (And it is; few bands allow themselves a "random" setlist as R.E.M. does, and a fan expecting "all the hits" or note perfect renditions of LP cuts will go away, at the very least, surprised.) "Maps and Legends" has also expanded in aural stature since its vinyl debut, throbbing and resonating with an anthemic force of epic proportions as the green-and-purple lighting scheme visually magnifies the wall of sound. "Kensey" is another slower piece, a bass-heavy, moody tale of (ahem) A Town Character. And "Auctioneer," "Driver 8" and "Life and How to Live It" fulfill the needs of the most ardent headbanger, completing the full circle with supercharged energy to spare.

It is worth noting some of Stipe's song intros, for they have become an integral part of an R.E.M. show. The age-old complaint is that the lyrics can't be understood, so on this tour he began giving brief explanations. "Kensey" was certainly the most popular in that respect, as Stipe had a number of "Chapters" with which to depict the sometimes hilarious, sometimes poignant, always fascinating Mr. Kensey, a Howard Finster "aide." The story might be about Kensey's mishaps at the bluejean factory; or it might be the ever-popular coffin story in which Kensey played dead in a coffin and had a friend drive him down to the local Piggly Wiggly. The friend would beckon a local woman over to check Kensey out, and when she leaned over the coffin he'd suddenly pop his eyes open and holler, "Boo!" (Michael: "She'd be doing backwards cartwheels in the parking lot—scared the shit out of 'em everytime!")

"Auctioneer" was prefaced by a description of some correspondence between Michael and Caroline where they decided that it was time to get away from all the bullshit and start a new nation. They'd need several things to get it off the ground: a battle hymn ("preferably more hymn than battle!"), a preamble ("We the people (pause) do not like (pause) green eggs and ham. We do not like them, Sam I Am!"), and a mode of transportation—the trains. ("Get rid of all the Chevvies, all the Fords, all the Toyotas.")

"Maps and Legends": "There was this man named Elija Pierce. He used to live in Columbus, Ohio. He had a barbershop and when he wasn't cutting hair he was carving little things out of wood. He died last year. The Columbus Museum of Art bought up all his little pieces of wood and now he's famous. This song is for him."

At other shows during the tour, Stipe might intro "Fall on Me" with a story about the acid rain descending over Canada. Or he would tell of the man who lived in a split level house (psychologically, that is) and left behind a closet full of books entitled "Life and How to Live It." Tonight Stipe took a biting political tack between "Green Grow the Rushes" and the unreleased track "Hyena":

"This is our last night. Very seldom do I get to explain things in such a manner as this. That song is taken from an old folk song. When the American soldiers went marching into Mexico they sang it. They sang, 'Green grow the rushes go.' That's where the word 'gringo' came from, and that's why we're called gringos by Mexican people now. Here's another gringo song. This one, and the last one as well, somehow involve the food chain. There's big fish and medium fish and little fish. Big fish is the United States. Medium Fish is Mexico. Little Fish is Guatemala. One eats the other one up. One gets bigger. . . ."

Also noteworthy was the presence of several chestnuts and two new gems. "Fall on Me" was a midtempo, Everly Brothers sounding tune (indeed, the evening's set included "Dream"), and gave ample proof that Mike Mills is no mere backup singer. "Swans" was reflective and lonely, the newest tune. Michael was still experimenting with the phrasing and timing of its lyrics, which were attached to a music stand brought out by one of the crew. A lovely, delicate ballad, "Swans" followed the sparse vocal/guitar–only version of "So. Central Rain" and gently waltzed and capered throughout the hall on the wings of acoustic guitars, never stopping to look back, but still imparting a tentative bit of melancholy that reinforced the sad images of the preceding tune. (Before the tears could roll, the electrics were donned and it was off into an instrumental "Ghost Riders in the Sky"—spaghetti surf's up, hodaddys.) The chestnuts included "Sitting Still," which is a happy song made happier by the addition of those folky "woo-ooh" Bill and Mike harmonies; "Time after Time," relaxing, and seeming to tie the band to their fans even more tightly than before as together we pondered the tangible energy transfer of the connection, an invocation of concerts both past and future; and the total surprise of the show, "Just a Touch," coming as it does from the deep R.E.M. past:

"Well, it's been eight long months and we haven't seen home. We're mighty tired and we're mighty alone: My feet (looking down, after gripping the mikestand, to see that it has been firmly taped to the floor by the crew between encores) are taped to the stage. [laughs] The crew think they're funny! They are 13 men strong . . . in the papers they talk about how we're reviving—they talk about the Minutemen delivering on the promise of hardcore. Which is shit! They talk about us ringing in the New Southern Heritage. Which is shit! So we decided to switch shit with the Minutemen. Now *they're* ringing in the New Southern Heritage and we're gonna bring on the promise of hardcore. In that vein, here's a lovely song from way back when. This one goes back about 500 years. . . ."

Yeah, it was a special evening. A loose, party feeling, like having the guys over to jam in your living room. All three Minutemen came out to help out on the cover of Television's "See No Evil"; Michael snarled the lyrics while a four-guitar army riffed mightily and the whole stage sang choruses with gusto. Mike Watt cracked up the band by singing a little song, then grinning and saying, "We are living in the material world, and we are just material dudes. This is the most real band I've met east of Hollywood!"

The "End Reconstruction" sign was brought out during the final encores. The entire house was dancing. Wine coolers were sprayed and ceremonially emptied over band members' heads. The crew, assorted friends, Jefferson Holt and "Fucking Trump" were all thanked.

Impressions Five: Charlotte

Hanging around after the show, a *Spin* photog fumbles to get his camera flash warmed up. Starry-eyed 13-year-old Ron Faulkner, the world's biggest young R.E.M. fan, gets his Hib-Tone 45 sleeve autographed and admires a Mike Mills bass string that was given to him. Lotsa Athens friends sit around in a circle, smiling and winding down. We check out some of Caryn's photos for the *BoB* article. Equipment is gathered; words

The group, 1986. *Photo © Stephanie Chernikowski.*

are taped to a lonely music stand. Mike Watt proudly wears Michael's paper hat. D. Boon sits quietly and happily in a chair. "Amazing show, loved it!" I enthuse, "Thanks, man, so did we, so did we," Boon says. I grin and shake his hand.

TOM MORTON

SOUTHERN ACCENTS (1986)

Melody Maker, *September 6, 1986*

Athens bakes in the Georgia summer sun like a clapboard gingerbread town, soft and sticky and sweet amid the orange groves. The houses range from Waltonesque single-storeys to gigantic Tara-like edifices, all pillars and flagpoles and Old Glory dripping past coitally in the aching heat. This is what proud locals like to term "little London," hip city USA, home to the B52s, 10,000 Maniacs, Love Tractor, Guadalcanal Diary (recently located) up-and-comers like the Kilkenny Cats. And, of course, R.E.M.

Mid-afternoon, and I'm in the Uptown Lounge, one of the two main rock venues in town, a quintessentially rawk 'n' roooall dive/bar, raffish and romantic with the odor of a hundred lost bands. I'm spilling Budweiser all over the floor, shivering in the air-conditioned iciness, when in rides Michael Stipe.

On a bicycle. With a screech of brakes, he halts next to the diminutive stage, leans his transport against a wall. Hi Michael. He looks normal. Considering that the last time I saw the great man in Glasgow he had peroxided, short hair, wristwatches in unlikely places and the word DOG written in felt pen across his forehead, this is something of a relief. He's very stubbled, be-hatted (disreputably), with wads of longish brown hair poking down over his ears.

He looks a bit like a less ravaged Tom Waits. He appears to have nothing written on his forehead. He is wearing one wristwatch on his left wrist. We arrange to meet later to conduct an interview, obviously not a task he relishes. I raise my bottle of Bud to him as he cycles out of the door.

Life's Rich Pageant, the new LP, is a fierce, sprawling testament to R.E.M.'s maturing genius. Compared to the meandering, mysterious indulgences of last year's *Fables of the Reconstruction, Pageant* draws on the myriad influences, components, myths, mysteries and magic evident in all three previous albums and sets them in a crisply recorded, vitally aggressive rock 'n' roll context. From the opening Stones/Velvets ferocity of

Stipe, 1986. *Photo © Stephanie Chernikowski.*

"Begin the Begin," through the soaring, anthemic "Cuyahoga" to the oddly charming psychedelic trash cover "Superman" (spot the Nietzschean overtones), this is easily the most approachable LP yet, as has been proved by its almost immediate playlisting on American FM radio. Producer Don Gehman (John Cougar Mellencamp, the Blasters) and engineer Greg Edwards must take huge dollops of credit for this.

But Stipe remains the enigma at the center of this newly commercial band. His lyrics have never been so clearly discernible as on the new record, nor so obviously addressed to contemporary America and its huge, escalating paradoxes. The plea of "Cuyahoga" to "put our heads together . . . start a new country up" is a cry from the heart of democracy for a return to mystical, pre-white settler roots. Yet the tortuous, almost Morrissey-like, perverse daftness of "I believe in coyotes . . . and time as an abstract" almost comes into the bizarre realm of past lines like "I dream of aborigines" from *Murmur.*

Michael, are you a pretentious bastard, or what?

"I draw from every situation, everything I come across. That's something I feel I'm really lucky in. I see everything and can apply it to everything else. I make a real easy correlation between things I don't think your average person can make correlations with. I'm always completely thrilled, wherever I am. Something will intrigue me, like a moth to lightbulb."

I sit and drink iced coffee in this unlikely bohemian café called, uh, True Confections, and ponder. But seriously . . .

"I find wonder in the most ordinary little everyday things. I really like sweeping. I get great joy out of sweeping—and typing. Typing is a real meditative experience for me. To sit down and type . . . anything. It doesn't matter what it is—I'll copy a book. . . ."

Hum . . . Sounds pretty damn hippyish to me. However, the problem with this kind of Stipe statement is that his undoubtedly bizarre ideologies are leavened with a mordant and sometimes impenetrable sense of humor. What about his infamous statement that the new album sounds "like two oranges being nailed together," as printed in *Rolling Stone*?

"That was a joke. I can't believe that they printed it—*Rolling Stone* is the stupidest magazine in the world. Basically there happened to be two oranges and a nail in front of me when I said that. I think a lot of the humor in R.E.M. goes unnoticed, but it's definitely there, there's a good amount of comedy. There has to be humor, even in the most dire situations."

I'm reminded of the Smiths, whose black depressive comedy has to be the most misunderstood extended joke since the Jesus and Mary Chain.

"Yeah, I think Morrissey's pretty funny. I enjoy reading his interviews. I saw him perform . . . in Brixton, I think. The first album, I thought it was . . . meandering. But there's a real lilting quality. . . . He's very funny on stage. I really enjoyed it."

Surely you invite misunderstanding, given the obscurantist approach you adopt to lyric writing?

"I just kind of present it. It's up to whoever listens to it to take it in. As I see it. I write the words and sing them the way I want to. I don't cater to anyone but myself and the other three members of the band. Those are the only opinions which matter to me, as far as how a song turns out in the end, how it's performed and what it means."

So you don't want to communicate?

"Well, outside of that, it's nice if people get it. It's really nice if people understand what I'm trying to get across especially with something like the material on the new record. I feel there's a good amount there—I would hope people would listen to it and draw something from it, maybe. But if they want to listen to it while they wash the dishes or if they just want to dance to it . . . that's fine."

Sounds like Springsteen methodology, that.

"I admire Springsteen. I think the only thing we have in common is a dick and two arms."

Stipe's "musical influences" are hard to pin down, counterpointing the more obvious rock historiography of Messrs. Buck, Berry, and Mills. Blues, folk, Appalachian front porch music, something called the Mackintosh Country Shouters, Mahalia Jackson, are all mentioned, but . . .

"I never really listened to music until oh, Wire and Television, that stuff from '75 and '76. I had no idea at all what happened in the Sixties. Most of the covers we do live, I've never heard the original. They just say well, here are the words, and I do them."

What about the effect of working with three other personalities in the band? Doesn't he ever feel the need to work outside of that? He's recently been co-fronting, with Natalie of 10,000 Maniacs (supposed girlfriend, rumor freaks), the Golden Palominos, a folkie contrast to the Hindu Love Gods. Peter, Mike and Bill's collaboration with lost hero Warren Zevon.

"Yeah, maybe. But not using words, but other things. With the band, I kind of have to keep myself in check because a lot of weight is put on the words at times. I'm representing four people and not just myself, so if I have a particular viewpoint—political or what have you . . . religious, colloquial . . . that the other guys don't share, it's really unfair."

Ever find that frustrating?

"I guess I do in a way. But a song, like 'I Believe' on the new album is . . . it says it all."

R.E.M. have now quite consciously rooted themselves in Athens, in the South with its plastic Last-Supper tablecloth religion, its social idiosyncrasies. How does this environment affect you?

"There's this history of Southern politeness. In New York, they're brash, they shout at each other and it's a game to see how much you can offend someone and how they'll offend you back. Down here it's politeness. They're incredibly polite. It probably goes back hundreds of years to when crazy Aunt Beulah May would tear off all her clothes and run around the garden naked. People were too polite to say anything. The point is that eccentricities are a bit more tolerated here than in other parts of the country."

Given Michael's proclivities towards driving about Athens in a yellow checker taxicab and garbled tales of a past life which included periods spent naked in the street, this is perhaps just as well. What about the religious atmosphere?

"I'm not religious in that way—I would say I draw a lot from religion—this is the very belt buckle of the Bible Belt. It's fascinating—in the same way as I find geology is fascinating. It's easier here to go watch people worship than it is to go look at rocks. It's fascinating from an outsider's point of view. But I have a sort of insider's point of view as well—my grandfather's a Southern Methodist minister."

Time to go. Tomorrow I meet Mike Mills, the chirpy bass guitarist who looks like one of the Kids from *Fame*. But there's two aspects of Michael's aesthetic tastes which interest me. First movies . . .

"I like films. I'm more visually orientated than anything else, but I'd rather go and watch the sun set. That sounds really hippy, but . . . there. It's different every night and you don't have to pay three dollars to see it. But I like films a lot—Wim Wenders, Fellini, Peter Weir."

Wristwatches?

"I have a really good one now. I'm going to try and hang on to it. It has two jewels. Most of them have 17."

Michael Stipe wanders off into the night with a very beautiful girl and a young guy in full Alice Cooper make-up and clothes. Stipe shakes my hand. "Is that the only bag you've got?" He indicates my camera, tape recorder, cigarette container with that hypnotic stare of his. Well, nearly. "I like a man who travels light." Quite.

Next day. To the R.E.M. offices, all hi-tech, computers and the coolest air conditioning yet. Geoff Trump, amiable and English tour manager, is saying things like "Get me the rider disc" to various members on staff. Manager Jefferson Holt apologizes for not showing up, he's hurt his back. Then wheech! We swoop off in a 1968 Born-to-Run Oldsmoble convertible to pick up Mike, who's as fizzy as a bottle of Lucozade, and . . . hungry. So am I. It's Rocky's pizzeria and . . . buffalo chicken wings all round. Heineken beer in iced glasses. Hangover? Vanishing. New Album?

"Really pleased with it."

Munch. What do you make of Michael's lyrics and the man's . . . approach?"

"Well, Michael's not going to write about love and cars and girls . . . we all have a veto. If there's a song or a decision that one person can't abide, it's out. The only thing that Michael did this time that I can't stand—the song on the record which begins 'Swan, Swan, Hummingbird . . .' on the sleeve it's called 'Swan, Swan H.' I didn't know he was going to do that, I hate it."

"He does things to be different, that's great, it makes us different from other bands, and I like that. But that's just a little too much, too far towards pretension."

We talk about Don Gehman, and the way his production approach has worked to the band's advantage ("Who else is there? We wanted someone who would make us sound like a band, really clearly and crisply, and he did that.") and then the conversation drifts back to words, and Mr. Stipe . . .

"He's being more topical than he has been, though for Michael, being topical is like, so what? Who can tell, you know? Some of the songs are more distinctly about something than others, but he still couches those ideas in such oblique phrases you really have to be lucky enough to stumble on where he's coming from."

The point is without Stipe, R.E.M. would be just another Southern punk band with a good record collection and a Rickenbacker 12-string. He's regarded in Athens as an eccentric among eccentrics, if somewhat . . . cultivated. The band seem to regard him with affection fused with headshaking perplexity. He may be just a bit of a poseur, but his oddity and absolutely left-field approach infuses the band with much of their charm and power.

Mike, on the other hand, is dead straight, friendly, honest and talkative. There's a story about how he nearly got into a fight with Iggy Pop at an Athens hotel, and ended up stealing his glasses. "Basically, I like to have a good time," says Mike. I can believe it.

We'll skip the bits about him once, long ago, being arrested for "cavorting nude with a young lady on a water tower." Meanwhile, R.E.M. are preparing for a mega-American tour, which sees them for the first time hitting the 9,000-seater venues in a few places. They're right on the verge. By the next LP, we could be talking stadiums here. Mike?

"I'm not worried. In lots of ways, it gets easier with a bigger crowd. I never thought we'd make the leap from small clubs."

Later that afternoon, I'm driving out of Athens, Buffalo Chicken bones still tangled in my teeth. On the way I pass six Baptist Churches and a very large water tower. I wonder. On the radio, they're playing "Fall on Me," the single from *Life's Rich Pageant*. Out there in America, the stadiums await. Here in the South, well, personally, I believe in coyotes. And Time is an abstract.

DANIEL BROGAN

R.E.M. HAS LITTLE TO SAY AND SAYS IT OBTUSELY (1986)

Chicago Tribune, *October 20, 1986*

Back in college, some friends and I delighted in making eccentric remarks that no one understood. We'd have gotten a lot of mileage out of "What is the frequency, Kenneth?"

Sunday, a band called R.E.M. played at the University of Illinois at Chicago Pavilion, and I couldn't help thinking of those days.

Plenty of people I respect are great fans of this band, and they've worked long and hard to convert me. And from all the interviews I've read, these four guys from Athens, Ga., come across as likeable, level-headed sorts. But while I sing along to the occasional R.E.M. single on the radio, I've been continually underwhelmed by their albums. To be sure, R.E.M. live sounds far more anthemic than on their moody, murky records. Nor does lead singer Michael Stipe mumble the way he does on vinyl, though he still won't be winning any public speaking awards. But even when you can understand him, there doesn't seem to be much in Stipe's purposely obtuse lyrics to latch on to.

Sunday—dressed like a campus bohemian in a top hat and black thrift-shop coat over a white apron—he began the show by singing the opening lyrics to "These Days" with his back to the audience. From then on he was a whirling dervish, dragging his microphone stand along with him as he paced the stage. For a time, this was entertaining. But it soon became routine as he ran through a set that included healthy doses of material from R.E.M.'s recent *Life's Rich Pageant,* as well as the band's three previous albums. Guitarist Peter Buck offered a welcome respite from Stipe's repetitive antics. In fact, for much of the show, I tuned out Stipe and concentrated on Buck's fluid but precise musicianship. At times, Buck reminded me of U2's *Edge* (especially on "Seven Brothers"). At others, his jangly riffs recalled the Searchers. And while his playing was always tasteful, I couldn't help wishing that he would have stepped into the spotlight for a few more solos. Drummer Bill Berry and bassist Mike Mills contributed equally solid rhythms. (Mills also took a lead vocal on "Superman," the band's second single from *Life's Rich Pageant.*)

No band, though, survives on instrumentation alone. Ultimately, it all comes back to Stipe, who seems less interested in saying anything than in making us wonder if he's saying anything. Consider this story he told midway through the evening as an introduction to "Swan Swan H":

"There's a man named Mr. Miller who lives in Gainesville and builds windows. He's 82 years old, and all his life he's had the ability to cure thrush, which is a childhood disease that was very prevalent during the Civil War.

"All he has to do is breathe into the child's mouth three times and the child is cured. Doctors have been sending children to him for years.

"He also has the ability to talk out warts, except that he forgot how to talk out warts. None of which has anything to do with the next song, except the Civil War part."

ROY WILKINSON

THE SECRET FILE OF R.E.M. (1987)

Sounds, *September 12, 1987*

Ronald Wilson Reagan, fortieth President of the United States of America and first stand up comedian of the apocalypse, has scored many notable achievements.

He's slept with a monkey, castigated trees for polluting the atmosphere, become a role model for zombies everywhere and now, perhaps most notably of all, he's got R.E.M.'s Michael Stipe to stop mumbling.

As 1987 draws to a close, it's time for the fifth R.E.M. album.

Their title is *Document* and the keyword is chaos. After their previous two albums *Reconstructions of the Fables/Fables of the Reconstruction* and *Life's Rich Pageant, Document*'s concise, affirmatory title is not accident. These are strange days and consequently this band has decided it's time for plain speaking and intelligible, decipherable singing.

These days, conversation fear must be overcome.

If the key to *Life's Rich Pageant* was "Cuyahoga" with it's longing for regeneration and optimism ("Let's put our heads together / Let's start a new country up") then a clue to *Document* can be found in "Strange" with its chorus, "There's something strange going on tonight/There's something going on that's not quite right."

Through *Document*'s first side ("Welcome to the Occupation," "Exhuming McCarthy," "Disturbance at the Heron House," "Strange," "It's the End of the World as We Know It [and I Feel Fine]"), the titles reverberate with a confused, ill boding portent. Something's wrong, the lunatics have taken over the asylum but it's too late to do anything but nervously laugh about it.

As the band plays on it's apocalypse tomorrow.

Peter Buck, the band's born again Rickenbacker kid and premier spokesman, is over here to work with Robyn Hitchcock but he's also taking time out to unravel this strange composite of resignation and defiance, an album where happily wound up amps spit at Armageddon.

"Sometimes you're on the merry go round and it's going out of control. You know it and I know but you look at the Government and they don't seem to know it."

"The last couple of albums have had stuff like this on them, especially 'Cuyahoga' and 'These Days.' I know that Michael felt a little more . . . he like the rest of us in the band are pretty pissed off by the way our Government's run. Y'know, the policies in Central America. We have loads of bombs over here in Europe and we don't want them over here any more than you all do."

On *Life's Rich Pageant*, if Stipe was confronting a celestial ceiling collapse with "Fall on Me," then with *Document* the walls seem to be giving way. The sky threatens to fall in.

I always took the line "buy the sky and sell the sky" from "Fall on Me" to be a reference to Ronnie's arch deluding Strategic Defense Initiative. It seemed that Ronald with the confused graft of biblical gibberish and haphazardly assimilated business speak that makes up his mind, would be just the person to confront the threat of a space born death attack by attempting to paper up the heavens with a billion dollar array of satellites.

Nowadays he distracts himself with a pattern of local aggression and apocalypse teeters on the horizon. Peter Buck, a self confessed "adult, fairly reasonable person," isn't too enchanted by Ron's increasingly errant last fling.

"It's not like it's a slide to cynicism but sometimes you do feel kind of helpless. All you have to do is turn on the television and be surrounded and inundated by complete lies from people who are supposed to be running the country. I think America is on a downward slide and is going to make some big, bad mistakes."

Document may be tempered by a feeling of inevitability but this shouldn't imply that the band aren't remonstrating. Check out R.E.M., political power brokers, and Michael Stipe, electoral advisor.

"Michael always says think local and act local—we have been doing a lot of stuff in our town to try and make it a better place. We work a lot for local environmental protection and we helped elect the congressman for our district. We supported him and did commercials for him."

The thought of Athens (city NE Ga., pop. 42,549) coping with an electoral address of Stipian obliqueness is a striking one.

"They used 'Fall on Me' in the background and Michael just spoke over it: This is Michael Stipe of R.E.M., vote for Whytchfowler for this reason. . . ."

"It was kind of funny. I was driving 'round Atlanta visiting my mom and then comes on the Big '96 Rock, the big local, dinosaur behemoth radio station and there's one of our songs and Michael explaining why you should vote for this guy."

Not that the involvement ends there.

"I've seen him get up at City Council meetings and say things. That's always fairly strange. Michael isn't the most linear guy. His lyrics are fairly representative of the way he is. The things he says in City Council are fairly amusing to say the least, totally befuddling to these old Baptist guys that run the Council.

"You have to attend the Council meetings if you want to complain about things. The latest one is the Baptist church wanting to put up a 200 foot tower to broadcast the word of the Lord . . . in my neighborhood. It's like, I don't want a tower there, they're already broadcasting from some-where else. F*** this."

R.E.M. have always found the notion of patriotism a problematic one. From the exhaustive American rock heritage file that is Peter Buck's mind to the cast of down-home, musical isolationists that Michael Stipe is continually finding and/or inventing, to the widescreen hints of American myth that runs through his lyrics, R.E.M. obviously love America. But as Stipe says their notion of patriotism is an ideal not a reality.

And now as '50s American dress imposes a retroactive sartorial impe-rialism on these isles, a bona fide '50s spirit is getting the upper hand in America. The reality of American patriotism is diverging ever further from R.E.M.'s ideal.

"Reagan is going to get us in all these little brush fires, little fights, because he's scared of communists. It doesn't make any sense at all. It's all coming back—commie hunting I'm sure will return."

"You're honorable, more honorable than me / Loyal to the Bank of America/You're sharpening stones, walking on coals / To improve your business acumen / Vested interest, united tie, landed gentry rationalize / by jingo, buy America"—"Exhuming McCarthy"

It's songs like this that highlight R.E.M.'s newfound desire to communicate very directly.

"Yeah, musically and lyrically that is kind of unusual for us. My favorite line is that *landed gentry rationalize*. Sometimes you just look around with disgust."

"Exhuming McCarthy" comes down on self-seeking in desperate times. As Peter says, poverty is relatively uncommon in America but as the recession bites, the purely selfish instinct for self-preservation is being rationalized into the ever acquisitive yuppie lifestyle, just as no one admits to voting for Ronnie, no one admits to being a yuppie. Yet they're everywhere.

"You can't believe how many people are really into that thing of making money. As if it means anything."

"I think that one of the things that Michael was writing about had to do with the whole flag waving thing. Though I like Bruce Springsteen, sometimes his songs get misrepresented as Ya Hoo America stuff. That's so disgusting to see a crowd of people waving flags and thinking your country is great when in fact we're going through a dangerous period—hiding their heads in the sand and trying to make money."

Songs like "Lightnin' Hopkins" and "Oddfellows Local" are more traditional R.E.M. fare. "Lightnin' Hopkins" follows the more usual Stipe lyric method of homing in cinematically on the subject, as Peter explains.

"I bought some Lightnin' Hopkins albums and came straight down to practice from the record store. We started playing them and Michael started singing about Hopkins.

"It's not really a tribute. In fact Michael told me to say that it doesn't mean anything, that it's utter bullshit. There's the weird verse about camera directions—it almost seemed like it was a film of someone filming a black person. It's kind of vaguely about being black. Since it was about Lightnin' Hopkins I put that shitty slide guitar on—I really am the world's worst slide guitar player."

"Oddfellows Local" returns to a favorite Stipe character type, the mythical railroad hoppin' bum or, in this case, the common or garden wino.

"There used to be Oddfellows Lodges all over the town, just like the Mooses or the Shriners.

"The song actually is about these winos who used to live down the street from us. They used to live in cars—we call them the Motor Club. These old guys would sleep in the cars and drink all the time. I think there was a guy called Pee Wee as well. Michael knew them because he lived

Mills, 1986. *Photo © Stephanie Chernikowski.*

right next door to them. Every once in a while you'd give them five bucks or drop off a bottle."

While making increasingly fewer interview appearances, Stipe maintains responsibility for R.E.M.'s visual representation. Designing the album sleeves, and directing the videos, he furnishes material that while hardly achieving maximum exposure for the band's faces has been critically acclaimed. As usual the sleeve for *Document* is a little obtuse and comes decked out with the familiar array of arcane inscriptions, a mysterious litany of names and titles.

"I think he gets it from Dr. Bonner's soap. Dr. Bonner is this crazy mystic who puts this peppermint soap out in this big bottle. The bottle has paper wrapped all around it . . . with this religious and visionary writing that the guy has and he's been doing it for about 50 years. He talks about the Pope, about communism and about one God, all faiths, yes man type stuff. I think that's where Michael gets his inspiration for all this stuff like Allied Five Document, Consolate Mediator, V Pres in Charge of Mike Mills and Ambassador J. W. Holt."

And as R.E.M. prepare to play their only UK date this year. R.E.M.ophiles everywhere will be contemplating Stipe's appearance. Will he be wearing a watch around his neck, will he have shaved his head or will he have dyed his hair blond and his eyebrows purple? Apparently not.

"He's got long hair. The shaving of the eyebrows was a particularly ugly phase he went through. This whole year he had really long hair and he looked really good. Then he wanted to shave his head and it was like, Michael, don't shave your head, you've got a funny shaped head. He looks healthy, he looks like Popeye."

As R.E.M. stands for rapid eye movement, the means by which unconscious brain activity is measured during sleep, it seems only fit to ask what Popeye dreams of. The answer's provided by their current single, "The End of the World as We Know It"—the dream features Leonard Bernstein, Lenny Bruce, Leonid Brezhnev and Lester Bangs.

"That was a dream that Michael had. It's kind of an apocalyptic dream. We did go to Lester Bangs' birthday party though."

The song goes on "Symbiotic, Patriotic, slam, butt, neck, right!"

Right Mike!

MAT SMITH

WELCOME TO THE OCCUPATION (1987)

Melody Maker, *September 12, 1987*

"You can't tell anyone you came here."

Michael Stipe mutters this as we pull up in the drive of his house, the humid night air alive with the chatter of crickets, brown recluse spiders and rattlesnakes. Stipe has learned the importance of protecting himself from the inquisitive glare of the unhappy, unbalanced and downright undesirables who turn up on his porch from nowhere, seeking words of wisdom or comfort from someone they see as the closest we've got to an Eighties rock 'n' roll guru.

For that reason the house is now strictly off limits, and, if it is possible to hint f*** off, then a notice, pinned on the door does so with characteristic Stipean charm. Once inside it's easy to see why. Common courtesy and respect for his privacy forbids any description of the interior—suffice to say it's a magical place. An R.E.M. LP cover brought to life.

The last train to Disneyworld left the station just as R.E.M. guitarist Peter Buck was waking that morning. Blinking his way across the bedroom he switched on the TV and was, once again, confronted by the Reverend Ike, who as usual, was frothing at the mouth.

"I want you to send me your money! And I don't mean that jingling kind cos that only makes me nervous. I want the folding cash! Cos I need a new Cadillac. God told me, I need a new Cadillac! I don't want my pie in the sky—I want my pie now!"

That was when Buck knew that R.E.M. had to make an album about America, 1987. America '87 and its surreal madness. Its attempts to revive the spirit of McCarthyism, its clandestine operations in Nicaragua and the blatant ones in the Gulf. The insatiable desire for money, murder and madness—everything that, to him, a young American, meant one thing—Disneyworld.

"It's a sideways look at the world and us. It has a kind of Orwellian wry humor. It's not that we're making light of America, it's just that I can't look at it the way Bruce Springsteen does. To me, America in 1987 is Disneyworld."

Buck pulls apart the slats on a Venetian blind and peers out into the Athens sun which is nudging 100 degrees. He surveys the quiet streets around the R.E.M. office, a last bastion of sanity in a country gone bonkers.

The evening before we arrived in Athens, R.E.M. had played an unannounced gig at the neighboring 40 Watt Club—rumors of which had shot round the close-knit community like a synapse, ensuring that the club was overflowing by the time they took the stage. According to eyewitnesses, they tore through a selection of new material and just one old song "Begin the Begin" from *Life's Rich Pageant*.

The experience had left them excited and obviously eager to talk. Even the infamously hard to pin down Stipe appeared relaxed, almost eager to please, if somewhat distracted by his friend's dog Joey, who he was looking after for the day.

R.E.M.'s last studio LP, *Life's Rich Pageant*, was characterized as much by the directness of the songs themselves as by Don Gehman's lushly textured production. The man behind John Cougar and the Blasters, Gehman grabbed R.E.M.'s intangible, intransitory meanderings by where their balls should be, and sculpted them into something very nearly approaching pop. Surprising, then, that *Document,* the revised title for *Disneyworld,* should be an almost complete about face, if anything, capturing the band in even heavier sepia tones than their pre-*Pageant* days. Was this desire to trip it all down and get back to basics a reaction against the highly polished sheen of *Pageant,* an unhappiness with a direction they'd not envisaged being pushed in perhaps?

"No, not at all," Buck explains, walking away from the window as the blinds snap shut. "Every record is a process of reacting against the prior one. I was really happy with *Pageant* but none of us wanted to make that record again. I think we made the perfect record we could in that style and the new songs, because of the way we wrote them, wouldn't have lent themselves to that big AOR thing.

"We always go into the studio with a set idea but it never comes out that way. It's hard to write to order. I think this time we wanted a really big sound with lots of chaotic stuff on top. Big in a way that Peter Gabriel records would be, but not as clean—full of weirdness, backwards stuff and noise."

Document is, at times, both more violent and more whimsical than any other R.E.M. LP to date, yet is less exact in the way it executes its intentions, displaying an almost cavalier attitude to any notion of conventional songwriting or playing.

"Well, we've been trying to write songs lately that are a little less form following," Mike Mills explains. "We're trying to write a little more musically nonsensical."

"Yeah," Buck interrupts, "I'm probably the worst for this, I'm the one who has to have a chorus in each song. But there are three or four songs in this LP which just don't have a chorus in the accepted sense, which is neat. Van Morrison has a lot of songs that don't have choruses and it's hard to work that into a rock 'n' roll perspective, but we wanted the songs to flow a little bit more and be divided less into anything like verse-bridge-chorus. Where's the bridge? Well the bridge is where the verse and chorus aren't."

So there was absolutely no intention of making a commercial LP then?

"I don't have a clue what commercial means." Michael Stipe deadpans as he's yanked into the room by Joey. "To me, commercial is 'Sledgehammer' or Gang of Four."

Stipe's vocals are pared down almost to a shout on *Document,* while

Buck's guitars screech and soar against them, defying the gravity of each particular song. In a way, Buck's guitar work plays much the same role on *Document* as Stipe's voice did on *Pageant,* and what few layers there are on the LP are stacked by him.

"It is our most male record," Stipe says, tongue in cheek as he disappears to fetch a bowl of water for his canine companion, never to be seen again that afternoon. Buck takes up the conversation.

"It seemed that on the last record, there was very little room for guitars because of all the keyboard parts. This time I got a bit greedy." He grins wickedly.

"It was a kind of release," Mike Mills continues. "We were coming out of the winter and we were itching to get it going so we really attacked it."

Document was recorded in Nashville with Scott Litt who Buck admired for his "Dare I admit? Big modern drum sound." For all its music biz connections Buck claims that Nashville was essentially a quiet town which soon succumbed to the R.E.M. way of doing things.

"Every night we'd finish at around one, go to a bar and meet the same five people." The band describe the sessions as easy going, a far cry from those for *Fables of the Reconstruction,* which from a safe distance, they now admit came close to causing a split within the band as well as a personal crisis for Buck.

"I think we were all kind of miserable," the guitarist explains. "I hate to say it, but it was raining every day in England and we were all going through these weird pressures and I think that every band goes through these times when you think: 'Do I want to be in a rock 'n' roll band?' We were at the point where we could feel ourselves getting sucked into the business. I was pretty much a wreck for most of that time.

"I was just drunk all the time. It's not that I didn't care, I was just depressed a hell of a lot and it showed within the band. I think we were thinking 'Why can't we just be hippies and say f*** the record? We don't want to do it we're going home.' In the end we worked through it. If we were to record those songs now, in a similar mental state to what we were in at the time, they would be very different. I do like that record. I'm not saying it was a failure. I mean, rock 'n' roll isn't showbiz, we don't have to be happy. F*** it. As weird as that album can get, that's how I felt every day. The thing that sums it up is that bit at the end of 'Feeling Gravity's Pull' where the strings come in and it goes down 'Neargh!' I probably looked like that too."

Document shares a similar intensity but, by and large, it's developed into an intrinsic theme rather than a state of mind. From the unstoppable droning folk of the LP's opening tour de force, "Finest Worksong," to the Thirties' WPA-style social realist murals which adorn the cover, its central themes can scarcely be denied. Much later that same night, in his favorite pizza parlor, Stipe puts it all into perspective.

"In America, if you can't make money, they think it's because you're a failure. The work ethic is really intrinsic to American thought and that has a lot to do with this LP. The idea that you can work and work and get what you want and then try for even more. It's the American dream but it's a pipe dream that's been exploited for years. I could get by without money, I've done it before. You can get by in this town without money, it's not a necessity. But it's kinda gross what money does to you. Businessmen say hello to me on the street now. They acknowledge me when I go into a nice restaurant. They let me put my bike in the kitchen at the best restaurant in town. I can wear a smelly tee-shirt and they'll take me to the best table. It's really gross."

The likes of the Reverend Ike and his ilk offering the promised land at a price also meet with due disdain, this time from Buck.

"That whole faith thing is something that goes through American culture like a knife. It has done for years. At the turn of the century I guess it was a big thing. Amiee McPherson and Father, er, what's that bastard's name? But he was a crook too. They all were. There's this American evangelical, Hucksterism, America's full of religious nuts. They all come here for that reason. They got kicked out of their own countries. My family came over from Sweden because they were agnostics and atheists. They came here to get away from that.

"That's why, when you compare our songs to writers like Flannery O'Connor and Carson McCullers, I'm flattered but don't quite make the connection. Flannery's characters are all struggling to reconcile their faith to a modern world where faith doesn't play any apparent part. In our case I'd say none of us have got any faith anyway. I don't believe in God."

In the past, many of R.E.M.'s finest songs have walked the fine line between patriotism and gentle celebration of certain elements of American culture. Yet, over the last year, Buck claims to have derived most pleasure from the tainted visions held by Big Black and Sonic Youth. Was theirs a view he'd been tempted to share?

"I dunno. I'm certainly not an apologist for America, though it would be a nice piece of land if you could wipe out most of the people. I think Sonic Youth's vision is very tongue-in-cheek. I don't think you can take all this America 1969 blood and Manson stuff at all seriously. I mean, they haven't killed anyone yet. It's real Alice Cooperish. They're probably just a lot more comfortable with that imagery than I would be. I'm not a blood and guts type guy. All the clothes that I like have skulls on them but, if I wore them, I'd look a dork. I just look at it all differently to them."

Nevertheless, the songs on *Document* are more overtly political and damning than anything they've put their name to before. "Welcome to the Occupation," "Exhuming McCarthy" and "It's the End of the World as We Know It" all rage with a seemingly uncontrollable anger. It's almost as if the passion and poignancy so prevalent on *Fables,* stirred by the spread of inhumanity and decay, had festered and boiled over into blind hatred.

"Well, generally, Michael is really worried about this conservative trend that's going on and the way that people in power seem to look at things." Buck ventures. "Right now Russia has the most sensible leader they've ever had and Reagan is just keeping the door open for more war. Reagan is a moron and that's all there is to it. I get upset when I think about him."

"End of the World" and "Strange," a cover of the old Wire classic, are also among the most powerful and strange vocal performances Stipe has ever laid down. Both are delivered in a speed crazy rush of emotion.

"I wrote the words to 'End of the World' as I sung it. When they showed me that song in the studio I just said, 'It's the end of the world as we know it and I feel fine.' I wanted it to be the most bombastic vocal that I could possibly muster. Something that would completely overwhelm you and drip off your shoulders and stick in your hair like bubblegum.

"'Strange' was a scratch vocal. I went in and sang it twice and said, 'That's it.' I didn't listen to it after that. They took it away and mixed it up and put some reverb on it. I just couldn't be bothered with it. I put a whole load of energy into the other songs and that one was just 'Ugh!' It's like spitting—you don't want to get it over your shirt but you wanna get it out and keep walking."

—

"We've never played before. It's gonna be awful—I can't wait!"

Michael Stipe is musing on the evening's entertainment. Athens' two rock clubs, the 40 Watt and the Uptown Lounge, offer the kind of nightly entertainment and guest appearances that, two or three years ago, would have had the average Brit rock critic salivating for more. Tonight, Stipe and a couple of friends are opening for his sister's band, Cowface. Unfortunately they are awful. Stipe whacking out a guitar drone while two beefcakes bash sheet metal with 10 lb hammers—a more testing Test Department.

A tortuous 30 minutes after it begins, an end is abruptly called and Athens' youth drift back to the bar, unsure whether to laugh or mourn the loss of their eardrums. Only Caitlin liked it and Caitlin, as anyone who's even been in a car that he's driving will know, is quite mad.

In the early hours of the morning, in a parking lot adjacent to The 40 Watt, Stipe unveils his reasons for all the recent extra-curricular activities. This last year has seen him extending his work with the Golden Palominos as well as producing an LP by Hugo Largo, the bassist of whom he met when interviewed by him in New York.

"As a band, what R.E.M. are capable of is still pretty limited when it comes down to it. There's a very set position where I exist. I could never get a sledgehammer on stage and hit metal with R.E.M. I've done it in the early days when we used to play biker bars. I'd wear this globe as a hat and I'd take it off and pound it on stage. The bikers thought I was insane so they left me alone. I think they kinda admired me 'cos I was this really skinny kid with funny hair.

"It's not really a frustration with R.E.M. If anything it's been opened up so wide to us that it's actually dangerous. But we're able to keep things intact and stay on top of each other. R.E.M. now is kinda like the statues that look out on Easter Island." His voice trails away, a trifle embarrassed at the veracity of the comment.

"I don't know why that came to me," he says. "It just did. I can't explain that one. I was trying to make some connection and it didn't happen."

Do you feel there's a responsibility as Michael Stipe to always try and be profound?

"Not really, no. I think my most artesian profundity comes when I have no idea and I'm just rambling. The best time to catch me is when I've had seven cups of coffee and I haven't slept in three days. I just vomit and, if you're there, you can catch the little chunks. I've read some interviews with myself and it's like I could not believe that I had said these things, they are so amazing. It's like Kafka or Jung. It sounds so incredible and underneath it says 'Claims Stipe!' And I just go 'Wow! Something's there after all.'"

The previous evening at a Mexican restaurant the waitress had voiced much the same opinion and had stared in disbelief when we told her we'd spent 10 hours on a plane just to talk to R.E.M.

"We see them in here all the time," she'd said. "Last week Mike Mills left his glasses in here and all the other waitresses were trying them on. It was really funny. Maybe we should have auctioned them."

Athens hardly trades on the reputation of its most famous sons. A tee-shirt here or a poster there modestly proclaiming "Infamous Athenians!" A far cry from the intensity with which Distiples, as they're called in Athens, study the band's output and lyrics, often coming up with the most amazing translations and interpretations.

"I guess I wouldn't have it any other way," says Stipe, slurping at an iced espresso. "If I had a band, I would want people to either love them or despise them. I would hate for them to just go 'Oh yeah.' In a lot of ways, I think people come to the band because they think that I have some kind of answer. I am kind of questioning things in a different way but I'm just as lost as everyone else. So when I'm expected to answer these questions and spout forth with humorous and philosophical anecdotes, sometimes it's difficult."

Stipe's reluctance to talk has led to Peter Buck and Mike Mills tackling most of the interview chores which they do with the geniality of old pros. I wondered whether if it was the inanity or the intensity of the earlier interviews that Stipe found so repellent.

"Well, I don't dislike doing them. It's just actually what comes out of them which is not to my liking. I enjoy talking to people except that it's always me, me me, which is kinda gross. A lot of times in interviews I come across as very sensitive or very dour because when I talk about myself it's like 'Ugh' I get too intense. I'm real reluctant to open up."

Does it hurt when people insist on calling you weird?

"No, I don't care. I've dealt with that all my life. I don't think anybody can hurt me really. I think they're disappointed when they find out how normal I really am. 'Cos I'm not weird."

The memory of a cold night in Glasgow two years ago flashed into my head. An everlasting vision of Stipe careering frantically across the Apollo stage, wearing watches all over his body and with the word "Dog" written in felt-tip across his forehead. This is normal behavior?

"Oh, I was so sick that night," he protests. "I couldn't stand up. I hadn't eaten anything but potatoes for a whole week 'cos the food is so bad in England. All I could eat was a sprig of parsley before I went onstage and I was vomiting and shitting. It was just awful. I felt like a dog so I took a felt tip and wrote it on my face. But I started sweating it off while I was on stage, which looked weird."

There are other rumors though, sightings of him reading books upside down for one! Could he remember the first time that someone remarked that what he was doing was strange or odd?

"You know my earliest memory as a child was when I was two years old and I had scarlet fever. I was hallucinating and I was having my picture taken. I had a sweater on and I was really miserable and there was this guy zooming in and out. To me that was weird but I can't remember people remarking that I was weird. I don't know . . . I think you block those things out."

The following morning he's up bright and early and already sitting by the phone in the R.E.M. office when we call. A pair of plastic sunglasses sit awkwardly on his head held together with a wad of Sellotape over the bridge of the nose. Along the sides he's glued strips of cardboard giving him the appearance of an Athens Terminator. In a truck parked in the street two stories below, 18 globes of the world are stacked neatly ready to be burned and bent out of shape in the video for "Worksong" that Stipe is shooting that afternoon. While he's not nearly as sensitive as he's constantly portrayed, Stipe is an incredibly serious and obsessive artist who never stops work, drawing inspiration from every waking moment and, often as not, every sleeping one. Indeed, he cites his dreams as an often frightening subconscious release.

"I was shot in one dream by this assassin who was sent to kill me. But I didn't die. I was shot point blank but he didn't kill me. In the dream, he was hired to kill me, but he couldn't do so until I looked him in the eyes. He tracked me for a long time and I finally got tired of it so I looked him in the eyes and he shot me. But I didn't die. So then I was wounded and went on for a while, got tired, looked him in the eye and he took an ice pick and stuck it in my temple and killed me."

Despite the unguarded descriptions of dreams, Stipe has learned to hold his tongue on the more mystical side of his nature. He refuses to be drawn into discussing the transgression therapy he is about to undergo, whereby he will be hypnotized and taken back to a past life.

"Well, you know it's really outside the band and I think it would infuriate them if I talked about it. We get enough shit about being hippies already, especially now my hair's long again."

That said, R.E.M. don't really care two hoots or too much about how they're perceived by others. Like every good band, they understand what it is they do that is so unique and are now sitting in a position where they can afford to indulge what their conscience tells them is right.

"Every decision we've made that has seemed to fly in the face of common sense has worked for us," Mike had said the previous afternoon. Peter Buck agreed. "You know, people say that we don't play the game but I don't know. To a certain degree we do things that are unpleasant to us, photo sessions and the like. It's just that we won't do things that we feel are deplorable or are against our ideals. They'd like us to have a glitzy video where we all sing and look sincere and where there's a pretty girl and we have to say 'Wait a minute. If we did that we'd look such pricks.' If you've got something people want you don't have to follow the game plan. Prince doesn't.

"Prince has weird covers and weird records. The new one sounds like a demo to me—which is partly good and partly bad. But at least he had the balls to do it."

Likewise, R.E.M. have turned down a prospective Radio 1 session scheduled for when they hit the UK this week.

"It's not like we won't do it," Buck explains, "it's just that we've got better things to do. If things hadn't have been so rushed maybe we would have found time."

Further example of their single-mindedness is the compilation LP, *Dead Letter Office*. From a marketing point of view, released dangerously close to *Document*, the LP works so well because it includes all the embarrassing bits other bands leave out. It makes you feel that you're listening to something that you shouldn't be which as everyone knows was one of the earliest appeals of rock 'n' roll.

"Yeah, well, we didn't have too many illusions that it would sell two million," Buck laughs. "It's a summertime album. Plus, if we put it out now we can have control over what's on it as well as the packaging. If we were to change record companies we wouldn't have that control. I was gonna leave out some of the ones that were more embarrassing but, ah, f*** it!"

What didn't make it on the LP?

"I really shudder to think!"

Dreams for the future include a reunion with Don Dixon and Mitch Easter, probably after the next LP, an attempt to buy the rights for the soundtrack of a cinematic version of Ian Bank's *Wasp Factory* and more production work for each member of the band.

"Basically, we're trying to learn how to produce," Mike says: "Also it's good to do other stuff besides performing. We can have a secondary career so, if the band should break up, we can always do that."

Horror of horrors you're not seriously contemplating . . . ?

"Well," Buck sighs, "I've always thought that a band should put out 10 LPs before they split. But the thing that always worried me is that we'll dry up. Everytime we finish an LP, that's what we think. And it's like 'God, this is it guys, it's finishing, enjoy it while you can.' There again, I suppose we could always play Las Vegas. Nostalgia for the early Eighties! Now that I could look forward to!"

THE NOTORIOUS STUART BROTHERS
A DATE WITH PETER BUCK (1987)
Bucketfull of Brains, *December 1987*

B.O.B.: Have you ever lived outside of Athens?

P.B.: Oh yeah, I lived in Atlanta for ten years and before that in Indiana and California.

B.O.B.: Where in California?

P.B.: East of San Francisco, out near Oakland; that was from nothing 'til about five. I lived outside San Francisco in 1966 and I remember going through and seeing hippies and stuff like that, I left there when I was about eight but I remember seeing hippies and beatniks lived on the block—that's what we called them before they were hippies . . . in '65; the guys had long hair and they obviously smoked pot—you'd see them on the front lawn in their underwear, doing paper airplanes and setting them on fire . . . good guys! I saw my very first live rock 'n' roll band, in the east of San Francisco, they were called the Postmen. I swear to God, the thing they remind me of is "Shake Some Action" Flamin' Groovies; they came on, they wore those outfits the Beatles wore in "Help". . . . the postman outfits, kinda like with the capes and shit. I remember they did "Tambourine Man" and "Ticket to Ride" and that's all I remember of the songs . . . I remember because I owned those records. It was like five guys, they acted and looked like the Byrds—12-string guitars, harmonies, all covers. For some reason they played our school . . . instead of having fifth period which was math or something they said "We've got a special treat" and it was 1965 I guess. They were cool.

B.O.B.: You remember that well, was that when you started thinking about a band?

P.B.: Well, I never thought I would do this—I didn't think I had a gift for it, I was a fan and I worked in record stores. . . .

B.O.B.: Do you still do that? We read that when you had time off you worked in record stores and got paid in discs.

P.B.: Yeah, I do it for fun, I just like working there. I always end up a hundred or two hundred dollars in debt! It's tons of used and rare stuff. . . . I'm not like an anal collector but I have thousands of records and that's what I've been doing with any spending cash since I was seven.

B.O.B.: Can we talk about the production you've been doing, like the Moberlys and Charlie Pickett?

P.B.: I did over an album's worth of stuff with them [Charlie Pickett], I think the tapes are real good—it's really raw, real bluesy. I was going "You guys are like a blues-rock band, I'm not gonna say 'this is outta tune' or 'you're singing flat'" so there's lots of out of tune guitars and chaotic stuff, lots of slide guitar, I like that.

B.O.B.: So what's your input in a production sense?

P.B.: I just say "That's a good song" or "That song sucks, lets not do it" or "Boy, that's a boring intro." I normally work with people who know what they're doing, so I just sit there . . . and I nod. What I do is more technical, making sure the drums sound good, the guitars have interesting tones, I readjust the amps and stuff. . . .

B.O.B.: *Are you an engineer?*

P.B.: No! I'm a horrible engineer. I could do it, but I'm really, really bad at it. I help run the board, but when I want to do effects and stuff I have to get the engineer to do the patch bay because I'm an idiot when it comes to that stuff. I know how to get sounds, I have to tell the engineer which kind of delay or reverb, how to pan. I'm easy to work with and I'm cheap, so that's the main concern to people I work with.

B.O.B.: *What were the Moberlys like? Tell us about that.*

P.B.: We had five days in the studio and then the board went down for two days so we didn't have as much time as I wanted. I don't have any interest in working with someone who's established and changing their sound, I'd rather work with someone who's not been in the studio a lot and I can help out. With the Moberlys, they didn't need any real help but it's good to have somebody at the board rather than just an engineer—and I do have a lot of good ideas.

B.O.B.: *How did you link up with them?*

P.B.: I heard one of their records 'cos I was staying in this guy's house in '82 and really liked it. I was doing a radio interview and someone said "why is Athens such a great town? There's bands everywhere!" and I said, we were in Seattle, "There's a great band up here called the Moberlys, I don't even know if they're together anymore." The drummer showed up an hour later and said "Hey, that was nice that you mentioned us, we're playing tonight—wanna come and see us?" I did and they were really great, I got up and played six songs, I just turned to ten. . . . I didn't really know any of the stuff. I said "If you guys ever want a producer, give me a call" and they did.

B.O.B.: *How did you come to play with Warren Zevon, that goes back a long way doesn't it?*

P.B.: I went to college with this guy who ended up managing Warren Zevon—he just called us and we did a demo. We did that record [the *Hindu Love Gods* "Gonna Have a Good Time Together"/"Narrator"] in 25 minutes, cost 96 dollars—paying for the tape, the cassettes and everything.

B.O.B.: What does Warren actually do on that?

P.B.: He just plays piano, he was just there. . . .

B.O.B.: Who's Bryan Cook [also plays on the above 45]?

P.B.: He's just a friend of ours. He likes to play, so we decided we'd form a cover band and do Troggs songs and shit like that and songs by the Sweet, Mud . . . we did a great version of "Tiger Feet"! We were doing the demo with Warren and he had 15 minutes off and said "Let's cut a record" so we called Bryan and said "come on over and we'll do two of the songs we did live" and we did those two. He was kinda bemused, Mike [Mills] was standing over his shoulder yelling out the chord changes. When he [Warren Zevon] got the record deal, we just went in and did it [his latest LP].

B.O.B.: R.E.M. are getting bigger and bigger all the time, how do you feel about that? Is it weird for you now, playing 8,000 seaters?

P.B.: To a certain degree, but it's not really "weird" it's just different. There was a certain pleasure to doing the clubs and I enjoyed that, and now were doing something else and I enjoy that too; I don't want to play hockey arenas—occasionally you do that, it's just the way it goes but we're trying to keep it down to manageable levels. If a city has a good hall, we'll play there twice . . . like in New York we're playing Radio City twice rather than Madison Square Garden—both shows sold out in an hour! Those hockey rinks are so impersonal, the sound sucks, rather than having rock 'n' roll people you have all these guys who would rather be doing basketball or something.

B.O.B.: I saw you play in LA last year, in Universal City—that was great, I loved that place!

P.B.: I saw the Smiths there, it was a really good show. I'll use this space to correct something: people used to ask me if I was influenced by Johnny Marr and that used to piss me off so much that I said really nasty things about the Smiths—but I do like the Smiths. When I came over to England people asked "Are you influenced by the Smiths?" and I was like "Fuck you! I've had two records out before the Smiths even started." So I always said nasty things about the Smiths, but I like them a lot, it took me a while to understand that—the first record I didn't really dig at all, from "Meat Is Murder" every record there's three or four songs that are just mind-blowing great. "How Soon Is Now" is one of the greatest songs ever and I just heard "Sheila Take a Bow"—it wasn't a single or a hit in America, I heard it on a compilation—that's a great song, reminds me of T-Rex. I'm sorry they broke up before I got the chance to admit that I like 'em!

B.O.B.: *Who else do you listen to? Who are the big faves?*

P.B.: Right now, just before I left home I was listening to this record by Dinosaur, Das Damen have made a couple of really good records, the new Sonic Youth record is really great.

B.O.B.: *I can't stand them.*

P.B.: I think it's tongue in cheek, the death . . . Manson obsession, I assume it must be. . . .

B.O.B.: *Do you not find dealing with those kind of images is dangerous?*

P.B.: I'm smart, I don't worry about it. For dumb people, I'm sure it might be a really weird thing. When Hinkley tried to shoot Reagan, because he liked *Taxi Driver*, it doesn't mean that was a bad movie to make. Manson is not someone I'm interested in, nor am I interested in death or anything like that . . . much. [Laughter] Death of course is interesting. It's not like they're writing just about those things, they use those images as a conscious metaphor for their view of society and it's completely valid. My mom reads a lot, but anything grim or nasty she doesn't like; to me—I don't care. If an author went out and killed someone, that would bother me but if they write about someone killing someone then big deal. Part of the thing you learn from books or records and movies is a view of life that isn't your own. Otherwise you just walk around saying "Have a nice day" to everybody, y'know? Nobody wants that. Then again, I'm not the type of person, and Michael [Stipe] isn't either—none of us are—that are going to write stuff like that. It doesn't make it bad, it's just not the way we are.

B.O.B.: *Everything's credited to all four band members. What's the normal way to write an R.E.M. song?*

P.B.: One of us might almost write a complete song, without the lyrics, and bring it in—but we find, lately, that the best thing we can do is go in without any ideas and just make noise. Basically, I like to play really loud. . . . [The conversation comes to a halt as Peter tries to decide whether to play a Jesus and Mary Chain or That Petrol Emotion tape prior to R.E.M.'s set later that evening.]

B.O.B.: *What's the new single in the States? Is it "The One I Love"?*

P.B.: Yeah. We didn't write it for that purpose but it seems to be more palatable to radio. We just write songs, who knows what the hell they're going to be. Over here "End of the World" is the single. I would like to have it be a hit over here just because it would sound really good next to Whitney Houston . . . it's definitely a mess, a chaotic mess of a record. Michael had vague lyric ideas and he just sung it once and that was it— one take, I think we overdubbed the choruses again.

B.O.B.: *It's all "L.B.'s"! Lester Bangs, Lenny Bruce. . . .*

P.B.: We did go to Lester Bangs' birthday party, and we did eat jelly beans and cheesecake, in 1980 just before he died. We'd never been to New York before and we decided to go and we went with this guy whose mum had a van and we slept in the van and got drunk every night. We were with Pylon, this was before we were a band—or maybe we'd just started rehearsing that week or something—and Pylon said "these guys haven't eaten in days, we're going to a party, maybe they could come and eat some food." Lester was so drunk, he just stood in the hallway and everybody would walk by and he'd call them names . . . he called me "a rotten cocksucker"; he's my favourite rock-critic. I think Michael wove that into his dream, or maybe his dream was woven into that?

B.O.B.: *"Voice of Harold" sounds like another stream-of-consciousness thing, was Michael Stipe reading an LP sleeve or something?*

P.B.: He did two takes and couldn't get the vocal; so he just walked in, grabbed this album off the shelf and was looking at the liner notes, said "Run the tape" and did it in one take!

B.O.B.: *Have you ever played that live?*

P.B.: "Voice of Harold"? No fuckin' way!! Every once in a while he'll slip in a line or two, he has no idea how it goes, he just did it.

B.O.B.: *Who comes up with the cover versions that you do?*

P.B.: We're real lazy, we never sit down with records and learn things—if we all vaguely know a song we just kinda do it. I love the Velvets but one of the reasons we do the songs is pure laziness . . . because we've all heard them. Like the Wire song ["Strange" on the *Document* LP]—to this day Bill and Mike have never heard that. We taught them the song and it's totally different to Wire's version. The thing is that Michael has to know the lyrics—I can fake anything and so can Bill and Mike. I've been wanting to do "Time Will Show the Wiser" by Emitt Rhodes for years. . . .

B.O.B.: *The same one that Fairport Convention did, that's great!*

P.B.: Merry-Go-Round [Rhodes' band] had a great version of it, it's on the B-side of some single, but that's a lot of work—we'd have to sit and actually learn it. "Academy Fight Song" is something we've been meaning to do for years . . . but I hear that Miracle Legion did it, we ought to pick another Mission Of Burma song though. . . . I love them, they're one of my favourite bands.

B.O.B.: *You said somewhere that you really liked singles, the trashy ethic of it, do you not find that you're thought of as an "album band"?*

P.B.: Yeah, sometimes it depresses me.

B.O.B.: *You make great singles, but basically they're taken off albums.*

P.B.: It's basically that it's such a pain in the ass to get us in the studio that when we go we cut an album rather than a single—I don't feel comfortable in the studio until I'm in a week. There are lots of songs we've written that should be singles. . . .

B.O.B.: *"Pretty Persuasion," don't you think that was an obvious single?*

P.B.: Yeah, but I really worry about that. We did a song we were thinking about putting out as a single between albums. We recorded it for the third album and it never came out, we called it "Theme from Two Steps Onward"—which means nothing. We did a real good single–ish version of that and, as a matter of fact, when we did *Reckoning,* "Rockville" wasn't supposed to be on the record—it was supposed to be "Wind Out" or "Burning Down" or something instead. We were going to put out "Rockville" as a single between *Reckoning* and the next album. I don't know how to make hit singles so what would happen is we'd put out a single that wouldn't sell and no one would hear it. Over here there is a singles market and the Smiths can sell singles but we never sell singles— it's like wasting songs. If we were having hits, if we were like Prince, I'd put out singles that weren't on albums because we're always writing stuff that doesn't fit on the records.

B.O.B.: What's your opinion of Prince?

P.B.: I think he's great. I saw him in like '83, I was one of the hundred white people in an eighteen thousand seat hall and then I saw him on the last tour, the "Purple Rain" tour where there was, maybe, two hundred black people in an eighteen thousand seat hall—it's weird how that changes overnight. When I went there were like piles of women, all black women, screaming to get onstage, I was going "There aren't any white people here, I thought white people were into Prince?" This was after "Dirty Mind"; next tour there's no black people, I don't know if he's not hip to blacks anymore, or what? I don't listen to him a lot but I really respect him. Him and us, we're the two weirdest bands in the Top 40 in America. There's lots of weirder stuff than us but nobody makes Top 40 with as weird things as we do and he does. He's weird, he's definitely out there.

B.O.B.: He's decided not to stop being strange, it'd be very easy to roll over, play dead and play "Purple Rain" for the rest of his life.

P.B.: Yeah, that's one of the reasons for this last record *Document*—we tried to make it a little bit "out there," we wanted to make it more weird because, y'know, we're successful now. Ideally, success means you can do anything you want but what it eventually seems to mean is that you gotta pay the mortgage, you bought a big house, so you gotta have another successful record so you make a record like the last one. We decided we wanted to make this one just a little bit more . . . I wanted people to buy it and go "Huh . . . what?" and it is fairly different for us. It's not like some big departure but it is fairly different.

B.O.B.: *The things on the B-side of the 12" over here, the two songs from McCabe's—what was that gig all about?*

P.B.: A friend of ours runs a record store and he was getting sued by somebody, or maybe he was suing someone, something like that. . . .

B.O.B.: *. . . a benefit.*

P.B.: It was more or less an excuse to play. Steve Wynn and I did a little duet set, Russ Tolman ex-True West, Peter Case. We went down and just played. I said before that we were going to use that song "Theme from Two Steps On" as a single—so we were going to have that as the B-side of the single. The tapes were all mislabeled, so we ended up in the studio without the song we're supposed to have as the B-side, it just wasn't there! So we wondered what to do and Michael said "Well, I've got this cassette of us" [recorded live at McCabes] and it wasn't even the original cassette, it was a dubbed cassette. . . .

B.O.B.: *It's great quality, sounds great on the record.*

P.B.: Well, it's an acoustic set so everything goes through the PA, the vocals and guitar. We did an acoustic version of "Work Song" and there's this great version of "So. Central Rain" that's like eight minutes long, the ending goes on and on, Mike's playing piano. . . .

B.O.B.: *Is that ever going to come out?*

P.B.: I was thinking I'd like to get it to a bootlegger and have him put it out. It's not something we want to come out as a real record because that builds expectations of something. But there's some really neat stuff on it. Because we are successful, any record we put out will be bought by a lot of people, because it's us, and I don't want to take advantage of people by putting out something that isn't representative of us. We work hard on the albums, and that would be a good record to put out but I don't think it's something I would want to put out for real. I wouldn't mind doing it through the fan club, doing a cassette, or having a bootlegger put it out, because that's something different, it's out of our hands. When we put out "Dead Letter Office" I had some doubts about that too, thinking maybe people would think we were trying to cash in, to sell records, but I kinda liked the idea of pulling together some of the bullshit and putting it out.

B.O.B.: How many did that sell in the States?

P.B.: Almost exactly what I predicted: 250,000 copies—because that's our core audience—they'll buy pretty much anything that has our name on it. What we were thinking was maybe putting out an EP of the live McCabe's show, 'cos an EP isn't the same as an album and people don't treat it as such. The acoustic version of "Work Song" isn't very good, but it's interesting—the kind of thing a fan might like—"So. Central Rain," the piano's out of tune—big deal! Mike hadn't played the song in two years because when we do it, we do it solo, Michael and I.

B.O.B.: That's just reminded me, you did a song in LA last year by Floyd Kramer—do you remember that?

P.B.: Yeah, "Last Date." That's actually going to be the B-side of some single in the future. We were real weird this year—we wrote tons of songs and threw them all away. We wrote ten songs last summer that we didn't use for this record—we wrote "The One I Love" last summer and that was it. All those others, we never even recorded them so they're just lost. So when we did this album we only did the eleven songs that are on the album—that's why the B-sides are live and stuff, I don't want them to have a B-side that is from the album, I think that's a shitty thing to do. I figured I'd rather go in and do something that's even half-assed that hasn't been released. . . .

B.O.B.: Like "King Of The Road"!

P.B.: Yeah, that was half-assed, but it was weird. It was one of those things that probably shouldn't have been done but everyone that heard it went "whaaat?!" So, we went in and cut "Last Date," the Floyd Kramer song, the day before we flew over here—in three hours. We definitely want to have nonalbum B-sides and at this point we didn't have anything left in the can so we figured we'd use that. Maybe during the soundchecks during this tour we'll cut a couple of other things.

B.O.B.: In terms of making albums, are you committed to doing one per year?

P.B.: I'd like to put out records closer together than we do now. The limitations as far as time goes, with touring and stuff, it's physically impossible to do that.

B.O.B.: *How long does it take you to cut an album usually?*

P.B.: About 7 weeks, but we have to write too and that usually takes a month of playing every day. We've got four or five new songs and a bunch of others that we're working on.

B.O.B.: *What happens when you get back to the States?*

P.B.: Our record contract with I.R.S. is up, so we'll probably spend some time talking to people. We're supposed to start rehearsing at the beginning of January, it'll be a little bit longer between records—we won't start recording the next one until about June. We're going to try and write 30 or 40 songs and get a really wide range of stuff. This album will be the first time we've had more than two or three weeks to write. . . . *Fables,* that album we wrote 15 songs in eight days, just getting together and "Boom!" knocking them out, having no idea what we were doing.

B.O.B.: *To us that was an amazing record, but a lot of people are really down on it, including the band to a certain extent.*

P.B.: I think it's a really good record, and I think it did what records should do, which is reflect the mood of the band. It's really a weird, edgy, depressing record, I mean that record depresses the fuck out of me. Partially because I lived through it, I remember that year and I didn't like that year much. To me "Feeling Gravity's Pull" is one of my favourite songs that we've done—that song particularly was just a picture of us at that point. I had a miserable time making that album, we were all miserable and mean to each other. . . .

B.O.B.: *You were about to break up?*

P.B.: Well, that's probably over-stressed, but if there ever was a point in our career where we thought we were sick to death of each other, that was it. We had just got off of an eight and a half month tour, we rehearsed for eight or nine days, wrote these fifteen songs, been home for a week and a half—the first time in a year. We flew over to London and it rained all the time, it's winter, it's snowing. We didn't have enough money to rent cars and shit so we had to take the tube, and there's nothing wrong with that but we were a mile from the tube station so I had to carry my guitar in the snow to the tube. I don't know who goes to Wood Green but the tube was crowded as shit so I had to stand up the whole way and then walk another mile to the studio. I wasn't sleeping, I slept about an hour a night and I drank all the time. If I didn't feel bad anyway, that was enough to make me feel crumby. That record just reflects that perfectly, it's a misery album in a lot of ways—but I like it, the songwriting's great, it's one of our stronger albums as far as songwriting.

B.O.B.: Have you ever considered doing a double album?

P.B.: I tried to convince everyone to do one around *Reckoning* because we had so many songs at that point. The ones that ended up on record are about 17. I wanted to do "Crazy" and put that on the album and we ended up doing another version of that, we did "Pale Blue Eyes," "Ages of You," "Wind Out," they were on there—they were recorded at the same time. I was going "Let's put out a 20 song double record." [At this point proceedings were brought to a close as Peter was called on to get ready for the evening's sell-out gig.]

That's it, that's an abrupt finish! I don't know if we covered everything we were supposed to cover . . . just make up stuff!

Part Three

SHINY HAPPY PEOPLE

ELIANNE HALBERSBERG

PETER BUCK OF R.E.M. (1988)

East Coast Rocker, *November 30, 1988*

Guitarist Peter Buck remembers walking down an Athens street with bassist Mike Mills the day it hit him that R.E.M. had an actual recording contract. "We were both broke," he recalls. "My girlfriend worked in a pizza place and she would slip us free food. We were walking downtown to eat and I said, 'Wait a minute—we've got a record deal! Ninety-nine percent of bands never get to a major label. We made it!' That's the day I said, 'I'll be able to do this for a while.'"

Since then, Buck, Mills, drummer Bill Berry and vocalist Michael Stipe have gone on to platinum albums and Top 10 hits, something they never foresaw when R.E.M. was rehearsing in an old church and playing biker bars. *Green* marks the band's transition to Warner Brothers Records. It is also a unique package—an atmospheric collection of songs in the R.E.M. tradition of nontradition.

E.C.R.: Are you actually able to separate yourself from R.E.M. during time off?

P.B.: I can put my guitar down and go home and just be the guy who lives in my house. I don't see myself as Peter Buck, Rock Musician. It's what I do and like to do. This year was supposed to be a year off, but we practiced six days a week. I think we've had maybe two weeks that we weren't; we *had* to be here doing things. That's fine. I like rehearsing. Time off for us is just time at home. If we spent six months here, great. That's six more than we had in the last eight years!

What did people originally see in R.E.M.?

When we came along in 1981, 1982, there weren't a whole lot of intelligent alternatives other than Elvis Costello and Richard Thompson, not a lot of people that you and I could listen to and say, "That's got thought behind it; it's a little different, not trying to sell records through image."I'm sure that's what appealed to the public and critics on our first album. We were new and different. I figured if we sold as many records as we sold of *Murmur* until we quit, which, when it came out, was 100,000—that's what I figured our audience would be. It's gotten bigger each time, and I don't know how or why.

When did that occur to you, and how have you dealt with it?

I'd much rather be appreciated than not, and if people over-appreciate us, then too bad. I think it's weird, but then again, I think we're all able to divorce ourselves from popularity. People think that—they think George Michael or Prince or who-ever are great. Essentially, we're all just guys with guitars.

Do you hear your influence on other musicians?

Not so much in Athens. It's the kiss of death to sound anything like us here. But other towns, I've seen myself on stage before. I always think it's a compliment. The Stones started out imitating Muddy Waters and became a great band. Kids who imitate us are mostly 18 years old, go on to something else, and maybe get more original.

Do you believe there is a theme to each album?

We tend to write songs in one big batch in a month-and-a-half. Musical and lyri-cal ideas come out in that time and reflect what's going on then. The last record had a lot of fire imagery, *Reckoning* had a lot of water imagery. But once we fin-ish a record, I never think about it again. It's old news. The next thing is on my mind. The day we send it to the company is the day it's out of my mind. I go on to whatever else I'm going to do.

Is there a middle ground in your audience?

A lot of people ignore us. Sure, there's a middle ground. The Butthole Surfers probably have no middle ground. I love them, but there's a lot of people who don't. People who tend to listen have strong opinions. I know people who hate us like you wouldn't believe, and some who think we're the greatest band in the world.

Which album was the hardest to make?

This one was pretty hard. The third one [*Fables of the Reconstruction*] was the hardest because we were at a point in our career where it was becoming a *career*. We could stay home and tour once in a while, or make a full commitment to be in a rock 'n' roll band. None of us were really sure. We'd been on the road for three years, so we wanted to stop before we got so sick of it that we didn't want

Berry, 1986. *Photo © Stephanie Chernikowski.*

to do it again. It's a lot of fun and I'd hate to lose that part of my life, although I'm sure I will some day—we'll just get too old for it.

What is the biggest misconception people have about you?

That we sit around and think sophomoric college thoughts, but the fact is not only that we're smarter than that, but none of us give much of a fuck. I take music seriously and I work real hard at it, but I'm just another clown walking around with a guitar. The worst thing you can do is take yourself seriously. You've got to approach everything with a sense of humor, whether you're polishing doorknobs, making records, or whatever it is you do. We look at it as "We're famous rock stars—b.f. deal, who cares?" This is a fairly funny thing to be happening to all of us and we acknowledge that. I never thought this would happen. I never looked for it, really.

What did you think would happen?

After a month or two, I realized we were kind of good. I figured we would play here and Atlanta and maybe once a year go to New York, kind of like what Pylon did, and play to 800 people, make local records, sell 4–5,000 copies, and play once or twice a month here in town. Each step along has been just that—a small step. I never thought we'd get past the point of doing *Murmur* and touring behind that with 400 people coming to see us and really liking us. I thought we'd be a cult band until we fell apart. It's an odd experience. At this point, it's, "Gosh, we're as big as a lot of people I used to go see when I was 13, 14, and think they were rock gods or whatever."

Could this have happened anywhere?

We weren't very good when we started, and if it had been New York, we probably would have been in the *New York Times* with a bad review the third day we played. There's a lot of immediate scrutiny, fighting for jobs. You've got to have the killer instinct to have a career in New York. Here, we just called up and asked, "Can we play Tuesday?" They said yes and we played. We had a year-and-a-half to write songs, throw songs away, test what we were doing, to get to the point where we were a decent band, writing good songs, playing well together, had something more than four guys making noise. In a big city, it would never have happened. We would have been faced with fighting for our life to be third on the bill at a big club and it wouldn't have happened. Having said that, I don't think we're quintessentially Southern or anything. Just being down here allowed us to do this, but you can't listen to our record and say, "They're from the South."

How has Athens changed?

As the town gets more people, it gets more upscale. As far as music, it's more professional, which is a drawback. If a band in this town has seen us and the B-52's, they know how to do it. We'd go see bands, there were 100 people there, we knew every one of them. We were outsiders, walking in fear of our lives in certain places. Now you can have a green mohawk and go into a fraternity and it's, "Hey, how ya doin'?" They're more tolerant, or at least have learned to live with it.

Can you imagine making records without touring?

Sure. As much as I like playing, touring is real hard and there will be a time when we make records and don't tour. Not for good, we're not going to retire, but maybe there will be a record where we don't feel like touring that year. I can see it becoming more sporadic, maybe playing certain big cities for three nights. I like the way Tom Waits toured last year—two nights each in nice halls, a lot of them, picking places rather than cattle calls in arenas. As you get older, the focus changes to writing, recording and rehearsing.

How did that attitude affect Green?

We were really focused and worked hard to make the record we felt we needed to make. It's a really strong record, which at the same time, isn't like an R.E.M. record. There are no typical R.E.M. songs.

What is a typical R.E.M. song?

Minor key, mid-tempo, enigmatic, semi-folk-rock-balladish things. That's what everyone thinks and to a certain degree, it's true. "Driver 8" and "So. Central Rain" epitomize to a lot of people what this band does. Everything on this album is in a major key, essentially, and that changes the tenor of the record. Minors are wistful, sad keys; majors are more aggressive and harsh. We wrote major key rock songs and switched instruments.

Is it hip to like R.E.M.?

About two-and-a-half, three years ago, it was. Now, we're unhip. Most of what I get, is people who really liked us, now that we're famous, they go on to more obscure bands. I'm the guy who hangs out in clubs, sees the little bands, and once they play the Omni [Atlanta], I don't care. I'd rather see someone who's totally able to fuck up and who knows what will happen? I like that.

What is the response to you in foreign markets?

Unfortunately, we had almost nonexistent distribution in Europe with I.R.S., which is probably the reason we left, because we like the people at I.R.S. We went to Germany and Green on Red outsells us three to one there. They're really good guys, but they shouldn't be outselling us. We should at least be equal. I get tired of going all the way to Europe and playing for an audience that's only G.I.'s.

Hopefully, Warner Brothers will rectify that for us. I want our records to at least be available.

Who are your fans?

I could give what seems to be the typical fan, but everyone's different. People who come up and talk to me are atypical. They're usually guitar fans: "What kind of guitars/strings/amps do you use?" It used to be easy to know our fans because they came to our shows and that was it. Now a lot of people come and don't necessarily like us. They come because it's the thing to do this week.

Does each album represent a different stage of growth?

I don't think about it. To me, we have a dividing line that starts somewhere before *Murmur* where I felt we were actually writing good songs and were a good band. After that, it was "How are we doing this year? Where are we going?" This year is another dividing line. We have a new record company, more time to write and work songs out, and made a strong record that's like another starting point. Records are diaries of what we did this year.

Are you still influenced by the music you grew up on?

I grew up on Iggy and the Stooges, New York Dolls, Velvet Underground. We sound a little like Velvet Underground, but not much. We certainly don't sound like Iggy, although yesterday we cut "Funtime," which we did on tour a year ago. We cut six songs, for B-sides and stuff. I don't play old records much except for old blues records. During the day, I put on a record that came out this year, or jazz—old John Coltrane and Miles Davis—you can't beat those.

Are things very different around you since the platinum album?

This is just what we do and sure, things change. You go through all these experiences and if you don't change, you're a moron! Things are different in my life, but they would be different if I was still working in a record store or had joined the Peace Corps or got thrown in jail. Sure, things are different, but I certainly can't complain. I enjoy what I do. I've been well compensated, much more than I ever really wanted. But it doesn't mean anything, certainly not in this town.

Does the publicity mean anything to you?

I take all good things written about us with a grain of salt because I see our good points and our faults. The reviews I get the most out of are thoughtful, bad reviews. When someone writes something that makes sense to me, I can say, "Yeah, we're weak in that area" and see his point. It doesn't bother me. It's just an opinion. I have lots of records I really love that suck!

What is the common link between the members of this band?

I don't want to hang around someone who's just like me, I can't think of anything more boring. We learn from each other. We all have the same thoughts on the way to live and the same acceptance of what goes on around us. We don't find ourselves at philosophical odds very often. We might disagree about what to play, when to tour, or what the cover should look like, but we certainly don't have goals that aren't in common.

Of course, we're different people. Everyone's different. Four people in a band, all the same, would be really weird. We all push and pull each other in and out of line and learn a lot.

Do you believe in limitations?

We can do whatever we want. Whether people accept it or not is up to them. I don't feel we have constraints whatsoever. If we wanted to sit on the floor and do acoustic versions of songs no one has heard, we could, if we had the songs. There are no boundaries and if that means less people come to our shows and buy our records, fine.

What about responsibility?

The only responsibility is to ourselves. If we all found God tomorrow and wanted to do a gospel show, we would do it. I never will—I'm an atheist. But if we drive people away because of the music we're making or what we're saying, fine. Don't come in. People who buy records and come to the shows consistently aren't buying a sound or a package. They're buying a vision which is our idea of what we're doing this year, where we want to be. They don't come saying, "I've got to hear this single." I don't think. Maybe we got some of those last year, but essentially people come see us do what we want to do, good or bad.

That's probably the core of the audience. It's not 10,000 each night who come for that. Three to four thousand want to hear the hits and that's fine. We don't give it to them. We don't do old stuff and sometimes we don't do new stuff.

But we don't feel there's any point in doing anything unless we can do whatever we want.

If that means sometime in our life span the audience number declines, fine.

What is the best thing about being in R.E.M.?

Buck, 1986. *Photo © Stephanie Chernikowski.*

Working with the other guys, being able to grow up with guys I respect and like, learn from them, work with them well. It's taught me to be more tolerant, more able to deal with people. They're like the guys in the office. I like working with them and it's nice, because a lot of people go their whole lives in a situation, whether it's business or music, and don't have that.

What else have you learned?

The business I never learned anything about and I don't want to. Self-knowledge is a very dangerous thing. People go see psychiatrists to learn why they do things, and I think a little self-knowledge goes a really long way. I prefer to do things. I don't jump in a hole 10 times in a row. I make stupid mistakes and go on from there. I certainly don't want to sit around and analyze myself. The thing I've learned most is how to work with people, deal with them. I've become quite whimsical in my older age!

SEAN O'HAGAN

ANOTHER GREEN WORLD (1988)

New Musical Express, *December 24, 1988*

"I TEND TO TRUST MY REPTILE BRAIN RATHER THAN MY RATIONAL THOUGHT PROCESSES AND, WITH THAT, THE INTUITIVE SENSE IN THE MUSIC COMES OUT PRETTY STRONGLY. R.E.M. INTUIT AS A BAND MUCH MORE THAN THEY ANALYSE. SO FAR, IT HASN'T SERVED US WRONG."

Horses

As a rule, the things people won't talk about are usually the most interesting/revealing aspects of their self. Today, Michael Stipe is reluctant to talk about his childhood.

Were you a weird kid, Michael?

"Erm. I wrote backwards right up until sixth grade. Perfect mirror image."

That's pretty weird. . . .

"It's quite common among left handers. This one teacher told me my brain would flip over if I didn't stop and learn to write properly."

So you stopped?

"Yeah. I had this recurring image of two fish inside my head, flip flopping over one another . . . ."

That's really weird.

"I can still do it, though. A little practice and I'm right back there in mirror image."

The all American alien boy picks a few place mats off the record company office table, arranges them in rectangular formation and does his very best to look uncomfortable with this line of questioning.

Were you a happy child?

"Pretty happy. I moved round a lot—Texas, Georgia, Germany. I flew, through childhood, didn't touch base a lot. That's all. I don't choose to talk about it too much."

Whatever, the young Stipe grew up to the soundtrack of his parent's record collection—"Film soundtracks, Gershwin, Mancini, 'The 1812 Overture' with real cannons."

He claims to have only owned three records as a young teenager—

At rehearsal, 1986. *Photo © Stephanie Chernikowski.*

Hayley Mills and Tammy Wynette on 45 and an unspecified Presley soundtrack—and to have been oblivious to the Britbeat colonialism of the Beatles and their peers.

"They meant nothing to me historically except as inescapable elevator music. I have no inclination to rediscover that 'cos I've done pretty well without it up to now. When I'm out of all this, sometime in the future, I'd like to investigate Captain Beefheart. I really respect him a lot."

In the mid '70s Michael Stipe had an epiphany. The earth moved, the sky fell in around his ears and his life was changed utterly. One day he was adrift, an introverted undecided kid with vague "photographic ambitions," the next, he was liberated; his imagination catalysed by a harsh, iconoclastic noise blowing down South from New York City.

"I guess I was kinda prepared for something 'cos I had this subscription to two magazines—the *Village Voice* and *Rock Scene*—one of those publicity offers. I dunno why I chose the *Voice* over *Women's Wear Daily,* though. Anyway, I was reading all this stuff on the Dolls, the Velvet Underground and Iggy and the Stooges so I started picking up eight tracks of their early stuff. I still have the first Dolls albums on eight track."

Was there any one particular artist or record that changed your life?

"Yeah. *Horses.* I got it the day it came out. It *killed.* It was so completely liberating. I had these headphones, my parent's crappy headphones and I sat up all night with a huge bowl of cherries listening to Patti Smith, eating these cherries and going 'Oh my God! . . . Holy Shit! . . . F—k!' Then I was sick. . . . That was the only record that really blew me away. I loved the first Television album, the first Wire album, all that stuff but *Horses* was the one. . . ."

Adjectives

Michael Stipe no longer listens to contemporary music—"'75 through '77 was the first and in time I ingested great chunks of music." He hasn't read a book in three years. Nor does he watch much TV or go to the cinema— "I'm pretty consumed by what I do."

Michael Stipe's world revolves around Michael Stipe.

And the music he makes in R.E.M. Which may be most of the reason why R.E.M. sound like no other contemporary rock band. You have to go right back to The Band's early work to find a group so in step *and* out of time.

With '87's *Document* and this year's *Green,* R.E.M. have stood alone, arriving at a point where popular acceptance, critical acclaim and consistent creative integrity have merged into a seamless whole. R.E.M.'s noise has grown from a Byrdsian folk jangle into a robust, melodic hard rock. And Michael Stipe's singing has gone from a mumble to a mesmeric, constantly starting and uniquely resonant instrument. The insistent *otherness* that courses like a vein through R.E.M.'s work is the sole, exclusive property of the singer.

Do you find yourself constantly at odds with the world, out of step with things, an outsider?

"Erm . . . I'm always trying to convince journalists otherwise—that I'm completely normal—but, yeah, I do. . . . A little, I don't think it's anything . . . um . . . special, just different."

You perceive things differently?

"Yeah. I do . . . I dunno. That's a hard call 'cos I'm surrounded by people who I'd have to say share that . . . erm, . . . perspective. I don't feel estranged or alienated in any big way. . . ."

From mainstream America?

"Oh God, yeah! We're talking a different universe, there. My idea of mainstream American culture is pretty tainted. I have a great joy in having been *delivered* from the mainstream. A great joy in deliverance. . . . "

In conversation, Michael Stipe is kinda how you'd imagine him from his songs, though a little more camp. Dressed in Oxfam chic, without the specs but with a pretty impressive pony tail, he veers between the willing boho and the awkward, gauche unwilling pop star.

Fidgety, preoccupied, always on the verge of wandering off, he answers questions with a slow, measured attention to language. His speech is peppered with strange nuances—"I've shed my Georgia accent in two days"—and slightly archaic words—"therein," "steadfastly," "often-times." At one point, he speaks of his fascination with language stemming from his "inability to grapple with it," a statement that contradicts the rich suggestion of songs like "Cuyahoga," "Finest Worksong" or "King Of Birds." "I've chosen my adjectives and verbs with care and I throw them together in as many ways as I can. This week's adjectives are 'deeply' and 'galvanising.' I'm using them a lot. Heh heh. It's a way to be serious *and* humorous simultaneously."

How do the others feel about this semantic mischief? Baffled?

"They accept me pretty much at face value. They edit me pretty well. I guess Peter's different. He kinda slots me into the Van Morrison tradition. Sometimes I think his great love for Van Morrison's music is the only thing that's kept him from strangling me over the years."

Books

So how come you've stopped reading books. Pretty drastic move, that. . . .

"WELL, I have some books in my case. I keep adding to them. Let's see, there's an Irish author called Christy Nolan—*Under the Eye of the Clock.* I gotta read that. What else, *The Mysteries of Pittsburgh.* And a book on architecture. Oh yeah I have a copy of *Economics as if the Earth Really Mattered* for my accountant. He might learn something from that."

Who's the last author you read in depth?

"Oh my God. . . . He's soo sappy and thick, I'm embarrassed. Lawrence Durrell. Before I traveled to Greece. His prose was so thick and tactile, no country could live up to that. I was incredibly disappointed.

Y'know Norman Mailer's *An American Dream*? Is that the one written from a sense of smell? Jeez, I had to put it down. Too suffocating."

Accidents

I read somewhere that you weren't too comfortable with technology?

"Yeah. That's right, I admit that. The lights even . . . they sorta bother me. . . ."

Are you afraid of technology? That's a pretty common response to the late 20th century: techno-fear. . . .

"Afraid—that's a harsh term. It's kind of a soft term, too, though. Easy. It doesn't apply. Not fear, more *distrust*, nah, misunderstanding. I still don't understand technology. How my voice goes in the studio microphone, through a process that ends with that same voice emerging out of something that resembles a place mat. Y'know? I'm not a Luddite. I understand the advances. . . . Give me a manual typewriter over a word processor, though. I get an: objectivity in my writing that comes from the sensation of hitting the keys, you know the '4' on the album sleeve—that's a typo, an error I left in. I meant to hit the 'R' and my left index finger hit the '4' instead. I left it in."

As a clue to a particular creative tendency? The idea that accidents have a meaning all their own, an *artistic* meaning?

"You got it."

Is that a recurring basis for your songwriting? I notice how, when you use a repeated phrase, you often alter it in a small, profound way— "Dreams compliment my life / Dreams complicate my life"—for instance?

"Intrinsically, I've learned . . . erm, for myself and a lot of other people—even if they don't recognise it and, if they do, they don't tend to admit it—that mistakes are often the most creative, no, *inspired*, part of anything I do. To be able to recognise that *and* enlarge on that. To make those mistakes and deliver whatever it is you're doing—I've been able to succeed with that. My entire style of singing—to cheapen it by calling it that—comes from that base. Not too many people have homed in on that before."

[He looks relieved and uncomfortable simultaneously.]

It's a pretty sophisticated approach though not in the accepted sense.

"It is? Thanks."

You don't think so?

"I dunno."

Well, your songs have a literacy all their own, a resonance and allusiveness that gives them a certain poetic literacy.

"A leprosy? a poetic leprosy of writing, is that what you said? Think about that for a minute."

Is your music's appeal mostly beyond language?

"I think so. I personally find language quite stifling and, simultaneously, liberating. That's what the leprosy of writing is all about. That phrase has made my day."

Songs

Have you written a straight narrative song yet?

"Yeah. I've succeeded a few times."

Name them.

"'Disturbance at the Heron House,' 'Harborcoat'—I thought that was a real simple narrative but no one else did. I had to tell someone what it was about a few days ago. God knows what that says about my narrative style. And 'World Leader Pretend'—I put the words on the sleeve 'cos I think that one song summarised the whole motivating idea behind *Green*."

How do you feel about *Green?* In many ways, it seems like your most realised album.

"Good. Good. If there's a mistake on *Green* it's 'cos I made it. The others have said the same. I don't feel that way about *Document* though we were pretty 'much in control. . . .' *Pageant* was real outta control. I had a lotta input but the mix still slipped away. The process was beyond us right up until *Green*."

Murmur sounds a universe away now, in comparison . . . ?

"You think so? That's interesting. Why?"

Well, the words for a start, they're pretty indecipherable.

"They're there, though. 'Radio Free Europe' and 'Nine to Nine' are complete babbling—they're the exceptions. The rest are right there. See, I feel that essentially *Green* is pretty much *Murmur* revisited. I went back there pretty intentionally and the rest did too though it wasn't a spoken thing. To me, everyone was carrying the idea that *Green* is very much exactly where we were at in the summer of '88."

Looking back, do you have particular songs that stand out for you?

"A series of songs that I think of as perfect? Yeah. In so much as my idea of perfection is that there is no such thing—an unattainable. I like the songs that came out exactly the way I heard them. That were delivered in a way that completely satisfies me and continues to do so. 'Perfect Circle,' 'Feeling Gravity's Pull,' 'Disturbance at the Heron House' . . . I have difficulty remembering without a track listing . . . 'King of Birds,' 'You Are

Everything,' . . . 'Welcome to the Occupation' and all the songs that go with it. . . . "

How do you mean?

"Well essentially . . . 'Occupation' is a rewriting of three songs that went before it. Mainly it's revisiting 'Green Grow the Rushes'—a song about Central America. I do that a lot. 'Oddfellows' is a debunking of 'Fables of the Reconstruction' which was pretty much my version of the storytelling tradition. Me playing the Brothers Grimm or Aesop. 'Oddfellows' destroys all that, hacks it off at the knees, strips the myth town to the harsh reality.

"A friend said 'There are seven songs in all of rock and roll and we play three of them. Over and over. Really well.' I thought that a great compliment."

Politics

Though you spoke out in support of Dukakis for President, R.E.M. aren't a band that immerse themselves in the body politic of America?

"No. We're a pop band. There's a real time and a place for everything. At the same time, we're aware of being looked on as examples. People look up to us and respect us for whatever reasons. There are times when you have to respond . . . my support for Dukakis was really a condemnation of Bush, a reaction, a statement. You do what you can. I was aware of pushing the limits of my job. . . ."

Who sets those limits?

"Well . . . I do. Ultimately. I weigh up the circumstances. I mean, there are subtler ways in which you can endorse things that people pick up on—taking Greenpeace and Amnesty on the road, having their stalls in the lobby during our shows."

Dreams

As a rule, the things people won't talk about are usually the most interesting and revealing aspects of their self. Today, Michael Stipe is reluctant to talk about his dreams.

Are your dreams a constant source of raw material for your songs?

"Yes . . . Erm, I don't tend to talk about that a lot, though. I can start sounding pretty eccentric."

Don't worry, it's already too late.

"Yes, I guess. . . . Whatever, I think dreams are pretty crucial to everyone. Certainly, to me they're as *real* as anything else."

Are all your songs, in some way, dream songs?

"Oh boy. I dunno. *Nah.* 'Get Up' is a song about the thin line between the real and the fantastic. Where you draw the line. But it's also a calling out to people song, so. . . . It gets pretty complex if you start dissecting them."

What about the collective unconscious? A song like "Cuyahoga" seems to deal with America, the collective dream, the myth. . . .

"Yeah. Americans are searching for a history that doesn't exist. In a really big way. That intrigues me. We're a restless people however much we try and placate our spirit. We're still pilgrims. In Europe, you can walk around and the sense of history that seeps out of buildings makes you feel not quite so big. You feel a great sense of place. In America, that sense of place is essentially a myth. Especially in the deep south. We destroyed a culture to build ours—that's what 'Cuyahoga' is all about, in a consciously naive way."

It merges the personal and the absolute pretty effectively. Another Stipe trait?

"Yeah. I'm glad you caught that. Especially the first person singular songs—they're very much a microcosm of something much bigger. The metaphor is usually quite clear if you're tuned in."

How would you describe the Michael Stipe approach?

"I tend to trust my reptile brain rather than my rational thought processes and, with that, the intuitive sense in the music comes out pretty strongly. R.E.M. intuit as a band much more than they analyse. So far, it hasn't served us wrong."

Lies

Tell me about your private life. I read somewhere that fans were starting to make the pilgrimage to Athens, Georgia to seek out Michael Stipe. I bet that's a real disorientating experience?

"No. That was really nothing. It's not a problem."

Is it an inconvenience?

"No. To be honest, I was lying. Nobody does that. Nobody knows where I live. Nobody bothers me."

Do you lie a lot?

"Depends. If I feel mischievous."

Are you feeling mischievous today?

[Michael Stipe doesn't answer.]

Sometimes the things people won't talk about. . . .

"*Horses*. I got it the day it came out. It killed. I had these headphones, my parent's crappy headphones and I sat up all night with a huge bowl of cherries listening to Patti Smith, eating these cherries going 'Oh my God! . . . ' Then I was sick. . . ."

BO EMERSON

R.E.M. (1989)

Atlanta Constitution, *April 1, 1989*

Minneapolis, Minn.—"Did you hear that sound?" asks R.E.M. drummer Bill Berry.

He is soaked in sweat, wriggling into a terrycloth robe in the back seat of a rental van, blasting through the snowy Minnesota night.

Minutes earlier, Mr. Berry and his compatriots had sprinted for the backstage exit at the Met Center sports arena in the Minneapolis suburb of Bloomington as 13,000 very happy customers cheered the finale of a two-hour plus concert. Now Mr. Berry and guitarist Peter Buck are out-maneuvering the traffic in the parking lot, as that high-pitched squeal reverberates in their ears.

"I noticed it right away," Mr. Berry says, "even at the first show in Louisville, it was sort of an 'E-E-E-E-E-eeeeee.'"

"It was three steps higher than last year," Mr. Buck agrees.

They're not talking about feedback. The sound is produced by the very young vocal chords of teenagers, and it follows the band from city to city these days—the result, they suppose, of having a Top 20 platinum album, major label supports, and your face in heavy rotation on MTV.

MTV, teenybopper fans, 13,000-seat arenas—what's going on here. If this doesn't sound like the little band from Athens, Ga., that you remember, you're right. Underground no more, R.E.M. has graduated from insider acclaim to mass appeal with the million-selling *Green,* featuring, "Stand," an instantly infectious hoedown that vocalist Michael Stipe cheerfully dismisses as a "dumb pop song."

"STA-A-A-A-A-A-A-A-N-D!" screams a young girl named Jeanne, dancing in the aisles at the concert hall. Jeanne starts screaming for "Stand" early in the Minneapolis show, and keeps hollering until the first encore. Jeanne loves this band, but she's not sure about their names. "Which one is Peter Buck?"

In performance, 1989. *Photo © Ebet Roberts.*

"It's sad," says University of Minnesota student Michael Wolf, looking around at the walls of this hockey rink, a big concrete bunker that contrasts sharply with the 5,500-seat Roy Wilkins Auditorium, where the band has played in previous years. "You look at people in the hall who've never seen them before," Mr. Wolf explains, "and you say 'I hate these people.' But then you think it's good that they've gotten the acceptance."

Mr. Wolf is a fan from the old days, before commercial radio would give R.E.M. the time of day. During the concert, seven hard-core followers like Mr. Wolf will stand up in the front row to make a silent request for a tune from the deep past—the *Chronic Town* EP, circa 1981—holding seven oversized cards that spell out "B-O-X-C-A-R-S."

Historically, there has been a special rapport between R.E.M. and its listeners. The fans send the band members postcards and curious works of folk art. The band responds with a special Christmas record for fans only and other nice gestures. Almost as fervent as "Deadheads," but more articulate, these devotees trade tapes bootlegged at live shows, and spend their vacations following the band on tour.

Bassist Mike Mills, whose round glasses and bowl haircut give him the look of the studious young Sherman from the "Peabody's Improbable History" cartoons, says R.E.M.'s success doesn't have to change things. "The relationship with the listeners hasn't changed, but there are a lot of new listeners with whom we have basically no relationship," he says. "A lot of people have only heard one or two songs on the radio, whereas in previous shows, it was people that knew us from touring and from the albums. . . . We're going to do our show regardless of who's listening. And the people that know us, will know what we're doing, and the people that don't know us, most of them hopefully will come around."

Of course, the show itself changes all the time. When four University of Georgia students got together to play for a friend's party in 1981, their band was mostly just fast and loud. But R.E.M. quickly developed its own personality, dominated by Mr. Buck's circular crosspicking (like a man playing a Rickenbacker banjo), Michael Stipe's rich, melodic yowl, and the irregular charm of their original songs. Critics toasted their debut album, *Murmur* (*Rolling Stone* magazine's 1983 album of the year), saying that R.E.M. somehow had made guitar, bass, drums and voice sound new again.

There is a light side and a heavy side to this band, and the two aspects seem to take turns dominating R.E.M.'s music. Folky sounds permeated *Fables of the Reconstruction* (1985), but that record also featured the heavy-metalish "Feeling Gravity's Pull." On *Green,* the rock and folk sides have become more polarized, represented by the uranium crunch of "I Could Turn You Inside Out" and such mandolin-enlightened acoustic tunes as "You Are the Everything" and "Hair Shirt."

The heavier side suits R.E.M.'s move to arena-sized halls, which, by the way, is a step that pains many of the old faithful. The band members are quite aware of this resistance. Mr. Buck is the man who once emphatically vowed to "never, ever, ever" play any venue bigger than 12,000 seats. Now reality has caught up with his promises. The hawk-faced guitarist shrugs off the change, saying that arenas are now the best way to accommodate the people who want to see the band.

R.E.M., with opening act Indigo Girls, has sold out two shows at the 16,000-seat Omni tonight and Sunday. To play for the same number of people at the Fox Theatre, where they performed four concerts in a row last tour, they would have to schedule a week of shows. "Four days was too many at the Fox last time," Mr. Buck says. "If you sit in the same place and play every day, you become stale, complacent."

Maybe some fans who've seen the band at the old 200-seat 40-Watt Club in Athens won't stand for the Omni. So be it, says Mr. Buck. "Being universally liked is something to be ambivalent about."

But if arenas are a concession, the band is not giving in to other corporate rock behavior, such as formulaic shows with fixed set lists. R.E.M.'s two-hour performance usually includes about 27 songs, and by the end of the first week of the American leg of the tour, the band had already played a total of 52 different songs.

"Our goal is to get it up to 100 songs by the end of the tour," says Mr. Buck, twisting open a Red Stripe beer in the dressing room.

"Whose goal?" says a dubious Mr. Mills.

"Fool's goal," comments Pete Holsapple.

The sardonic Mr. Holsapple is the official "fifth Beatle" for this tour, playing guitars and keyboards on songs that require more than four pairs of hands. "I'm the satellite guy," he says. "All the stuff on their records that can't be replicated by the four of them, I fill in."

Mr. Holsapple was with the late, lamented dB's, a Winston-Salem, N.C., band that opened for R.E.M. during its last tour. The dB's were one of many underground bands that members of R.E.M. have staunchly championed. True to form, R.E.M. has two up-and-coming Atlanta bands—Indigo Girls and Drivin' N' Cryin'—and the English cult figure Robyn Hitchcock opening the concerts on different legs of the U.S. tour.

Their willingness to tour with lesser-known groups seems to bear out Mr. Holsapple's credo, which is: "If R.E.M. wins, everybody wins. . . . I love seeing R.E.M. succeed," he says. "No success would be too much for these guys." Like the managers, roadies and technicians who work in the extended R.E.M. organization, Mr. Holsapple is impressed with the good temper of the band, not to mention their willingness to work hard. "R.E.M.'s karma seems to be great," he says.

This work ethic, stated in songs such as "Get Up" and "Finest Worksong," permeates the R.E.M. organization. Manager Jefferson Holt, who is suffering from a 103-degree temperature, flies from his Athens home to Minneapolis and comes to the Met Center in a wheelchair, to meet with the band and discuss the upcoming European tour.

"Is that Jefferson?" an onlooker wonders, as Mr. Holt is rolled through the Met Center corridors. "No that's F.D.R., going for his fourth term," Mr. Holsapple quips.

By all accounts, this Minneapolis show is the best of the tour's first six cities. The ticket-buyers stay on their feet, arms in the air, through old chestnuts ("Wolves/Lower"), mid-period anthems ("Begin the Begin") and the obligatory cover version of Pylon's "Crazy." Twin Cities legend Bob Mould, late of Hüsker Dü, joins the band for "See No Evil" and "Crazy," and is welcomed warmly by his hometown fans. Messrs. Berry, Buck, Mills, Stipe, et al., exit grinning. Afterwards, Messrs. Buck, Berry, Holsapple and Hitchcock rocket over to a downtown club called First Avenue, where some of *Purple Rain* was filmed. All but the drummer get together in the two-roomed club's smaller room, playing tunes by the Band, the Byrds and the Beatles. This pick-up unit, dubbed the Worst Case Scenario, also assembled itself after the March 6 Chicago concert, to play a benefit at a club called the Cubby Bear Lounge, presenting what Mr. Buck calls "the history of 1965."

The evening winds down with a bowling party at Lariat Lanes, where even the elusive Mr. Stipe joins into the middle-brow festivities. Are they happy with their new lives? Can a former thrash band from Athens play arenas and still have a good time? As they knock down pins and scarf pizza into the early hours of the frozen morning, this quartet seems to be

Billy Bragg, Natalie Merchant, Michael Stipe, 1990. *Photo © Ebet Roberts.*

quite relaxed indeed. "Let me put it this way," says R.E.M. attorney Bertis Downs. "I've never seen Michael Stipe bowl before."

Aside from better cheese and cold beer in the dressing room, things haven't changed much, Mr. Mills says. "A lot of people will tell you that it can't be done," he says, bowling a neat strike in a 150 game. "They say that you have to alter your show for that fringe audience that has never heard of you before now, but I don't think that's true. I think that you can win over the fringe audience by doing the things that have gotten you as far as they're gotten you."

JIM WASHBURN

SPONTANEITY MISSING IN R.E.M.'S CONCERT AT PACIFIC AMPHITHEATRE (1989)

Los Angeles Times, *October 20, 1989*

For the last couple of years, ever since R.E.M. graduated from cult college band status to "America's best band" or whatever critics called them for a few weeks when they first hit the big time, it's been tough to tell just how much the group has pulled a mainstream audience into its musical dream-scape or how much the band itself had been pulled into the waking every-day world.

R.E.M. concerts often have become a tug of war as the band flirts with the conventions and emotional triggers now standard to rock shows, or actively confronts and attempts to defuse those standards. While there seemed a certain hint of arrogance to it, it also was fascinating to see singer Michael Stipe interrupt a show to call the audience "a herd" or chastise the unfurrowed minds that choose to bellow, whistle and hoot through every quiet song.

Such admonishments have now, in their own way, become a convention of R.E.M.'s performance. Indeed, at the group's show at the Pacific Amphitheatre Wednesday night they were chiefly dispatched by filmed messages projected behind the band, from the tongue-in-cheek "Hello [your city here]. Are you ready to rock?" to such pronouncements-from-on-high as "Understand that change begins with the individual." Unfortunately, much of R.E.M.'s actual performance Wednesday seemed as pre-programmed and rigid as the filmed messages. While the 27 songs showed that R.E.M.'s music is still a unique, insular thing, much of it was rendered common by a shortage of immediacy and life in Stipe and the band's delivery. In that regard R.E.M. seemed downright jaded compared to opening act NRBQ, even though that group has been toughing it out on the club circuit since the '60s.

Maybe playing nightly to people who do persist in bellowing, whistling and hooting can affect one's faith in the power of the music one is playing. Whatever the case, the edge was missing from much of R.E.M.'s show.

Limited in its musical range, the group still had always played previously with an engagement and adventurousness that suggested the music could fly in any direction at any time. Though now using with a broader tonal palette—augmenting its guitar drone with former dB Peter Holsapple on keyboards and second guitar, and working congas, dulcimer, accordion, mandolin and amplified chair (used as percussion by Stipe) into the mix—the music often seemed flattened by its lack of spontaneity.

Looking just a bit like Elton John in a suit, cap and sunglasses, Stipe opened with a less-than-rousing "Stand" from last year's *Green* album, following with scarcely more involved versions of "The One I Love" and "So. Central Rain." In place of the somnambulant swirl Stipe once moved in, his broad stage gestures and shimmies seemed contrived, and perhaps parodic. A parody was evident in Stipe's repeated use of rock-critic clichés to introduce songs, beginning several with "This is a song for personal and political activism."

Things picked up with "Turn You Inside Out," the *Green* album's ode to personal responsibility, which Stipe dedicated to the Exxon Corp. and delivered, Tom Waits-like, through a bullhorn. There were moments when the band's old drive seemed present: the confrontational/inspirational "These Days" and "I Believe" and clarion-call "Finest Worksong"; the beautifully melodic, rarely performed "Perfect Circle" from the 1983 *Murmur* album; and a passionate "King of Birds," dealing with change and the passing of generations, dedicated by Stipe to the exiled students of China. But such times were exceptions in the long show. The rhythm section of bassist Mike Mills and drummer Bill Berry seemed tight but constrained, while guitarist Peter Buck rarely matched his antic stage leaps with his playing. The net effect: Where the band once tried to pull audiences into its dream, it now seems content merely to relate that dream from a distance.

DAVID FRICKE

MOMENTS IN LOVE: *OUT OF TIME* (1991)

Melody Maker, *March 23, 1991*

THE WORLD IS COLLAPSING / AROUND OUR EARS / I TURNED UP THE RADIO / BUT I CAN'T HEAR IT.

These are the first words out of Michael Stipe's mouth on this, R.E.M.'s "difficult" seventh album, and they ring with a truth that he could not have possibly imagined when he first wrote them. In a week when George Bush has sent his Rough Riders chasing Armageddon over Arabian sand dunes while the body count keeps rising in America's inner cities, the release of a new R.E.M album seems like a minor wrinkle in the new world order. Even the remarkable shift in R.E.M's own sonic order—however dramatic and confounding it may be in the context of their past work and recent success—seems small noise indeed amid the numbing aural bombardment of hourly fear-and-loathing news reports and repeated Top 40 spins of Whitney Houston's Super Bowl rendition of "The Star Spangled Banner."

But, *Out of Time* is actually the kind of whisper that, with time and continued exposure, makes you want to scream. For joy. It is a record about (if Saddam will pardon the expression) the mother of all battles— the war of hearts—and the music is dominated not by hallelujah power chords or howitzer drumming but by the hushed strumming of acoustic guitars and mandolins, the bittersweet sawing of chamber strings and the doleful burbling of a Hammond organ. There are times here when Stipe sounds like he's down on bended knee for the final count. "This could be the saddest dusk I've ever seen," he laments in the bleak, beautiful "Half a World Away"; the chorus to "Low" simply goes "low, low, low."

Yet all through the album, you can hear in his voice and the band's gently shimmering performances the kind of troubled but welcome relief that comes with confession and the indomitable hope that daylight is just around the bend. You can practically hear dawn breaking over Heartache Ridge in "Near Wild Heaven," a peppy Stipe/Mike Mills confection that glimmers with echoes of classic Sixties' Britpop and the choral *Pet Sounds* majesty of the Beach Boys. Even Stipe's despondency in the harrowing "Country Feedback" ("It's crazy / What we could have had") is not absolute; "I mean this," he insists against the sweet 'n' sour backdrop of the weeping pedal steel and the police-siren sustain of Peter Buck's guitar, "I need this . . . " *Out of Time* is not just a poignant survey of love's scarred battlefield; it shivers with the promise of reconciliation renewal.

At the risk of perpetuating the old R.E.M. bugaboo about jangly guitars (which are largely absent here) and the band's debt of influence to The Byrds, *Out of Time* is, in some ways, the R.E.M. counterpart to *The Notorious Byrd Brothers*. There is definitely a cosmetic parallel in the use of strings and brass, the expanded role of Mike Mills's previously-occasional keyboards (Mellotron and harpsichord, among them) and the subdued but effective undertow of the guitars, which are often muted or unplugged entirely. More importantly, like *Notorious* on which McGuinn and what was left of the original Byrds sculpted a work of timeless folk-rock wonder out of fierce personal disorder and scrambled musical intentions, *Out of Time* is a stunning baroque beauty fashioned from dark, frank lyric testimony and the willful chaos of the band's switched-instrument fever.

No song captures that fragile elegance and expansive nerve more dynamically than "Losing My Religion." While its urgent chorus and pervading sense of minor-key dread echo "The One I Love" on *Document*, the mournful strings and Peter Buck's raindrop-on-a-tin-porch-roof mandolin heighten the pained intimacy of Stipe's unresolved battle between eroding faith and accelerating obsession. "Texarcana," a driving ode to love lost and hope eternal sung with boyish esprit by Mike Mills, runs a damn close second with its motley but moving compound of aching strings, strident guitar arpeggios and barely audible pedal steel. As implausible as it might look on paper, the song rather sounds like what Gram Parsons might have come up with if he'd been raised on a diet of Nick Drake. The Alpha Band and recent Replacements.

Out of Time, really, is the album R.E.M. tried to make in 1985 with *Fables of the Reconstruction*. The general "fun" quotient is higher here as well. You can't but help but laugh along with "Shiny Happy People," a bizarre mix of waltz-time strings, rippling guitars and some of the most hilariously hippy-dippy words Stipe has ever committed to record (and he swears they're not meant in jest). There's also the incongruously funky "Radio Song," which features Mills doing his Booker T thing on organ, Buck salting his guitar part with a taste of David Bowie's "Fame" and a guest appearance by rapper KRS-1. Anyone craving a return to the less complicated days of *Reckoning* or *Document* should definitely be sated by the closing track, "Me in Honey," an enervating guitar-fuelled duet by Stipe and Kate Pierson of the B-52's.

Out of Time may ultimately prove to be more of a detour than a landmark declaration of future intent. There's already talk of R.E.M. returning to the studio and going the two-track, live in-your-face route. Which would be no mean thrill either. But with *Out of Time* they have at least proven-to themselves as much as anyone—that they have not exhausted the possibilities of being R.E.M. or of rock's capability for surprise and candid reflection. This is a complex and daring album, and it may not be easy to love. But, to paraphrase Stipe in "Country Feedback": they *mean* it, you *need* this.

DAVID FRICKE

LIVING UP TO OUT OF TIME/ REMOTE CONTROL: PARTS I AND II (1992)

Melody Maker, *September 26, October 3, 1992*

"IT'S JUST NOT AS SWEET AS YOU WOULD EVER THINK IT IS."

On an unusually balmy afternoon last January, in Athens, Georgia, while the town bars and sidewalk cafes absorbed the seasonal crush of University of Georgia students returning from Christmas vacation, Michael Stipe sat behind a desk in the R.E.M. office and talked about one of his least favourite topics: being famous. He fidgeted in his chair, looked wistfully out the window every now and then as if he were silently lamenting the loss of another sun-blessed Georgia day to the business of being in R.E.M., and lugged absent-mindedly at the brim of his baseball cap, a custom job emblazoned with the name of a new film he was working on. The title: *Desperation Angels*. Perfect.

"The very weird religion of celebrity in the United States really scares me," Stipe said with a nervous shudder. "It's like we're creating gods, fake heroes, because we don't have any real ones. We're having to create our own little versions of Zeus because we feel we don't have any. The government has failed us, religion has failed us, what do we turn to? Celebrities.

"That's probably a commonly held pop viewpoint. But it's weird being a media figure. I used to be able to walk through black neighbourhoods and not get recognised. Now I do. That's actually a real compliment, because our audience is primarily white and I like that crossover. But it's wild to be recognized everywhere by somebody."

He took a sip of tea. "But the record, the voice, all that stuff—to me, once it's pressed and it's out there, it's not me anymore. I'm proud of it and it's an extension in a way. But I kind of feel that once it's out there, it belongs to everybody. That's when the separation has to occur. I can't think about why it does what it does."

Or, he might have added, to whom. At the time of that conversation, R.E.M.'s latest album, *Out of Time,* had sold 10 million copies worldwide.

The Pyjama Game

Nine months later, almost to the day, it's Peter Buck's turn to wonder about the numbers and consider the burdens. The guitarist is in Los Angeles juggling phone calls, band business and an interview while awaiting his curtain call on the set where R.E.M. is shooting a video for "The Sidewinder Sleeps Tonight," the prospective second single from the band's new album, *Automatic for the People.* He is bored, impatient and doesn't really care who knows it.

"It's video hell," he says with the weary resignation of the eternally damned. "I'm doing interviews. I've gotta talk to some guy in an office in New York. And that's just today. I'm not complaining at all."

Not much anyway.

"It beats a day job. But things like this. . . ." His voice trails off. "Mike [Mills] and I were talking about it today. We never wanted to be actors, in the last two years, I've never looked at any of the videos. I think I saw maybe half of one of them. And I don't read any of the interviews or reviews. I really don't care. I try to do what I want to do, which is write songs and play them."

Which is what he did just the other day. While Stipe was busy with preparations for the "Sidewinder" shoot and the business of R.E.M. continued to roll in its gently inexorable way, Buck went into a studio with T-Bone Burnett to record material for the next album by Burnett's wife, art folk diva Sam Phillips. When R.E.M. arrive in London in October to ride the obligatory press merry-go-round, Buck is determined to do a day in front of a tape recorder with long-time friend and collaborator Robyn Hitchcock.

This is also a man whose attitude toward perfunctory industry backslapping is best illustrated by his appearance at the Grammy ceremonies in New York last February; when he walked on stage to accept R.E.M.'s three gold statuettes dressed in pyjamas. Not only faux-formal jobs custom made for glamorous pop star occasions. This was a pair of everyday Irish-green beauties—decorated in a gambler's motif with darts, dice and playing cards—that he wears around the house all the time.

"Actually, I sleep naked. But when it gets cold, I build a big fire in the fireplace, get my guitar, maybe a bottle of wine, put my pyjamas on and play. That's a great day for me.

"I went to the Grammys under protest. My mom and wife really wanted to go. I went, but I did it for them. And I said, 'Okay, if I'm going to the Grammys, I'm going to wear my pyjamas.' Everybody just started laughing and I said, 'I'm f***ing serious!'

"Then, the day before, we were in the limo and everyone was going, 'Now, Peter, I know you promised to wear your pyjamas, and we really hope you do, but if you don't we're not going to think you chickened out.' Those were fighting words. I was bound and determined to wear my pyjamas."

The jammies, it turned out, were a big hit. After R.E.M. received their awards and the TV network cut to a commercial, the Mistress of Ceremonies, actress Whoopi Goldberg, yelled over to Buck, "You in the pyjamas! They look great!"

"It depends on how seriously you take yourself," he insists a little impatiently, as if it pains him to belabour the obvious. "We don't have bodyguards. We never have, I never will. I drove here today in my rent-a-car jeep. I just take control of my life and don't worry about it.

"I've got a varied life outside of the business, and certainly outside of promotion. That's the thing. If you want to keep doing it, when you get to my age—not that I'm ancient or anything—but so many people go, 'Oh, I don't want to do all this.' So don't f***ing do it. For us, there is no reason in the world why we should have to do anything other than the creative aspect of being in R.E.M. Michael is interested in the videos and he'd probably do something like this anyway, even if he wasn't in the band. I'm not, and I'm not in them very much.

"I'm not trying to sound selfish or spoiled. But to keep doing it at the level we're doing it, we have to concentrate on writing songs, where we want to go with the band. I think this is our best record. And the reason it's that way is because we don't give a f*** about anything else."

Peter Buck has a very hard time trying to comprehend what 10 million records sold really means, what it looks like. Even when his brother went to the trouble of figuring out the exact amount of physical space that 10 million albums would take up, he couldn't believe the results.

"My brother worked out that if you took your record collection and lined all the albums up, if you were driving 60 miles an hour, it would take you an hour to drive past 10 million of them. Think about it—that many records would stretch from Athens to Atlanta.

"I used to think 200,000 was mind-boggling. I've never seen 200,000 of anything. Maybe the people on New Year's Eve in Times Square. But those people are all on a little television screen."

He pauses, still a little rocked by disbelief.

"The way to deal with it," Buck says with as much finality as he can muster, "is not to worry about it."

Co-produced by R.E.M. with long-time studio collaborator Scott Litt, *Automatic for the People* is the kind of album that no slave to the numbers would ever dare make. It is a careful attention and a willingness to surrender yourself to the anguish that always precedes hard-fought, lasting joy. It is certainly not the album of fast *Document*-brand, guitar-driven rockers that R.E.M. promised after they'd gotten *Out of Time* out of their system. Peter Buck, Michael Stipe, Mike Mills and Bill Berry have, if anything, strayed even further from expectation.

Where *Out of Time* was a startling drop in volume and mood from the arena-friendly angst and politicized clamour of *Green, Automatic for the People* seems to move at an even more agonized crawl. The album opens with two startlingly sombre ballads—"Drive," a dark, ironic examination of disconnection and self-determination scored with acoustic guitar, acoustic fuzz guitar and bittersweet strings (one of four orchestrations done for the record by ex-Led Zeppelin bassist John Paul Jones); and "Try Not to Breathe," a death-bed elegy in waltztime, sung in the voice of an old man looking back at his life and heightened by a soul-wringing, happy-sad blend of back-porch picking and insistent guitar distortion.

The ballads, in fact, define the record. "Everybody Hurts" is an achingly beautiful stab at chamber soul—a Memphis torch song dressed up as a pop-art hymn, with kitchen-sink orchestration and a stunning Stipe vocal. "Nightswimming" is Southern Gothic romance incarnate, simple reverie and innocent days so deftly arranged that even with its full complement of plantation strings, it sounds like just Stipe alone with his thoughts under the stars.

There are rockers, but only three. One is an out-of-character but on-the-money election year diatribe, "Ignoreland," aimed directly at the space where George Bush might have once had a heart. The other two—"The Sidewinder Sleeps Tonight" and "Man on the Moon"—are smart pop pay-offs with broad hints of "Stand" and "Shiny Happy People" in the sing-along clinches. Yet amid such stark, determined introspection, they seem pleasantly alien, strategic lifts of tone and spirit to prepare you for the next plunge.

Automatic for the People is a sober but purgative experience, an album about hurt, insecurity and desperation—and how there's no tunnel so long that there isn't a light on at the other end. As Stipe sings in "Find the River," the album's elegiac finale, "Pick up here and chase a ride / The river enters to the tide / All of this is coming your way." Even the album's blackest song, a grey droning ballad spiked with extra amplified crackle on the cello, has a title that best captures the album's real intent: "Sweetness Follows."

It might just be overcompensation, but Mike Mills is convinced that, for R.E.M., the bucks—the big ones, anyway—stop here. "This is not the same record that *Out of Time* was," he says matter-of-factly during a conversation a couple of days before the "Sidewinder" video shoot. "I think it may be a better record, but I don't think it's going to sell like *Out of Time*."

"When we made *Out of Time,* we knew it was time to make a bigger record. Not as in a 'big' hit record, not in the sense of selling a lot of copies. I just mean in the sense of encompassing a lot of things, of having new things jump out at you. It was the first time we felt comfortable with something like a full string section.

"This is not a big record in that way," he insists. "It's smaller, personal, more intimate. It's not gonna have the splash that the last one did. Everybody I've talked to likes it a lot. But they're not sure how much."

Buck has no such doubts. "This album is not the record you would be making if you were planning the Big Follow-up. But it's a strong record. Ten years down the line, everyone's perceptions of this band are either going to be different or gone. And the only thing that's going to be left is a pile of records. And I think this one is going to look real strong in comparison to the others.

"We wanted to be different. We felt we'd followed the trajectory to *Green* as far as it would go. *Green* was a logical outcome in terms of the *Document*-style sound. From *Life's Rich Pageant* on, those records were more guitar-driven; the sound was getting bigger. It was more rock 'n' roll-ish.

"But when we started out, we didn't even want to say we were a rock 'n' roll band. I always had trouble with that, What the hell are we? We aren't rock. We aren't pop. So we said we were folk-rock, which is probably why we got saddled with that Byrds business."

"The very weird religion of celebrity in the United States really scares me. It's like we're creating gods, fake heroes, because we don't have any real ones. We're having to create our own little versions of Zeus because we feel we don't have any. The government has failed us, religion has failed us, what do we turn to? Celebrities."—Michael Stipe

"What do we do? We write songs. And I can do that on any instrument. Now we're just songwriters who make records."

Filling the album was never a problem. There were only a couple of extra, briefly considered candidates like "Think Tank Decoy," a leftover from the silly list for *Out of Time*, and "Star," after the lush, twisted love song "Star Me Kitten"—itself a drolly-coded reference to Stipe's otherwise unembarrassed and easily decipherable chorus "F*** me kitten." According to Mills, "Automatic for the People," despite its implied dig of R.E.M.'s own reduced commercial expectations for the records, is of quite humble origin.

"It's the slogan from a soul food restaurant in Athens," he explains. "I wasn't there when it was suggested, but it's great. When they're dishing up the food, you say, 'I want some pork chops.' And they go, 'Automatic!'"

Stipe's Rich Pageant

Last January, Michael Stipe stood in the Globe, a popular Athens hangout for students and a favoured R.E.M. watering hole, raving about some new R.E.M. music he'd heard earlier in the evening. "We had our first practice of the New Year tonight," he exclaimed, "and it was like, 'Wow!' We had great new songs, the music sounded real good. It felt great to know that we still had it in us."

When pressed to describe what the music sounded like, the best he could do at the time was, "pretty f***ing weird. More acoustic, more organ-based, less drums." He was pretty wired about one particular work-in-process, though. "The other guys gave me this new song that is so beyond 'Stand,'" he said, grinning, "that it makes 'Stand' sound like a dirge. I mentioned it and they all started laughing. But it sounds like that song 'The Sound of Philadelphia' by MFSB. It's really out there!"

There is no official record of whether that song survived that weeding process or, if it did, in what form. But Peter Buck remembers some of those early practice and writing sessions quite vividly. There was one evening, two weeks into rehearsal, when Buck, Mills and Bill Berry wrote the music for both "Sidewinder" and "Man on the Moon," "Try Not to Breathe," which was a wistful Appalachian mountain ballad before the band spiked it with electronically doctored background vocals and short, sharp shocks of bayonet feedback, was another early birth. And "Star Me Kitten"—a glacial beauty draped with liquid background "aaaahs" copped in no small part, Mills admits, from 10cc's "I'm Not in Love"—popped out of the R.E.M. song oven in nothing flat.

Some songs took longer to ripen. "Nightswimming" was put down as a demo with just bass and guitar during the final stages of recording *Out of Time,* the version on *Automatic for the People* is that very same demo with additional strings arranged by John Paul Jones. "Drive" dates back to the very last day of mixing for *Out of Time.* "It wasn't actually in the running for that album," Buck says. "When we're mixing or doing over-dubs, we all sit around with guitars and just play. I put this thing down on tape and then Mike added some stuff. We though it might be a good B-side for that album. But Michael didn't even hear it until eight months later.

"I had it on a cassette of demos and I always fast-forwarded through it. I thought it was the most boring thing I'd ever heard. Then, all of a sudden, Michael had these lyrics, which defined the song for me." Buck admits that R.E.M. had little or no chance of delivering that promised album of *Document*-style piledrivers. They made a yeoman effort to write some fast songs in initial rehearsals but come up with less than half a dozen possibilities. Only one made the final cut, "Ignoreland." And of the estimated 30 songs that Buck, Mills and Berry did put together for Stipe's lyrical consideration, only 14 were actually recorded.

"I can never tell what's going to inspire Michael," says Buck. "Like 'Me In Honey' on the last record. That was literally a riff Mike played once. I put this guitar line over it and Bill added a drum beat. It was maybe 30 seconds long and it was on the end of a cassette tape of five real songs.

"And Michael fixated on that. Just 30 seconds, one chord. He went, 'That beat, that key, D flat. I've got a song for it.' So I said, 'What about another chord for the chorus?' He said perfect. We broke up the riff in sections so that each verse was a different length. Then he worked it out on paper, scribbling out lines. And I thought, 'Weird, how did he get all of this out of one chord?'"

R.E.M. have always operated, in songwriting as in everything else, under the proposition of one man–one vote. "We're a democracy," claims Buck. "Or we're Communists. I can never decide." But he concedes that, as a lyricist, Stipe can rarely be persuaded to follow where he does not want to go. That was unfortunate for three songs in particular, "mid-tempo folk-rocky things that could have fit really well on *Life's Rich Pageant,*" according to Buck. "But he didn't finish them." (One of them was ultimately completed with Natalie Merchant of 10,000 Maniacs on vocals and donated to a forthcoming charity record benefiting the National Abortion Rights Action League.)

"To a certain degree, what we give him defines what he does," says Buck. "And if we ever got to the point where he was tired of what we were giving him, we'd have a problem. But we still get excited about surprising each other. 'Oh, I can't wait until they hear this!'"

Even with a record as emotionally fertile and sonically elegant as *Automatic for the People,* Buck still can't help lamenting the ones that got away. "There were a couple of his that I loved so bad, I wish he had finished them. He had one called 'The Devil Rides Backwards on a Horse Called Maybe.' It was a great title and it fit the chorus too. But he couldn't come up with a second and third verse."

Buck still can't figure out why Stipe never completed the job. "Sometimes, he'll come up with something so good, you just go, 'God, Michael, I wish you'd finish that.' That 'Devil Rides Backwards' song was one of those.

"I still hope in the back of my mind that he'll go back to it someday. Two more verses," Buck sighs, "and it'll be perfect."

Remote Control

"It doesn't look like we're gonna do it this time." Mike Mills is talking about a tour—and how—there isn't going to be one to go with the band's new album, *Automatic for the People.* Eighteen months ago, when *Out of Time* was released, R.E.M. had promised to step off the album/tour tread-mill for just one record, to gather their wits and ideas before taking it back to the stage. You can now file that promise under "good intentions."

"We're just gonna wait a little while longer," Mills says, a little sheepishly. "One more record. Still, it's funny. I feel like I've been on the road enough to have toured. We recorded this record in the four corners of the U.S."

Just about. Written and rehearsed in R.E.M.'s basement sanctuary in Athens, Georgia, then recorded in demo form at the band's favourite local facility—John Keane's cozy studio on a leafy street just a brief stroll from Chez Buck—*Automatic for the People* was cut in Woodstock, New York; Daniel Lanois' studio in New Orleans' French Quarter, Miami and Seattle, where they were quite unperturbed by the Sub Pop–Nirvana–Pearl Jam uproar. There is some guitar fuzz to be heard on *Automatic,* but largely as a dramatic foil to the elegant whisper-ballad symmetry of the arrangements and the compelling tension of Stipe's lyrical fears and prayers.

"The thing that separates this record from *Out of Time*," says Mills, quite proudly, "is that we just have some of the weirdest songs in the world on there. It has some real screwball writing on it."

Automatic Transmissions

"Drive": A dark, fragile beauty, with shy, simple strings and the delicate plucking of the acoustic guitar spiked with Buck's abrasive fuzz punctuation. A song about bending under a heavy load, but never breaking. Also, the first song Michael Stipe has ever written that actually has the words "rock 'n' roll" in it.

Buck: "Pylon wrote this song, 'Hey, kids, don't rock 'n' roll,' which I always loved. I don't know, it just came out of Michael. It's probably the least wave-your-list-in-the-air type song that we could write. So it's kind of appropriate that it has that line."

Mills: "This isn't a 'down' record. Every song on it, even though some of them are about death and life as you've lived it, has a hopeful ending. Or a hopeful message. 'Drive' is just telling kids to take charge of their own lives. [Pause.] Among other things."

Buck: "It's a subtle, political thing. Michael specifically mentions the term 'bush-whacked.' But if you want to take it like 'Stand,' that's cool too. You like to think that you can appreciate these songs on any level you want to. I have a lot of records I listen to when I'm just doing the dishes.

"Like the Ride records, I really like Ride a lot. And I have no idea what the songs are about. And I really don't care. I don't even worry about it. Lyrics are the last thing I listen to, unless someone is hitting me over the head with it."

"Try Not to Breathe": A waltz for the aged, a look back at a hard, but hard-fought life, the calm acceptance in the death-rattle shake of the tambourine and the angelic answer-chorus by Mike Mills underscored by the grim finality crackling in Buck's distorted interruptions.

Buck: "An old man, imagining death. Chord structure-wise, it could be some kind of mountain ballad. But then it has electronically altered background vocals and feedback in the bridge, to give it an unsettling feel.

"Just for those people interested in minutiae, we were doing the demo, and I had the mic for my guitar right up against my mouth. I was kind of huffing. So John [Keane], the engineer, said, 'You're making too much noise.' So I said, 'Okay, take two. I'll try not to breathe.' I just meant that I wouldn't breathe during the take. But Michael heard it and said, 'Oh, that's a nice title.'"

"The Sidewinder Sleeps Tonight": Sounds like "Stand" going way off the deep end. Stipe negotiates through the word-busy chorus ("Call me when you try to wake her") with relaxed aplomb and even permits himself a giggle in one pass. He even has a bit of fun at the expense of the Sixties hit, the Tokens' "The Lion Sleeps Tonight."

Buck: "We actually paid them for that. We didn't want some guy, down the road, going, 'You owe me two million dollars.' So we called them up and said, 'We're calling it "The Sidewinder Sleeps Tonight" and the singer kind of paraphrases the line.' In any court of law, we couldn't have been nailed. Because the song doesn't have anything to do with it. But you don't want someone to feel that you're stealing from them."

Mills: "It's about somebody who doesn't have a place to stay. Part of it is also about what man can do that machines can't. The rest of it—I don't have any idea what it's about."

Buck: "I don't know what that snake imagery is all about. I don't even need to know. I'm just like a fan. 'Okay, whatever the snake is to you . . .'"

"Everybody Hurts": Athens soul-time, a Sixties-style Memphis hymn transformed into a tenderly sculpted, universal wail, blushing with strings and one of Michael Stipe's most powerful, unaffected and crystal-clear vocals ever. Al Green could take this one to church.

Mills: "Bill [Berry] wrote most of it. He came in with the chords on guitar. We were actually playing with Bill on guitar, Peter on bass and me on drums. It sounded terrible. We thought, 'This sucks. Let's demo it, playing our own instruments, play it right.'

"We never thought Michael would do anything with it. But it turned out that he really liked it. That was one we never thought would make it on to the record."

Buck: "It has a little bit of that mid-Sixties Stax feel But then it's shuffled through us. Like the bridge is in a way-weird different key. We're not Otis Redding. But given that, we took some of the influence, that music we loved for years."

"New Orleans Instrumental No. 1": Successor to "Endgame." Resonant acoustic stand up bass, toothpaste fuzz guitar and stairstep electric piano. Written at Daniel Lanois' New Orleans studio and a short but vivid musical soundtract for lonely boozehounds walking through the French Quarter after the tourists and sailors have finally retired for the night.

Buck: "It was two in the morning. There were a couple of bottles of wine around. We did the track of 'Drive' there and it turned out so well we kept it. We'd done some overdubs and played with things. Then Daniel said, 'Why don't you just write some songs here?' I sat down with a bottle of wine and wrote three things. This is one of them. Another one is going to be a B-side, New Orleans Instrumental No. 2, for completeness sake.

"I would never claim to say that we captured any of New Orleans. But I really wanted to conspicuously try and get a late night horn feel, that muted trumpet feeling. Whereas the other instrumental sounds like a deranged piña colada commercial."

"Sweetness Follows": In its way, the album's theme song, a bleak droning ballad that promises redemption in the end. The distorted cello, played by Knox Chandler of the Psychedelic Furs, careers through the song in a defiantly anarchic way, like a gentler cousin of Bob Mould's modal guitar shriek in Hüsker Dü.

Mills: "Peter wrote the bulk of it. Actually, it's mostly a demo. There's no bass on it at all. It's all cello, played through an amp."

Buck: "I did that a lot on the record, putting weird, harsh things underneath which undercut the song. 'Sweetness Follows' would be too saccharine if it didn't have that discordant cello back there."

"Monty Got a Raw Deal": A real sleeper, sneaking up on you like "Losing My Religion" in jester's clothing. The "Monty" is the late, star-crossed actor Montgomery Clift, who was condemned to glitter only on the screen. According to Mike Mills, the life's wordplay on American game show legend Monty Hall [*Let's Make a Deal*] may have been just a coincidence on

Stipe's part. Or maybe not. Inspirational verse: "Movies have that movie thing / And nonsense has a certain ring."

Buck: "I wrote it on bouzouki in New Orleans. Someone was having a party next door. I was up late, couldn't sleep. We put it down in one take and Michael said, 'Oh, that's my favourite song.'

"The Montgomery Clift thing came because there was someone who was a photographer on the set of *The Misfits* who came by the studio. He had photos from it and he was talking about it. How much of the song is real, how much of it is about Montgomery Clift and how much is about home, I couldn't tell you. But we saw those pictures and, while we were recording it, Michael was talking about it."

"Ignoreland": A song for George Bush, Papa Reagan and the Republican Party Hate Squad, delivered with all the urgency and venom they deserve.

Mills: "Michael's rolling against Republican politics. The opening line is, 'Bastards stole the power from the people / Who suffered from the Us-Me-Them Years' something like that, wrecking all things virtuous and true. And the last verse is really great—'I know that this is vitriol, no solution, spleen venting / But I feel better having screamed, don't you?' It's really great."

Buck: "You need headphones to get all the words, but they're understandable. Michael's singing through an amp on that. He wanted to get that cold anger in his voice that you get with natural distortion. And the song is written in Neil Young's tuning. Not that he owns it. But the E's are tuned down to D, like in "Cinnamon Girl." I admit it, he's the one I learned that tuning from."

"Star Me Kitten": Liquid love, a troubled relationship poured over a light coating of molten Hammond organ with 10cc background harmonics. The real choice is, as you probably know by now, "F*** Me Kitten."

Mills: "It's a very twisted love song. Those are the hardest words to catch on the whole record. And Michael's just saying. 'Yeah, relationships are tough and ours may not be the best, but go ahead. What are you waiting for? F*** me!'"

Buck: "I don't care about the word 'F***.' I use the word in conversation. But if it means that some kid in Idaho can't hear it, can't buy it at the K-Mart. . . .

"Actually, this really sounds like name-dropping, but they were shooting this movie in Seattle and Meg Ryan came by and she just loved the song. But she said, 'You know, when I grew up, if the word "F***" was in the title and it was on the cover, I couldn't buy it in my town.' And we thought, 'That makes sense.' You want to reach people. You don't want someone to arbitrarily say, You can't hear this.'"

"Man on the Moon": Very infectious, and deeply strange. An irresistible, upbeat pop song populated by, among others, Charles Darwin, Moses, Elvis Presley, wrestling manager Fred Blaissie and the late gonzo comedian Andy Kaufman. Nice touch; Michael Stipe's comic Elvis-style gurgle in the vocals.

    Buck: "Lyrically, I don't know where this is coming from. I just think it's a surrealist version of heaven. Michael came in with it, asked what we thought and we said, 'Don't change a word. It's perfect.'"

"Nightswimming": Sweet Southern Gothic, with lush—but not over-wrought—strings. Originally recorded during the *Out of Time* sessions.

    Buck: "We used to go swimming at night after rock 'n' roll shows in Athens. We'd all go see Pylon or the Method Actors, then pile into a bunch of cars and go swimming in this pond. I think it was on private property, but we never really got into any trouble. It was all very innocent; we were only 19 or 20 years old."

"Find the River": The closing prayer.

    Buck: "It's a great way to end the record."

Home, for Now

R.E.M. played only one live show this year, a benefit concert in Athens for a local mental health charity. They started out with acoustic guitars for "Fall on Me" and the Robyn Hitchcock song, "Arms of Love." Then they plugged in for a stirring reprise of "Finest Work Song" from *Document* and old 40 Watt Club–style covers of Them's "I Can Only Give You Everything" and the Stooges' "Funtime."

    "It was fun," raves Peter Buck. "We taped it on cassette and it sounds wonderful. So maybe we can use something from it on a fan-club B-side.

    But the show wasn't so much fun that it changed the band's mind about touring.

    "Right now, we're making these records," says Buck, firmly, "and I want to make another one."

    He laughs, a little embarrassed, when reminded of the band's promise to resume live work after sitting it out for *Out of Time*. "You just can't tell," he says. "You have to play it intuitively, and for us, that just seems the right thing to do."

R.E.M.'s conspicuous absence from the road has given rise to grim rumors about Michael Stipe's health. The combination of his taste for the ascetic look—short hair, week-old stubble, slightly sunken cheeks—and the AIDS-in-rock phobia sparked by Freddie Mercury's death, has caused scuttlebutt merchants to write Stipe's obit, just because he can't be bothered to haul ass all over the globe and relive the exhausting *Green* arena experience.

Mike Mills' response to the rumors is a short simple, "Bullshit." Buck, no less annoyed, goes into a little more detail.

"What can you say about it? We've all been tested. We have tons of insurance, millions of dollars worth. Not that it's somebody's business, or that I care one way or the other what people think. But I know Michael passed the test just two months ago. And one of the reasons we know this is we have this God-like insurance."

He laughs. "I could probably get a gun and kill a hundred people and I'd be covered. We're at this level, we're a corporation. But you know, as bad as it is to have all these rumors, if it makes kids think a little bit more about their actions, that's fine with me."

What will it take to get R.E.M. on the road again? And when? Mike Mills isn't sure. "We did everything we could do in arenas on the *Green* tour. We have a great time doing it. But we don't just want to go out and duplicate that. And we're not going to play stadiums. I don't see that happening, even if we could.

"It may just be that these songs weren't the ones that kicked us in the butt enough to get us on the road," he says. "We just want to disappear from the business for a while anyway. Take a few good months off. By not touring on the last record, we were supposed to have some time off—completely off.

"But we had none. Zero. We went straight from making the record to doing the press, doing videos, then right into writing songs for the next one. Even when our days were free, we were still going in nights to write and rehearse. This time, we're going to say, 'No band business for the next fix or six months.'

"Which doesn't mean we won't get together to write songs," Mills adds reassuringly. "That's something that never stops."

STEVE MORSE

SURPRISE! NEW LP TAKES UP ACOUSTIC CHALLENGE (1992)

Boston Globe, *October 2, 1992*

Georgia rockers R.E.M., arguably the country's most casual superstars, are doing the unexpected once again. Not only is their new album a quiet, acoustic-oriented retreat from the limelight, but they're not going to support it with a concert tour. It's the second straight album that R.E.M. won't tour behind, though that didn't hurt their last one, *Out of Time,* which sold 10 million copies to become the biggest seller of the band's 12-year career.

"I love touring, but is touring the right thing to do for the band right now? We all think it isn't," guitarist Peter Buck says from R.E.M.'s office in Athens, Ga. "I can't imagine touring with this new record and focusing the set around 12 songs that are mostly passive and slow. So we're going to do another record and then tour."

The new album, *Automatic for the People,* is due out Tuesday. It's largely "moody and dense," as Buck says in a recent interview, but it most definitely rewards repeated listens. Like a latter-day Van Morrison record, it insinuates itself slowly, thanks to singer Michael Stipe's stream-of-consciousness lyrics (notably some anti–George Bush rhetoric in the song "Ignoreland") and a melodic weave of Buck's acoustic guitar and mandolin, plus string arrangements on three tunes by Led Zeppelin's John Paul Jones.

The album is, by and large, insular, with very few guests. Call it chamber folk-rock, if you will. It's nowhere near as playful as *Out of Time* (which contained the hit singles "Losing My Religion" and "Radio Song"), but it's not a sad record, either, despite song titles like "Everybody Hurts" and "Try Not to Breathe." Sonically, it does make sense as the next step.

"You forget what a real musician-type instrument an acoustic guitar is," says Buck, who hasn't featured his electric guitar in three years. "You can't cover up an acoustic guitar with fuzz. It's a matter of you having to play it right. I also like the sound an acoustic guitar makes. But I just got a huge Marshall stack and a Les Paul guitar, so maybe the next record is going to be more rocking. I think that's our plan—to make more of a rock 'n' roll record and go on the road."

Don't look for a tour, however, before 1994.

"When we do tour, we'll have a complete new body of work that basically has never been played live," says bassist Mike Mills in a separate phone interview. "It will be a new thing rather than just a continuation of the same old album/tour, album/tour thing. It'll be fresh for us. It'll be fresh for the people. I just think it's going to be a better idea that we wait a little longer.

"We'll then have three records that we won't have toured behind," Mills says. "That's 30-something songs and we only play 20-something in a night. So we'll be able to play all these songs you've never heard live before. Of course, we'll throw in some of the old ones just for occasional fun, but basically it's going to be a clean slate."

This is strange talk from a band that once toured constantly, building from an alternative, college-popular band (back in 1981 when the song "Radio Free Europe" first broke), to a mainstream band that sold out arenas in 1989. Along the way, they also played a lot of surprise club dates, turning up in such Boston-area clubs as the Rat and Charlie's Tap.

"The fact we were on the road for the entire year of 1989 had something to do with it, because by the end we were more than ready to stop," says Mills. "But I think it's more that we didn't want to go out and do the same thing again. It would have just been like the last arena tour with slight changes in scenery and a few different songs. We want to wait until everybody is really fired up and ready to go and committed to touring. If you go out and just give a half-[baked] show because you don't want to be there, then you're just taking people's money."

After 1989, some rock promoters even eyed R.E.M. as the next stadium act, but that's never going to happen, Mills says.

"You won't see us in stadiums. There's only one reason to play stadiums and that's to make a lot of money. It's absurd. Half the people can't even tell who's up there. And they have to watch these big television screens. That's gross. That has nothing to do with music at all."

Not that R.E.M. hasn't performed within the last few years. They did a benefit in February in Athens for a friend who lacked medical insurance and a few dates in Europe last year. Buck, the most live-oriented player in the group, has done numerous acoustic gigs with Georgia friend Kevin Kinney. Buck also sat in nearly every Wednesday in 1990–91 in Athens with a country band, the Normaltown Flyers, who just released their own album.

"I did it for free, except for all the beer I could drink," Buck says.

"But I've liked not getting paid. I haven't got paid for a gig in three years and I've probably done 100 of them."

Buck, Mills and drummer Bill Berry also found time this year to record an album with '60s garage-rock relics the Troggs, whose "Wild Thing" remains a rock classic. The new album, *Athens and Andover* (Rhino Records) stars Troggs singer Reg Presley and has some fun but time-warped moments. "It's kind of a neat record," says Buck. "And Reg's obsessions are the same. He's still writing about women in hot pants."

R.E.M.'s new album, due to Stipe's poetically oblique lyrics, is naturally more complex. Some songs don't work, such as the quirky, Randy Newman–like "Nightswimming." But most do. There's even an ambient, Brian Eno–like instrumental in "New Orleans Instrumental No. 1" (recorded at Kingsway studio in New Orleans, owned by U2 coproducer Daniel Lanois); and touches of comic relief in "Man on the Moon" (about comic Andy Kaufman) and the TV spoof, "Monty Makes a Deal," with this line tucked amid an accordion texture: "Nonsense has a welcome ring."

The most lasting memory, though, is the assault on George Bush's conservative doctrine. The new single, "Drive," talks about being "Bush-whacked," while the song "Ignoreland" is even more negative toward Bush.

"It's a total anti-Reagan/Bush diatribe, but it's also a message to America. That's what 'Ignoreland' is—America," says Mills. "It's people who only get their information from sound bytes and television, and who don't really bother to research the presidential candidates; or ultimately the more important ones, who are your local candidates." Nothing on the album jumps out as an immediate hit single, but that doesn't faze R.E.M. "We're an album band anyway," says Buck. "Are we big enough to drag our audience along to a record that isn't a radio-ready Top 40 hit? It doesn't matter one way or the other. But I think our fans are into the band enough that they're not going to need a dance-pop, Top 10 single to buy the record. . . . Our fan base will be there. I'm not worried about it. As long as we do good work, we'll be fine."

ALLAN JONES

FROM HEARSE TO ETERNITY: *AUTOMATIC FOR THE PEOPLE* (1992)

Melody Maker, *October 3, 1992*

Reviewing R.E.M.'s astonishingly sombre new single, "Drive," in last week's *MM,* David Stubbs confused the Marlon Brando movie *The Wild One* with the Sam Peckinpah western, *The Wild Bunch*. This was an interesting juxtaposition.

Both films, after all, examine a specifically American kind of nihilism. But where in *The Wild One,* Brando's biker is compelled forever to remain on the road, even if he's not going anywhere, *The Wild Bunch* is a film about what happens to a particular kind of American hero when the road runs out and they come to the end of the line. At which point, the best they can hope for is to check out on their own terms, confronting death with dignity, finding redemption in the manner of their dying. Which is what, finally, this album seems mostly to be about. *Automatic for the People* is the sound of Michael Stipe and R.E.M. raging against the dying of the light.

It's almost impossible to write about the record without mentioning the recent grim rumours concerning Stipe's health. Variously, he's said to be dying with either AIDS or cancer. Elsewhere in this issue, Peter Buck vehemently denies these stories. This is good news, of course. But *Automatic for the People* still seems extraordinarily preoccupied with dying and death and how we face up to those final moments between absolute light and absolute darkness. To which extent, it's an often staggeringly brave attempt to somehow describe the unimaginable.

Around the time of *Document,* there was a definite whiff of apocalypse about some of R.E.M.'s music. The most blatant example of this drift was provided by the alliterative crunch and musical headbutt of "It's the End of the World as We Know It (and I Feel Fine)." But the sense of things coming apart was also unnervingly apparent on tracks like "Disturbance at the Heron House" and "Oddfellows Local 151." These songs were charred, spare, characterised by an atmosphere of burned-out desolation to which the group return here.

The grim truth behind much of *Automatic for the People* is that death isn't always glorious. For most of us, it's slow and agonizing and we end our days hooked up to drips and tubes, life leaving us in small desperate gasps. Most of us like to think that given the choice, we'd prefer to go out in a blaze of glory and screaming fury like Peckinpah's outlaws in *The Wild Bunch*. But few of us are that kind of hero, and Stipe is touching in his recognition of the fact and *Automatic for the People* celebrates a different kind of heroism.

If the pared-down intimacy of *Out of Time* was a surprise after the stadium-sized strum of *Green*, the further musical reductionism of this LP may come as an even greater shock. As David Fricke remarked in his feature last week on the making of the record, *Automatic for the People* moves at an agonizing crawl. For sure, there are choruses here that ring in your ears like Christmas and some of Buck's guitar feedback is like being hit by lightning. But the sound overall is Spartan, uncommonly naked, deeply brooding. Even the orchestral arrangements that are employed on several cuts are full of turmoil, a sense of dark foreboding.

The sullen morbid grandeur of the magnificent "Drive" is typical of the album, but barely prepares the listener for some of the cheerless depths charted elsewhere. "Try Not to Breathe," for instance, is a deathbed lament, Stipe giving exhausted voice to the reflections of an old man looking forward to death, calm in its final embrace. The poignant backporch instrumentation is briefly reminiscent of something like "You Are the Everything," but the track is given an acutely disturbing edge by Buck's coruscating guitar distortions which are like something creeping through your house at night, frightening and ghostly.

Not everything here is so uniquely blasted. There's a certain playfulness to "The Sidewinder Sleeps Tonight" and the gorgeous spaced-out bossa nova of "Man on the Moon" (an eccentric love song to the dead American comedian Andy Kaufman, with walk-on parts for Charles Darwin, Moses and Elvis Presley). "Ignoreland," meanwhile, is a full-scale sonic broadside aimed at George Bush and his Republican party reptiles, Stipe delivering a vicious lyric with all the poisonous spite he can muster— which is plenty.

These, however, are random shafts of light in a landscape that is otherwise drenched in shadows and touched by the pale hand of mortality. Loss and grief pervade the album like a haunting. "Readying to bury your father and your mother / What did you think when you lost another?" Stipe sings in a wracked folkie croak on the harrowingly beautiful "Sweetness Follows," a song about watching, helpless, as someone dies, played out over a vicious droning cello and writhing chunks of feedback.

"Sweetness Follows" is the blackest, bleakest moment R.E.M. have committed to record. By comparison, even this album's other beleaguered ballads are lifted by a redemptive passion. "Everybody Hurts," for instance, is a stirring hymn to human resilience in the face of all the awfulness the world can throw at you. It begins like a classic soul anthem, Stipe's fantastic vocal testifying over tabernacle organ chords. When the strings flood in, however, pitched against Buck's electric guitar, I'm reminded of "Astral Weeks" with feedback.

The same kind of aching beauty evident here is echoed by the record's closing tracks, "Nightswimming" and "Find the River." The former is a song about the loss of innocence, days long gone and the people, the friends and lovers, who have gone with them. It's almost insufferably moving, with another stunning Stipe vocal and a final horn solo quite heartbreaking in its loneliness. "Find the River," as Buck remarks, is a perfect conclusion, an elegiac farewell, the sun setting for the last time on a worried, dying world, the bruised loveliness of Stipe's voice drifting towards an eternal stillness, the sleep at the end of time.

Amazingly, initial reactions to *Automatic for the People* in this particular vicinity have been mixed. People whose opinions I am usually in enthusiastic agreement with have said they find it hard going, glum. They can't hear any songs on it. Psshaw to them. *Automatic for the People* is R.E.M. at the very top of their form.

Listen to it, and let it stone you to your soul.

Part Four

BANG AND BLAME

R.E.M.'S BEST ALBUM SIDE? BAND MEMBERS SAY IT'S NOT "AUTO-MATIC" (1994)

Chicago Tribune, *November 27, 1994*

Here's a rundown of R.E.M.'s nine studio albums, with comments by Peter Buck (B), Mike Mills (M), Michael Stipe (S) and Scott Litt (L), who took over as the band's producer beginning with the *Document* album. Star ratings are by rock critic Greg Kot.

Murmur (1983 ****), *Reckoning* (1984 **$^1/_2$) and *Fables of the Reconstruction* (1985 ***) established the band as jangly, enigmatic folk-rockers.

S: "*Murmur* is a great record to a lot of people, but to me it seems like another person made it. It was 11 years ago, but to me it was 811 years ago."

M: "*Murmur* is just these excited kids having a great time discovering rock 'n' roll, and *Fables* is these suddenly old men discovering the tragedies of life. We grew up a lot in those two years. We were on the road constantly, dealing with what it meant to be a band, and it was a very rugged learning experience."

S: "*Fables* reflects that time of utter craziness, uber insanity."

B: "*Reckoning* has 'South Central Rain,' which is still one of my favorite songs. It's one of the first ones that Michael (Stipe) captured that elliptical way of writing that still managed to say something specific and tangible."

With *Life's Rich Pageant* (1986 ***) and then *Document* (1987 ***$^1/_2$), the band became more outspoken in its lyrics while turning up the guitars.

M: "At that point we were in the midst of all the Reagan-Bush b.s. and things just had to be said. We were discovering that we had a platform to rail from. It was just us exercising our influence muscles, and using it to do what we thought was good." Producer Don Gehman "brought that out of Michael [on *Pageant*]. I love that record, because we were really powerful live at that point, and those are some of the best live songs: 'Cuyahoga,' 'These Days,' 'Begin the Begin.'"

B: "The first side of *Document* is the best album side that we ever did. And then you flip it over and get the weird stuff."

155

Green (1988 $**^1/_2$) was a transitional album. It went platinum and established the band as an arena act, but some of its more experimental tracks didn't work.

L: "*Green* led directly to [the denser arrangements on] *Out of Time*, but I don't think it was formulated as well as the subsequent records. It had some clunkers. But we did 'Turn You Inside Out' with Keith LeBlanc, the Sugar Hill [hip-hop] drummer, and opened up some different ideas. In R.E.M.'s music there's always something going on from the waist down, there's a little bit of swing and sexiness to it."

With *Out of Time* (1991 $***^1/_2$) and *Automatic for the People* (1992 $****$), the music took a dramatic turn inward. Where *Out of Time* was a lush tapestry of acoustic instruments, *Automatic* was sparse and even more emotionally wrenching. In contrast, *Monster* (1994 $***^1/_2$) is the band's hardest rocker yet.

L: "It was scary when we finished [*Out of Time*] because we had no idea how people would take it. The only thing we knew was that 'Losing My Religion' was a really easy song to listen to again and again."

B: "*Automatic* is the album that I think will hold up best, the one people may think is pretty good 10 years from now. I was driving through the desert with a friend listening to it and saying, 'We should probably break up. This would be a good place to stop.'"

JIM SULLIVAN

NEW SNARLING FREQUENCY *MONSTER* MARKS BAND'S NEXT STAGE (1994)

Boston Globe, *September 25, 1994*

How, might you wonder, can R.E.M. still be like a punk-rock band? Sure, the first single/video from the band's new *Monster* snarls out of the speakers with lots of noisy tremolo guitar and even more attitude. But we're talking about the veteran grand masters of alternative rock, a Warner Bros. act who in recent years have been automatic multimillion sellers every time they get around to putting out a new album.

"We came out of the punk-rock movement, even though we weren't punks by any stretch of the imagination," explains R.E.M. guitarist Peter Buck by phone from an Atlanta hotel room.

"The idea of punk wasn't buying a leather jacket and having green hair. Punk pretty soon turned into a series of rules that you followed to join a certain crowd. Everyone likes to join a crowd and we don't. We took the ideals to heart. We latched onto a lack of rules, the idea that you can do it yourself, and don't have to depend on some big machinery. Of course, we're signed to Warner Bros., which does have a lot of big machinery, but as long as you do the work outside of the business end of it, I think you're doing all right."

R.E.M., which releases its 11th album on Tuesday, has played by its own rules. The group—since its late-'70s inception in Athens, Ga., composed of Buck, singer Michael Stipe, bassist-singer Mike Mills and drummer Bill Berry—slowly built up an audience. Buck jokes, "Nobody knew who we were for 10 years." Not quite true, but their steady surge preceded alternative rock's big 1991 breakthrough. So, then, what did R.E.M. do? Rush to capitalize?

Not exactly. R.E.M.'s 1991 album *Out of Time* and the 1992 album *Automatic for the People* sold 10 and 8 million copies, respectively, but R.E.M. supported neither with a tour. In fact, they haven't toured in five years. The whole "alternative" rock breakthrough, from Nirvana to Green Day, happened more or less around them—they were more of a ghostly video presence than a working band. Alternative rock has gotten harder—more punk, if you will—and now so has R.E.M.

R.E.M. will launch their "Monster" tour overseas early next year. They aren't expected back in the United States until mid-1995, when they'll mount a hockey arena or summer shed tour.

No stadiums, says Buck: "I have real trouble with those big places. Preferably, I'd like to play in front of 150 people in a blues bar in town, but that ain't gonna happen."

From a musical perspective, Buck explains, the paramount concern in R.E.M. is to not bore yourself. Do not repeat yourself. Do not settle for what is expected of you. The mandolin flavorings and folk-rock shadings of earlier efforts are largely gone here. With *Monster*, R.E.M. has come up with a fierce, guitar-driven rock record—in a sense, an abrasive little number.

"Good," says Buck. "That's what we were going for."

You won't be calling Buck the Jangle King on this one. Yet you may once again be sifting through the layers of guitar to decipher lyrics. The album's first single/video "What's the Frequency, Kenneth?" is not atypical of *Monster*: a "Sweet Jane"–like power surge; a clanging, tremolo-laden guitar hook that stutter-steps across the terrain; enticing, oblique vocal lines like the lead-off "'What's the frequency, Kenneth?' is your Benzedrine / I was brain dead, locked out, numb, not up to speed."

Yes, Buck says, the title comes from the mantra two New York muggers chanted when they beat Dan Rather in 1986. Lyrics are all Stipe's doing. R.E.M.'s re-appropriation keeps the never-explained non sequitur alive in pop-culture circulation.

Musically, there's a terseness, a seriousness, a hardness to much of *Monster.* R.E.M. breaks from form, much the way their peers U2 did with *Achtung, Baby* and *Zooropa.* And there's Buck's electric guitar ripping every which way—a Sonic Youth–like drone/wash in "Let Me In," a churning, clanging presence in "Star 69." "We've said for years that we were gonna make a rock 'n' roll record again," says Buck, "and, I dunno, it just seemed to work out that way this time. I think getting away from playing, doing videos and stuff, just taking time off, we came back feeling refreshed. I felt like a teen-ager. I was sitting in our little rehearsal studio with a big pile of amps and electric guitars. It was, on a visceral level, very pleasurable to just turn it up and play really loud. We tried to stay away from all the 'hallmarks' of the R.E.M. sound—no ringing guitars. . . . The songs are, by and large, a lot simpler than has been the way of our songwriting over the years. We really pared things down to two or three chords. It had some tremolo, some songs that came out of that sound."

The middle of the disc is the most R.E.M.-like part. "Strange Currencies" has a quiet, Velvet-y sound and a yearning, sensual tone, with Stipe singing "I want to turn you on, turn you up, figure you out." "Tongue" is languid and romantic, featuring a churchy organ underlying it, and Stipe's sister Linda on vocals. "Bang and Blame" begins with the familiar, winsome-sounding verse much like "Losing My Religion," but then slams into a tough "Bang, then blame / It's not my thing so let it go now" chorus.

Lyrically, there's a sense of quest and confusion—if you can pick it out. "I think the lyrics are a lot more focused," says Buck. "But there's a lot more stuff going that's covering them up. Basically, it's kind of a weird record. There's lots of space, but there's also a lot of indistinct things and there's a lot of noise. The lyrics on the printed page are really strong, but it's a matter of having to put your head into the speaker and figure things out."

There certainly seems to be some issue of sexual ambiguity, with Stipe singing "Make it charged with controversy / I'm straight / I'm queer

/ I'm bi" amid the swaggering, metallic grind in "King of Comedy." The song itself is a knock at artist as commodity; it would seem Stipe is inviting one to play the guessing game, while he's denouncing the star-making machinery.

"Well, it's not first-person personal," offers Buck, by way of comment. "I know Michael just throws a lot of stuff in. You know, the sexual identity stuff is not his personal thing. [But] I think he kind of likes to keep them guessing, too. . . . Sex, identity, obsession, media. It's more character playing on Michael's part. Sex is in there a lot, a lot of sex songs."

Buck looks back fondly on the path R.E.M. has taken—from the club circuit, working up to mid-size theaters to the arenas. "If I was gonna plot a career course, which would be a scary thing," he says, "I would have done it just like this. I was talking to Krist [Novoselic] and Dave [Grohl] from Nirvana a while ago and they mentioned they didn't spend huge amounts of time in clubs. It was good for us. We did club dates for five years and we did medium-level places for another four."

Buck says the band has always measured success in uncommon terms. "One of the reasons we may have lasted so long," he says, "is that our main goal was to be really good songwriters and do challenging, exciting work. If you can do that, then you can kind of just putter along. I mean if selling records was that important to me, we would have been considered failures for over 10 years. I feel real good knowing that several million people will hear this record in the first couple of weeks and that we'll probably sell our tour dates out."

So: Does *Monster* have to top the sales of *Automatic* to be considered a hit in their eyes? "I'd be lying to you to say that I don't care at all. But I don't care that much. We're at the point where we're gonna sell a fair amount just because of who we are. As long as we think the record's where we want it to be and it's a good record, I don't really worry if it sells a few million more."

DAVID CAVANAGH

TUNE IN, CHEER UP, ROCK OUT (1994)

Q, *October 1994*

R.E.M. held a four-day band meeting in Acapulco. On the agenda: What do you give people when you've already given them everything? Answer: A back-to-basics rock album called *Monster,* and, bugger it, a world tour. David Cavanagh went to LA to hear the minutes, talk Cockney rhyming slang with the guys, and to feel Michael's head. In this exclusive tête-a-tête, Stipe announces, "We're going to throw ourselves to the dogs for 10 months."

On a big vertical stick 15 feet above the Psychic Shop on Sunset Boulevard, Bullwinkle looks at Rocky. His expression rapt, his antlers taut, his mindset de-tuned from Los Angeles's neon-exotic Medication Superhigh-way, he fixates with moosey adoration upon—what the hell is Rocky, anyway?—a species of small blue beaver, or a unique, pastel-shaded squirrel. The cartoon pals grin foolishly, frozen in plastic, and the lunchtime heat is glorious.

Directly across the street, at the bottom of a verdant hill that leads up to the secluded Chateau Marmont Hotel, four shifty-looking chaps are eyeing the traffic. One of them, whose baggy dungarees are of marked rural aspect, has bushy eyebrows that traverse his face like the final quarter of a cat's tail. Another sports glasses and new, thick hair. A third is tall and talks constantly. And the fourth . . . God, the fourth.

Skinny torso flexed under a drab T-shirt with a star design—functional, Soviet—he has shaved his head to within a rasping millimetre of his scalp, *après* John Malkovich in *In the Line of Fire,* and is eating French fries with the manner of a man who has never before seen food. He has orange varnish on his fingernails.

A car slowly makes its way down the Chateau Marmont's driveway and perches at the intersection, waiting to pull out. The driver glances at the small roadside gathering. Hmm, he probably thinks: four no-marks getting their photograph taken. He effects no double-take. But Orange Nail-Varnish has seen something.

"You've got a flat, man!" he shouts, pointing at the car's right front wheel.

The driver shoots him a concerned look and cruises out into Sunset. Shouting Boy shrugs and goes back to his chips. Michael Stipe, it's good to hear your voice.

Stipe talks. Stipe converses. Stipe forms sentences. Stipe even shouts. What Elysian astral plane is this? It's LA, it's Sunday, it's tea-time and R.E.M. are in the studio completing the mix of their new album. If you're not there, the place to be is Room 19 in the Chateau Marmont, where a playback is taking place of the six songs they have finished so far. The Warner Bros. suite is lined with six large speakers, connected to a giant mixing desk, into which a tape is slotted. A sheet of paper is flashed around, with the words "R.E.M.—Monster" written across the top, and a list of song titles: "What's the Frequency, Kenneth?" "I Took Your Name." "Bang and Blame." "Crush with Eyeliner." "I Don't Sleep, I Dream." "Strange Currencies."

One immediate puzzle. A San Francisco band called Game Theory had an odd, very abrupt track on their 1987 album *Lolita Nation* called "Kenneth—What's the Frequency?" And Game Theory's producer, Mitch Easter, co-produced R.E.M.'s first two albums, *Murmur* and *Reckoning*. Are R.E.M. helping out some old mates here, with a lucrative cover version?

No, they're not. As Peter Buck's first blaring chords to "What's the Frequency, Kenneth?" strike up, it's palpably a new R.E.M. tune. It's also very loud. Just as they promised, R.E.M. are a rock band once more, with a garage-like feel, a dose of what might justifiably called "attitude," a built-in, guess-the-next-chord-yep-spot-on, Ezi-Learn facility, and lashings of sexy tremolo. Electric guitars. Feet on the monitors. No songs about AIDS, death or the White House. A total change of strategy. The gravitas of *Automatic for the People* is in storage. We are entering a Melancholy-Free Zone and when the first R.E.M. tour in five and a half years kicks off in Australia after Christmas, word has it Peter Buck has been informed that, should he see fit to bring his mandolin, he can expect to wake up one morning and find it in two pieces on the carpet outside his hotel room.

In one sense, it's all a bit of a shame. *Out of Time* and *Automatic for the People* were superb records, and that kind of beauty is just not on their flat-plan any more. On the other hand, you've got to laugh. The Jesus & Mary Chain would reject a couple of these songs for not being complicated enough.

In honour of this sea-change, the R.E.M. media tourniquet has been loosened sufficiently to permit two interviews—conducted in pairs and of 40-minutes duration—before *Monster* has even been properly completed. Stipe, who did no interviews for *Automatic for the People,* has agreed to take part, speak, converse, form sentences, etc. etc.

After four listens, the songs are fixed in the memory, verbatim and note-for-note. A couple of them are in real danger of getting on your tits. You drift out on to the balcony and look out over the neat little garden and out on to Sunset. What was that line Stipe had growled so enjoyably on "Crush with Eyeliner"? "We all invent ourselves . . . and you know me." He got that half-right.

It's Monday at the Chateau. Peter Buck saunters into the room and immediately rejects the alcoholic temptations within the fridge. Dowsing his throat with the contents of a blue bottle of sparkling water, he enthuses paternally on the subject of his freshly-hatched twins, Zoe and Zelda.

"The doctor goes, Ohhh, at your age [he's 37], probably take about six months." He grins with libidinous, nuff-said satisfaction. "First time. And twins is definitely the way to go, I think. You get it all done at once."

He, his second wife Stephanie and the twins checked out of the Chateau some time ago, after finding they were unable to order pizza at three in the morning ("The guy goes, Oh, we're awful busy down here, sir. *Really?*") and instead shipped into the lavish Four Seasons, where their fellow guests included the Argentinian football team. Even Buck, who loathes sport, admits he had heard about Diego Maradona's five-drug downfall. He just didn't know Maradona was Argentinian.

"I don't take sports seriously," he says dismissively, "although I like that Scottish thing where they throw the poles. I'm down with that."

Jefferson Holt, R.E.M.'s manager, enters owlishly and immediately heads off to the bedroom to make a phone call. Buck, too, picks up a phone. Their voices start talking at exactly the same time. Are they on the phone to each other?

Bill Berry ambles in, looking like a character at the end of the bar in a Sam Peckinpah movie, and politely says hello. He models late 19th-century farming chic: cap, dungarees, look of distraction.

"I bought property just outside of Athens and moved an old house out there," he explains. "I'm a hay farmer now. I have to worry about rainfall and fertiliser, keeping oil in the tractor. But I get on the tractor and it's like all my problems go away. It's been great therapy for me."

Do your neighbours know who they're living next to?

"Yeah, but they don't give a shit. They know that we sell records, but they've never heard of them. I'm not in a country band, so. . . ."

Buck, too, has known the great outdoors. Last summer, he and his wife went on safari in Africa.

"I went to Kenya and Tanzania," he grins. "Slept in tents. I was sitting in the tent at three in the morning and I heard this *rrroooowwffff*, and a hippopotamus brushed by the tent. They make weird noises."

Berry turns to him: "So did y'all conceive there?" "No, no, right afterwards. It was actually the day after the MTV show. I could tell you the time of day. . . ."

Can one forget about being in R.E.M. on safari? Buck laughs matter-of-factly. "I can forget about being in R.E.M. while I'm on stage."

The linking theme of *Monster*, Berry explains out on the balcony, has been illness and lack of sleep. Buck has been a proud victim of the early morning Twin Alarm Call ever since the great drop. Stipe has had a tooth abscess. Mike Mills was recording "What's the Frequency, Kenneth?" at two o'clock one afternoon when he complained of a strange pain in his side. Come midnight, he was lying in a hospital bed, recently divested of his appendix. Berry himself came down with very bad flu. All of this amounted to a fortnight of lost studio time. Then there was the suicide of their friend Kurt Cobain in April. . . .

So what happened to the mandolin, Peter? Did you step on it?

"Packed it away. And there are no acoustic guitars on it either. It's funny, the last record, they had to force me to play electric guitar, basically. This time around, all of a sudden it seemed like the right thing to do. We're all really excited about playing electric instruments and using Marshalls and Les Pauls. So the mandolin's in a closet somewhere."

Has there been a general rediscovery of rock 'n' roll in the band?

"I never stopped thinking that we were a rock 'n' roll band. I guess we were getting to be a quieter rock 'n' roll band. I mean, we started off playing bars for drunk people who were dancing. Those days are gone, but it's part of what we do."

Do you know that Game Theory used a similar title to "What's the Frequency, Kenneth?" on one of their albums?

"Oh, you're kidding! Really? Well, you know where it comes from? There's a famous newscaster in America, Dan Rather. He's very stolid and sincere—really straight guy—and he was beaten up one day. And he claimed that two men ran up to him and started pounding him mercilessly and then they'd stop and go: 'What's the frequency, Kenneth?' and then beat him some more. (Laughs.) It didn't make any sense. It's like, What the fuck are you talking about? What exactly is going through your mind here?"

In retrospect, do you know why *Automatic for the People* sounded as solemn as it did?

"It was a reflection of where we were, as people. I don't know if that sounds unclear or not."

(It does, and one point is often overlooked. While ghastly rumours that Michael Stipe had AIDS gathered momentum, the restless Buck's own life was far from wonderful. As his first marriage ended, Buck famously ballooned out, drinking heavily and retreating from view.)

"I pretty much literally spent two years in bed," he says. "All I did was drink wine and lay in bed. I'd get up and practice every night, and then go back to bed. I never left my house. And then I figured out what I wanted to do with my life, and did it. I made a lot of changes. But it was kind of fun. I'd recommend it to anyone. If you feel depressed, take a two-week vacation and don't leave your bed. Order pizza, drink wine. It's a great thing."

No one in R.E.M. seemed thrilled around the time of *Automatic for the People*. Interviews were spent parrying deep, death-related questions and dodging rumours about Stipe. As to the album itself, it wasn't that the songs weren't fun to play as a band, more that many of the songs were never played as a band at all.

"The last album was kind of like, dare I say, *The White Album*. It was a weird record. We didn't do a whole lot of playing together. We never played 'Sweetness Follows' or 'Nightswimming' as a band. Bill and I aren't even on 'Nightswimming.' I'm not on 'Find the River.' Mike's not on 'Sweetness Follows.' Bill wrote 'Everybody Hurts' and he's hardly on it. But with this album, we recorded a lot of it on a soundstage and we all had monitors and people would be in a studio and it's this airless, anti-septic room and you know that you're getting down to work and you have to be real serious about it. This was, we'd go and tune up, and play, order pizza . . . More fun than it's been in quite a while."

You must have been aware that huge sections of the population were hoping for a loud, electric R.E.M. album?

Berry: "My wife sure was."

Buck: "I have a lot of Italian friends and I was there—in Sicily, actually—last summer and they were pulling me aside and going, Now, Peter, it will be a *rrrrrock* record. You will *rrrock*. You will *rrrock* and *rrroll*. I'm like, Yes, we'll do that, yes."

That's not a bad accent. Can you do Cockney?

"Aaaah . . . no. Cockney's really tough, although I wish there was a book on the rhyming slang, because that's just so fascinating. We're impressed by Cockney rhyming slang."

Well, put it this way. You've just had a couple of dustbins.

"Which would be . . . ?"

Dustbin lids. Kids.

"Oh Yeah! That's good. I like Stroke-on-Trent, for gay. Hehhehheh. Mike and I were watching this show—I guess it's called *Only Fools and Horses*—and not only could I not understand about half the dialogue, but the other half was in this rhyming slang, and we're like, What the fuck are they saying? It's fascinating. I guess it's in cultures where people feel marginalized, like African-American slang, which is purposely so that us honkies don't quite get it."

You distinctly acted [as a barman] in the video for "Man on the Moon," after always saying you never would.

"No, see, I've been a bartender. It's really not that hard. You hand beer to people and take change. Y'know, I didn't have to emote. I liked doing it, too. Running a tab for some of the regulars, y'know. I could be a bartender again, so long as I didn't have to mix Piña Coladas. I'm not interested in that."

Is it true you rescued Alex Chilton from life as a bartender in the '80s by getting him a booking agent?

"No, not at all. I think that maybe the fact that a lot of us in the South respected him and liked his past work helped him. But I've met the guy, like, 20 times and I still don't think he knows my name. Alex gives less of a shit than almost anyone I've ever met. I do remember when we played this place called Tupelo's Tavern in New Orleans, he was the janitor there. And he went in our dressing room, drank every single beer that was there while we were on stage, and then insulted us afterwards. It's so funny that all those Creation bands discovered Big Star two years ago. You talk to all these Scottish guys, they're like, [awful accent] Och, I've just discovered this *grreat* band."

Berry: "He does the Italian better."

Can you remember what touring was like?

Berry: [sighing] "We're just now forgetting the bad parts."

Buck: "The playing is great. There's someone who was in Duke

Ellington's band who said, They don't pay me for the playing, they pay me for riding the bus for 23 hours. I mean, we're friends and we like, none of us were that traumatized by it, we just thought it'd be better for the band to not do it. And I feel that there was a great growth thing for us to concentrate on making records and letting ourselves realize that there aren't any rules that we really have to follow. For better or worse, we've invented the way we go about doing this."

Were there ever specific acts of violence on tour?

Buck: [to Berry] "Didn't I throw a plastic jug at Mike once? I seem to remember that in Arizona. And then he threw a chair at me. But no, we've never really done that. Not to say that it wouldn't have helped at times. I still think Mike deserves a good thrashing."

Berry: "Mike and Michael had some pretty bad friction going there for a while, on one of those tours."

Buck: "We weren't being very nice to each other around '85. We were just mean to each other. We didn't really talk. I seem to remember seeing most of that year from the bottom of a glass. If I had to go back and change something, I think I'd make us see a group therapist."

Is it true R.E.M. had a four-day conference in Acapulco last year to decide whether or not to carry on?

Buck: "It wasn't to discuss *whether* to carry on, it was to discuss *how* to carry on. It was a meeting to decide stuff. Tour? Probably, yeah, so that's good. Make a record? How do we go about it? Cut it a bit more live. . . . It was just a matter of quantifying our desires. It was great. We used the Warner Bros. house, which was ideal. We'd water-ski, or swim all day, have a two-hour meeting over Piña Coladas and, er . . . it doesn't sound too bad, does it?"

In Acapulco they sketched a gameplan from 1994 to the end of 1996, although that's not as adventurous as it sounds. This album's tour will take them right through to the end of 1995.

Buck: "Then we're talking about doing something ambitious. We've got a lot of songs. We wrote 45 songs for this record. We've got a whole album's worth of acoustic stuff that we demo'd that is pretty nice. Then another idea is maybe doing a live album recorded in a hotel room."

Do you think Kurt Cobain's suicide was a personal decision, or was rock 'n' roll partly to blame?

Buck: "No . . . that was Kurt. I have trouble even talking about it. I don't . . . [sighs] . . . That was Kurt. It wasn't a surprise. As a friend, you wish there was something that could have been done. But everyone tried.

It wasn't like this poor kid was abandoned. I know people that work at his record label, and I know his booking agents. There were four interventions in the last two weeks he was alive. Everything that could have been done was done. That was a thing that he planned, and it sucks and I wish that something could have been done, but he didn't want it to be done. I think about it every day and it's hard to deal with."

Did R.E.M. as a touring band attract the same coteries of hangers-on and ne'er-do-wells as other bands?

"No, that never really happened with us. We don't get groupies, we get teenagers who want to read us their poetry—which I'd much rather have. At least you meet people who are kind of interesting. We've never had that leather-clad, with-the-whip thing. That's just not where the band is. The drug-dealer thing was never really there. None of us were into that."

Berry: [puzzled] "Does that even happen any more? For anybody?"

Buck: "I think maybe Guns N' Roses and that ilk of bands probably get a lot of that."

A lot of English bands do too. Apparently, Ned's Atomic Dustbin are very glamorous to American girls.

Buck: [slowly] "Ned's Atomic Dustbin? Are you telling me that *Ned's Atomic Dustbin* get groupies? Uh . . . I'm going to have to take your word on this one. I don't get it. Although I do notice that English bands seem to have some attraction over here that certainly isn't reciprocated in England. You don't pull up to Colchester and have 16-year-olds throwing themselves at you. It's not like we're virgins, but that doesn't happen. [Pause] Ned's Atomic Dustbin, huh? Really. [Sigh] There you go. [To Berry] If only we were English."

Berry: [hesitantly] "So, Ned's Atomic Dustbin, is that a reference to a child, then? Didn't you say that dustbin, er . . . "

Buck: "Do you remember going to England the first time in '83? I'd never been out of America—none of us had except Michael, who'd lived in Germany when he was six years old. I had no idea what to expect. I thought that it would be mohawks, old buildings and warm beer. Guess I was right, hehhehheh. But all I knew was literature. I knew more about 1880 from Dickens than 1983. It's funny, we thought we were all men of the world who knew all this shit. We didn't know anything. I remember the first time we went to New York, there was me, Mike and Michael, with a map of New York, and we're in Greenwich Village and we have the map on the ground, and it's about six feet wide and we're kneeling on it, trying to figure out where we are. And this street guy comes up and he looks at us and goes, Man, you've got the map upside down."

Will it be just the four of you on stage when you tour?

Buck: "Mostly. We'll probably take one other person. Not Peter Holsapple, no [close-to-honorary fifth member, played on the Green tour and *Unplugged*]. He's got a new band and he's got a kid and he's living in New Orleans. So that's fair. It sounds like a lot of fun, but I don't think being an extra member of a band is all that fun. It's lucrative, but you don't have creative input. I wouldn't do it. Oh! [To Berry] We should give someone's address to send demo tapes to. Let's give Mike's home address. Let's see if we can ruin his life."

Blissfully oblivious in the next suite along, Mike Mills is resting his fluffy new hairstyle in a comfortable armchair and there is one cigarette butt in the ashtray, with a packet of Drum tobacco next to it. Michael Stipe, even at this stage of the game, rolls his own. In January, he shaved his head; the subsequent months have seen limited grow-back of a suspiciously serrated-looking surface of stubble atop the cranium.

"No, it's nice. Here, feel."

(Rizzzz, rizzzz, hmm, short-haired cat mixed with slight hint of facecloth.)

Mike Mills leans over and feels. "Mmm. That's nice."

Stipe is ordering food. Aside from fries and ketchup, he urgently desires a complicated order of fruit and vegetables that features celery, and possibly cherries. He is wearing National Health glasses. He sits, not in an armchair, but on the floor. He continues to wear orange nail varnish. So far so Stipe.

But God bless him, when the talking starts, he goes for it. There's none of the enigmatic silences and deep-throated "uhhhhh . . . [long pause] . . ." that many have come to know and fear as the Michael Stipe experience. He speaks briskly, invariably answers without missing a beat and is extremely easy-going. He's also tactile, self-deprecating, zany, bouncy, courteous, linear, unpretentious and precise. He may be hungry, but he sure ain't weird.

This album sounds pretty direct and sexy.

Mills: "Mmm. Very much so. That's what it's all about. Playful, sexy, fun, loud, all those things."

Unlike *Automatic for the People.*

Stipe: "Yeah. Sure. *Automatic for the People* was downright depressing at points. Not depressing, no. Always with hope. But, you know, pretty sad [laughs]."

And why was it so sad?

Stipe: "Probably the subject matter. Most of the record was about mortality and dying. Pretty turgid stuff [laughs again, louder]."

Were you surprised by its success (1.8 million copies sold in the U.K. alone)? A lot of people wanted to hear those songs about mortality and dying.

Stipe: "Yeah, I was surprised. [Shrugs] They're good songs, though, overall."

You use a lot of modern business slang on this new record. It's quite menacing. Phrases like: "I wrote the sales pitch," "I'm up to speed," "cop an attitude." Do you like that language?

"Yeah, it's great as a writer. [To Mills] Do I use it in real life?"

Mills: "Sometimes. It's colourful. It's expressive."

Stipe: [muttering] "Up to speed."

Do you ever think, when you're writing the songs, These words are going to be sung all over the world?

Stipe: "Yeah! This guy told me last week—my best friend from Athens is from Morocco, from Marrakesh, and he told me, Oh yeah, you guys, everybody in Morocco loves your music, everybody sings 'Losing My Religion.' And in Portugal, people cry when 'Losing My Religion' comes on the jukebox. That's great; you know, that's kind of beautiful. [Laughing] In Israel they refer to that song as 'Oh Life.'"

Mills: "Yeah, because they don't know the English, so they come up to the DJ and say, Play 'Oh Life'! Play 'Oh Life'!"

Stipe: "Obviously, there are other songs in our repertoire. But I guess that was our . . ."

Mills: "Big international pop nerve-toucher."

Stipe: "So people are going to sing it. That's cool. I like that idea."

On *Monster*, they explain, they have left blank choruses at the end of certain songs, where in the past Mills or Berry would have chimed in with a fifth harmony, so that R.E.M. fans can sing away, just like karaoke.

Stipe: "It makes it interactive. If you promise you won't fucking put that word in this interview, right? No, but I mean, I love it when Joan Jett leaves out a chorus and I can sing along."

When you tour, won't you miss the privacy you've become accustomed to?

Stipe: "Yeah. Sure. But it's a trade-off. We're going to throw ourselves to the dogs for 10 months and that'll be that. Come back and live a normal life."

How much do people really know about you two? Could you put it in a fraction?

Mills: "In terms of facts, facts are easy to know. As far as people . . . no, there's very few people who really know us. People can rattle off any sort of biographical information about us, but that's not the same thing."

Stipe doesn't answer. One was afraid of something like this happening in a democratic interview process. It's now time—rudely and unfairly—to try and squeeze Mike Mills out of the conversation. Maintaining unwavering eye contact with Stipe, you proceed.

What do you think people will make of the line on "Crush with Eyeliner" that goes: "We all invent ourselves and you know me"?

Stipe: "I'm sure they'll have fun with it. Well, you know your idea of me. I kind of hope they'll turn it in on themselves. They can hold me, or us, up as whatever they want us to be. But hopefully it'll go a little bit beyond that. Obviously, I'm having fun by throwing shit like that in there."

Do you find your voice goes down an octave when you do interviews?

"Well, I don't know. I hear myself on tape and I hate my speaking voice so much. I hate my accent, except when I'm in Georgia and it gets a lot broader, much more like how I grew up. But people tell me that my voice is completely flat, that there's no inflection or intonation, and that, if they're hard of hearing [laughs] it's very hard for them to hear my voice."

Did "Everybody Hurts" succeed the way you wanted it to?

"Yeah. Absolutely. A young woman walked up to me in a club in New Orleans and said that that song kept her from killing herself. Now, the song alone did not do that, but at whatever point she heard it, it had a great impact on her life. I thought that was the greatest compliment that anyone could ever pay me about a song like that. That's exactly what it was intended for. I like writing those songs that hit that universal chord. Everybody can feel like: this is me. And not in a false way. When I was a teenager and I heard love songs on the radio, I would think: this is me. I would hear them again a month later and I'd think: I've been fooled. And I hated that. We didn't write love songs for 10 years because of that. When something comes along like 'Everybody Hurts' and it's really genuine, or

'Fuck Me Kitten' on the other side of the spectrum—totally genuine. Not necessarily from, I mean, certainly not from my experience. But that song speaks of something that I think everybody at one point or another has been through. Same with 'Country Feedback' on the darker side. I like hitting that universal chord. That makes me feel accomplished as a writer. That makes me feel tapped in."

How well did you get to know Kurt Cobain before his death?

"Um . . . tough question . . . really. [Pause.] Kurt loved our band. He loved what we had done. He loved what we represented. And I think he wished he had more of that—incredible management, incredible foresight, whatever it is. Because we'd never really planned any of this. I never expected to be in this position. I'm dodging the question, aren't I? [Pause.] We hung out a number of times. He came and stayed at my house once. We talked a lot. We spoke a great deal right before he died. And I knew him well enough that it was a deeply painful loss, not only because he was a brilliant songwriter and musician, but also personally, because I really had a great deal of respect for him and liked him a lot."

Can we pre-empt the inevitable rumours? How healthy are you at the moment?

"I'm extremely healthy."

Why didn't you make a statement when people were speculating that you had AIDS?

"This might be really naive, but my number one reason was—this is incredibly naive, in retrospect—but I really felt like there are a lot of people who might respect me, for whatever reason, because of the music or just because I'm a celebrity, that thinking that [the AIDS story] about me might impact them in the way they handled their own private affairs, or in the way they thought about people who were HIV positive or who had AIDS. And number two, I felt like it was a ludicrous claim and I didn't feel like sinking to kibbles-and-bits journalism to even respond to it. It was spawned from a ridiculous series of little things and I didn't feel like it was worth answering."

Was there one person who started it?

"Not that I can tell. I wore a hat that said White House Stop AIDS. I'm skinny. I've always been skinny, except in 1985 when I looked like Marlon Brando, last time I shaved my head. I was really sick then. Eating potatoes. That's before yuppies brought spinach salad to every restaurant in the known world. [Pause.] What were we talking about? Oh yeah, how it started. I think AIDS hysteria would obviously and naturally extend to people who are media figures and anybody of . . . [pauses for 16 seconds, maintaining steady eye contact] . . . indecipherable or unpronounced sexuality. Anybody who looks gaunt, for whatever reason. Anybody who is associated, for whatever reason—whether it's a hat, or the way I carry myself—as being queer-friendly."

Do you like your sexuality being indecipherable?

"Yeah. I kind of like gender-fucking. We've done it from the beginning. I think the songs should be heard by anybody and not necessarily have a male voice. I have written certain songs from what I consider to be a very female perspective, where the protagonist of the song was, in fact, female. 'Sweetness Follows' is the most recent and obvious example of that. To me, it's a very female song. [Pause.] I like fucking around with that stuff. Blurring the edges a little bit. I don't really like binary thought, no matter where it lands. And I think sexuality is a really slippery thing. I think a lot of people agree with me."

You've refused to sign autographs for some years. [He invariably balances this by offering instead to shake hands.] Could you explain why?

"It just got to be a pain in the ass. I'd have to sign cocktail napkins in bars and stuff when I wanted to watch bands. I'd try to be very friendly about it and say that I'd only do it for charities—it makes the autograph worth more money. Of course, everybody always says, I'm a charity. And I'm like, You don't look like a charity to me. But it became very distracting. I'd always be down like this [autograph pose]. I'd rather look somebody in the eye if they're going to confront me with their opinion of what I do."

Do you have a bodyguard?

[He shakes his head.]

Have you ever needed one?

"Oh, when it's announced that I'm going to be somewhere and it's a huge public thing. Usually it's not my choice. Whoever's putting on whatever it is will provide someone for me, just to prevent anything from happening. When I did the Presidential Inauguration. When I go to benefit concerts. Anything like that, it's usually a good idea to have someone there. I'm a little guy, you know. . . ."

He stops suddenly.

"It's 2:22," he says in a deep, uninflected voice. "You've got to shake hands when it's 2:22."

He shakes Mills' proffered hand, to the bassist's amusement, followed by mine. He then signals that it's OK to resume.

Do you ever wish you could step outside yourself and see the Stipe enigma that everyone else sees?

"The enigma? Yeah . . . I could answer that really cynically, but I choose not to [laughs]. I think a lot of it, frankly, is the way I'm presented by the media. A lot of people will pick up on the little weird things. Somebody famous once, about 100 years ago, made a comment about fame. They said—and I'm really super-paraphrasing here—that you could pick any single person in the world and put them under the microscope that fame brings, and they would seem like the most eccentric and the most bizarre and strange human being alive. And I really think that's true. We all have our weird little things about us. Mine are just magnified and blown out of proportion by the fact that I'm a pop media figure."

Do you ever have to choose your words carefully, knowing they will be quoted around the world?

"I'd like to. I'd like to think that I'm that in control of any conversation or situation. But I'm not. I'm not as smart as people make me out to be. I'm a high-school graduate and a magazine reader."

Your quote about Grant Lee Buffalo's *Fuzzy* album was used all round the world. Were you happy about that?

"I kind of warned them that my name carried some weight. I said: Consider the ramifications of this, but I'd love to do it. I'm a huge fan. Grant and I steal from each other, readily and regularly. We swap ideas. I can't listen to music when we're writing, because I do steal a great deal. I absorb like a well-made paper towel. I have to be really careful. So I don't listen to music, since last September."

You haven't heard any music since last September?

"I can go see bands live. You can never hear the words, so I'm not directly stealing. But when I sit down and listen to tapes, it's really easy for me to lift things. For some reason, the line is drawn at recorded music. The recording process is a mysterious and bizarre one to me."

Can you remember what touring was like?

Stipe: "It was horrifying."

Mills: "It's about two hours of fun interrupted by 23 hours of boredom and insanity."

That's 25 hours.

Mills: "Exactly."

Stipe: "You're goddamn right. I would up that a couple of hours, personally."

Just for argument's sake, "Shiny Happy People" starts playing on a ghetto blaster out on the lawn. What do you do?

Stipe: [carefully] "I shut the window. I beat my head against the door. I ralph."

Is it going on the imaginary box set?

"Not if I have anything to do with it."

Mills: "Maybe we'll put the instrumental version on the box set."

Stipe: [sarcastically] "Mmm! Thanks a lot!"

"Shiny Happy People" is not playing on ghetto blaster as the party strolls down the hill towards Sunset. In fact, the Strip is quiet, the Chateau Marmont itself so secluded that when John Belushi decided to die here, in one of the villas, no one knew anything about it. Besides, Michael Stipe has other things on his mind. He jiggles impatiently.

"You'll never guess what I saw on top of the Marlboro Man sign last night?"

What?

"An owl. The biggest owl I've ever seen."

It's extraordinary news. An owl. The biggest he's ever seen! And he must have seen thousands! But no one in the band pays him a blind bit of notice. He continues down the hill, unfazed.

MICHAEL OLLIFFE
R.E.M. IN PERTH (1995)
On the Street, *January 17, 1995*

Walking along the main drag of Hay Street, there is a special vibe. The people of Perth seem to be honoured that their city has been chosen. In one sweep around the mall, three different R.E.M. songs waft out of the stores. David Johnston, guitarist and vocalist of local trio Ammonia, notes that at the record store where he works, R.E.M. are clearly the week's best sellers.

The Thursday of Ammonia's performance at the Grosvenor Hotel, the venue was ludicrously packed before the band had unpacked its gear, a situation due entirely to a rumour that R.E.M. would be playing a warm-up show that night. Peter Buck's wedding the previous day had ruled that out, but it didn't deter hundreds of punters from chanting "R.E.M.," over and over, for half-an-hour after Ammonia had left the stage. The vibe was strong.

A rumoured 180 media people had gathered in Perth to cruise on that vibe, their very prescence making this an Event in the truest sense of the word. Yet R.E.M. would argue that they are simply a rock group, and what's all the fuss? The fact is that R.E.M. are much greater than their self image, and are revered and respected by millions.

If R.E.M.'s power could be gauged, it would have to be measured by the devotion of their fans. While they gather new converts with every release, there are also legions who have followed their every move from nearly the start. The world that R.E.M.'s fans share is a powerfully evocative planet, where every shard and sliver of emotion is dredged from the depths of their collective soul. This is the sort of affinity that R.E.M.'s fans have with the songs. These are people who identify with rich tapestries of emotion, who understand the place from which these emotions are born. The message is not always clear, often deliberately clouded, but at its core is raw feeling and empathy which forms the basis of a reciprocal relationship.

For 15 years, R.E.M. have maintained this fellowship with their audience. From *Chronic Town* to *Monster,* their attitude has remained immutable. Here is a group so conscientious, so thoroughly committed to creativity that serving up anything less than the finest, most inspirational moments of music would amount to failure. Yet they never falter.

The oppressive conditions that had enveloped the recording of *Monster*—illness, death and confusion—might have ruined a lesser group, but the resulting work justified R.E.M.'s belief in their own worth. Their hearts are nailed proudly to their sleeves, they are both vulnerable and invincible. And now they are here, in Perth.

The Interview

Prior to R.E.M.'s first proper live performance in over five years, Michael Stipe seems remarkably cool. His mood is one of excitement, not dread. The thrill of touring, it seems, is still there for him and the urge to get out and do it is growing stronger and stronger.

On 1989's Green tour, Stipe tore his way across stages, writhing and jumping like a man possessed. Back then, he was the world leader pretend. But repeating the glories of the past is beneath R.E.M.; their world is one of constant evolution, not only in their music but also in the live arena. When asked about the changes that would eventuate with a new show, Stipe's reply indicates that he wants to keep things as loose and as vibrant as possible.

"You know what," he smirks, "we haven't done it yet, so I can't really tell you. It's kind of a new thing for me. It's been five years since we last toured, so I've got no idea what it's going to be like. My plan for the full tour is just to stay in key, and try and keep the pitch right."

Coincidentally, R.E.M.'s tour begins on Friday the 13th, but it's something that doesn't seem to unnerve Stipe in the slightest. "Isn't that great?" he beams. "It's good luck, actually. My grandfather was born on Friday the 13th, and if he hadn't been born, . . ." Stipe trails off. For a guy about to embark on a world tour, he's coming across as ridiculously casual. Does he even remember life on the road and the rigours of a touring lifestyle?

"No, I mean I've been travelling since the last tour a lot," he replies, consciously separating the travel from performance. "But I tend to go somewhere and stay there more than a day. I don't really remember. I did it for ten years of my adult life, so I think it should be cool. I'm just really excited to be doing it."

As for pre-tour rehearsals, Stipe seems to have acquired a taste for good old fashioned rockin', something which he describes with great relish. "They were pretty rowdy," he laughs. "We rehearsed in New York for a while, and we rehearsed in Atlanta for a while, and then Ireland. They were just a blast."

Stipe gleefully relates the process of rocking up some of their more easily-paced numbers from *Out of Time* and *Automatic for the People*. "The only song that I know that is really working is 'Try Not to Breathe,' and that's just got this guitar on it that is really, like, fucked up. I really like that song.

"Having never performed these songs, it's like visiting an old room where you used to live, like ten years later, except you don't live there anymore and there's different furniture. So it's kind of cool to do those songs, particularly some of the stuff off *Automatic*. It's good to change it."

It's been five years, and weighing up the trepidations of performing live again, it's easy to imagine Stipe being a little concerned about getting back out there. "I'm pretty clumsy," he says. "So I always think I'm going to fall. But when I walk on stage I kind of just go for it. I think it's also the adrenalin. It's a natural kind of drug and it's much better than heroin."

In something of a pre-tour gesture of support, Stipe was the recipient of a goodwill message from one of his heroines. Stipe has often cited Patti Smith as one of his greatest influences. "Yeah, you know, I've blindly stolen from her for the last 15 years [laughs]. She wrote me a note that I got at the airport in LA just before we left. She was just saying, 'I hope you have a good tour and thanks for all the nice things you've said about me.'

"I was a walking boner for about eight hours," he chuckles. "I mean, I really think that she is one of the premier artists of my lifetime."

While we're on the subject of boners. Stipe was recently quoted as saying that infiltrating the consciousness of his audience through his lyrics is "the supreme boner."

"It really is," he says of his desire to deliver something personal to his audience. "And it's not like it takes a lot of intelligence to learn how to articulate your thoughts to people. There's a little more than just clever word play involved."

One of Stipe's most recent lyrical concerns has been the previously avoided terrain of the love song. On *Monster* tracks such as "You," "I Took Your Name," and "Strange Currencies" successfully bypass the clichés to act as a counterbalance to more formulaic examples of the genre offered by other artists. When I suggest that R.E.M.'s songs act as something of an antidote to these music atrocities, Stipe is amused.

"The antidote? That's a bit of a cross to bear! Like all the other songs I've written are just totally fucked up?" he challenges. Well, no . . . "I disagree too. I feel like I'm following a time-honoured tradition, and to know where it's coming from; that to me is like some sort of emotional fascism."

Certainly, when it comes to conveying emotions, R.E.M. can take many cakes. With them there is no deception. Even when you can't quite put your finger on exactly where Stipe is coming from, you inevitably arrive at a conclusion using the song's mood as a guide. It's open and honest. Isn't it?

"Yeah, I think so. I don't have the typical American male hang up of not being able to show my emotions. I just kind of go for the jugular. I despise that whole false emotionality that you find in Steven Spielberg movies. You can either hate it for what it is, or you can say, 'Alright, I'm going to go along with it,' and allow yourself to be manipulated emotionally, and that's okay. It's like jacking off.

"I mean, hopefully I'm not adding to all that," he continues. "Hopefully, somehow, I'm side stepping that whole thing. Somebody told me recently that the first time they heard 'You Are Everything,' they were laying back in the back of a car, looking at the stars. That was the most powerful thing; it was this Hispanic guy who just stopped me in a restaurant."

Another of *Monster*'s primary concerns is Stipe's assessment and condemnation of popular culture and consumerism. "I'm not a commodity," he asserts on "King of Comedy," as well as targeting corporate structures:

"Make your money with a suit and tie," and more inclusively, "Make your money with exploitation." Stipe observes the machinations of industry from within, challenging the suggestion that R.E.M. are mildly involved.

"Mildly?! We're smack bang in the middle of it!" he proclaims. "I'm just looking at the kinds of conditions we're living in, and looking at myself and seeing where I can fit in. With something like 'King of Comedy,' it's a very cynical view of things commercial."

Then, of course, there is Stipe's dissection of the mass media along with the clueless figures who bandy about brands names such as Generation X to describe youth culture. "'What's the Frequency, Kenneth?' deals with media, not so much consumerism," explains Stipe. "Well, in a way it's like the buying and selling of a generation, which is exactly what the song is about. Once again, I'm smack in the middle of it, I can't escape it."

Tied in with this is R.E.M.'s tendency towards political activism, something that has become a staple of their public image. On *Document,* "Exhuming McCarthy" deals with paranoia from the conservative right, while simultaneously denigrating the policies of the Bank of America and the general economic catastrophy which the Republican administration dealt out during the '80s. *Green* quite obviously dealt with environmental issues, with "Stand," "You Are Everything," "Pop Song '89" and "World Leader Pretend" being liberally or lightly threaded with their "right on" politics.

Stipe's reasoning for the political angle is obvious enough; when everyone else is apathetic and your immediate world, not to mention the global community, is threatened by greed, the only way out is to fight against it.

"Our political activism and the content of the songs was just a reaction to where we were, and what we were surrounded by, which was just abject horror," Stipe says. "In 1987 and '88, there was nothing to do but be active."

Be that as it may, Stipe is exceedingly reluctant to wear the Voice of a Generation tag. "I don't like the position we are forced into, like Eddie Vedder or Kurt Cobain. Not only is it hard for the person and their band, but for anyone else. I mean there are millions upon millions of black and Hispanic people in the U.S. who have never heard a Pearl Jam song."

When R.E.M. graces your town, you ought to be listening very carefully. It's no minor coincidence that the name Michael is Hebrew, meaning "he who is like unto God." This, perhaps, is a tag that Michael Stipe could wear; not as a deity, but as one in possession of genuine, god-like qualities. An original rock 'n' roll monster.

The Show

When Died Pretty checked in with a writhing rendition of "Stops 'n' Starts," the tone for the evening was not just set, but encased in concrete. Died Pretty are essentially protruding, forceful and passionate. Peno's poodle strutting, his contorted displays of flailing limbs suggested a peacock in heat.

He is not merely a singer, and Planet Ron has moved into its own galaxy. During a performance, Peno seems blissfully oblivious to everything around him, tracing complex shapes and weaving his taut frame across the stage.

"DC" was moving to the nth degree. Where Peno's voice climbs, Brett Myers' guitar follows, and Johnny Hoey's keyboards swell and flow to gesture you towards a pinnacle of perfection.

"Harness Up" provides the balance; the glowing up-vibe contrast to the preceding emotional rollercoaster. Peno becomes playful, making masturbatory motions. "Godbless" then has its airing. It is potentially explosive, and finally it hits. The crescendo drags us back up to one of those Moments, the grinding rhythms hammering out to a remarkable climax.

As a finale, we remain suspended at celestial heights with "Sweetheart." The slow burn groove trickling into rapturous applause with Myers strangling his favourite instrument, draining every last fractured note from it. The summation is simple: Some groups can achieve more in 20 minutes that thousands of other ensembles will achieve in several careers. Died Pretty are definite candidates for the Colossus Club.

Grant Lee Buffalo are equally as edifying. Exciting and ameliorating, with Grant Lee Phillips exuding passion like he bought the right to it, probably in exchange for his soul. We are eased gently into the set, which gradually builds upon Died Pretty's opening sortie, and then scales it with tempered ferocity. Paul Kimble attacks his bass as if it were an enemy, punching at the strings and careering around his stage territory like a rock 'n' roll dervish. Grant Lee Buffalo put out in every way possible, they hid behind nothing.

Their performance is truly blistering in parts, magically serene in others; always incredibly compelling. "Mockingbirds" is perhaps the finest example of a song that can instantly galvanize an entire audience. Kimble's floating melody elevates Phillips' cherubic tune into sacred realms. There is simply no phrase accurate enough to afford such an experience a proper description.

This was also the case with "Fuzzy." Grant Lee Buffalo's music gives you strength, purpose, and fulfillment in the space of four minutes. Peroxide genius? Bleached brilliance? Probably both. "Lone Star Song" can probably be placed within this frame, to be hung squarely on your heart for bold display. Simon Wooldridge once claimed the song was bigger than the state it is about. He was right.

You wouldn't be condemned for believing that "support" acts should not be this good. You always expect to be underwhelmed by the undercard, before being overawed by rock's overlords. But this was not the case with R.E.M. It was indeed a case of substance and quality triumphing over mere image. By granting two such bands support slots for the tour, R.E.M. have only advanced their own cause. They have increased our perception of them as genuine, unflinching quality merchants, giving us a totally engaging and enthralling experience.

Grant Lee Buffalo didn't merely warm up—they burned. They caressed our souls and dug deep trenches in our chests into which they poured their music, causing us to fall hopelessly in love with them. They opened their arms and the embrace was warm and fuzzy. Perth concurred.

Stipe propelled the evening into history, striding out wearing a black beanie and white oval sunglasses shielding black eyeliner. A fashion refugee.

He confined much of his movement to relaxed strolls, foldback balancing acts, cheeky grins and reclusive crouches. "What's the Frequency, Kenneth?" with its accompanying precision and strobe freak-out, was our grand hello. R.E.M. presented themselves boldly, as a revitalized and energized six-headed monster. Two extra guitarists filled out the sound, creating a richly textured guitar mesh that was engulfing.

Mike Mills bobbed and swaggered, sporting a bright red suit with flares to shame a million Stone Roses fans. Peter Buck whirled and kicked, looking well chuffed to be rocking once more, while Bill Berry gleefully pounded out the beats. The title of The Greatest Rock 'n' Roll Band in the universe was looking sewn up.

Four songs in and the night was ascending rapidly; R.E.M. had three albums' worth of material to give a proper airing, and they set about making up for lost time. "Me in Honey," *Out of Time*'s concluding track, swam through the room. Mills' rolling bass providing the spark for the inevitable combustion. Big Bang theories need not be confined exclusively to the sphere of science. A whole other world emerged from this thunderous opening.

Stipe's current on-stage persona totally abandons his Green tour theatrics, leaving him to wander as he pleases. Yet he still manages to erase, deny, and avoid all the clichés. Following each song, he would tear the lyrics from his music stand, and donate a souvenir to the front rows. His first words to the audience came six songs into the set. He was playful and endearing, following his "How's it going?" salutation with "So we're here, here's another song," instantly cueing Berry to lead the band into a rocked-up version of "Try Not to Breathe."

"Tongue" was an unmitigated success, with a disco ball being employed to its fullest extent. The venue suddenly filled with glittering, technicolour orbs, as Stipe rendered his falsetto ballad with tenderness, then finished with a rattling presentation of *Document*'s apocalyptic rocker, "It's the End of the World as We Know It (and I Feel Fine)." As the visuals bombarded us with question marks, Stipe ranted his litany of names and phrases with poise and style.

Stipe's apparent aloofness throughout proceedings was a feature of the performance that needed questioning. For someone who is renowned for his limitless energy on stage, he seemed terribly sedate. Maybe, as he states on *Monster,* he was just making it look easy.

But this is a minor gripe. The set was heavily laden with mid-tempo and slower numbers; not exactly pogo action. Disregarding Stipe's relative inactivity, he seemed to be thoroughly enjoying his time on stage, throwing suggestive looks and mischievous stares to the punters.

With a great proportion of the songs coming from the last three albums (unsurprisingly), R.E.M.'s performance proved, if nothing else, that they deftly cover the entire spectrum of moods, and deliver them with startling clarity and consistency. Whether it be reflective balladeering ("Let Me In"), camp glam rockisms ("Crush with Eyeliner"), or political posturing ("King of Comedy" and "Pop Song '89"), Berry, Buck, Mills and Stipe drill it straight into the mind and soul.

Epilogue

The trucks moved out last night, the two days and then some of R.E.M. fever already beginning to fade. Adelaide is next, and one by one the Australian cities will rabidly greet our guests from Athens, Georgia. After this country has been conquered, the rest of the world will have their turn. And perhaps never again.

It has been a remarkable few days, forming a collection of unforget-table moments that have already been registered in the memory. Meeting Peter Buck for a whole minute, granting me sufficient time to take a pho-tograph. Seeing one of the greatest (no—three of the greatest) bands in the world twice in two days. Tomorrow there will have to be time to assess the previous days' blur of activity. If it ever sinks in properly, I'll probably never erase the smile. But, hey, that's not such a bad way to be.

JUD COST

R.E.M. INTERVIEW: BREAKFAST WITH BUCK (1995)

The Bob, *1995*

On the eve of what may be R.E.M.'s last full-blown world tour, I sat down for an hour with Peter Buck and chewed the fat on what's come down with the Eye Movement crowd since he and I last did an update at the end of 1993. One major event in Buck's life since last we spoke occurred in May of 1994 when Stephanie Dorgan presented him with twin daughters, Zoe and Zelda. On the R.E.M. front, '94 saw the release of the very noisy new album, *Monster.* Of all the reviews I've read, the only phrase that sticks is the one claiming that at this point R.E.M. might be incapable of recording a bad album.

One thing they've done recently, which gets two thumbs up in these parts, was to hire Young Fresh Fellow mainstay Scott McCaughey to join them onstage for the entire 1995 tour, slated to run from January through November and visiting Europe, Asia, Australia, New Zealand and South America, as well as every nook and cranny of the U.S. McCaughey joins Los Angeles club musician Nathan December—himself a replacement for the band's original choice, former Minor Threat bass player, Brian Baker—to help beef up the live sound.

If you waded through most of the meaty interviews R.E.M. did in the big league music press, coinciding with the release of *Monster* last fall— more magazine cover shots for a group than I've seen at one time since the heady days of the Beatles—the *Bob* thought you might enjoy something a little more homespun. Think of this chat as something that took place over a leisurely Sunday breakfast, even though it didn't. With that in mind, pour yourself a cup of coffee and pull up a chair. Buck and I were just discussing a CD for which I've done the booklet notes. Oh, and pass that basket of bran muffins over this way, if you would. Thanks.

The Bob: *Glad you liked the* Count Five *CD.*

Peter Buck: Well, as you know, I'm really into free goods—especially that kind of stuff, as you can tell from our new record. It's really our garage record.

Last time we talked, [late 1993] the Giants and the Braves were locked in a life and death battle down the stretch. And now, suddenly, no baseball. Does that bum you out?

Oh, no. I think it's kind of funny actually, that people set their worlds by it. It's no more real than music is. Mike has Braves season tickets, and he was looking forward to the play-offs, so he's really bummed out. But, you know, if they took every athlete on earth and sent them to colonize the moon, I would never know for a month or two.

My idea of journalistic hell would be to have to interview athletes. I love watching them play, but they don't have anything to say.

Well, at least with music, you can say that it's about something. With sports, it just is.

You told me the other day that you never read any of the interviews you or the rest of the band does.

I read the record reviews, because I always like to see what people think of the new album. And I do read the other stuff occasionally, if it's well written. I try not to read stuff about myself, because I don't want to have to think about what I'm saying. Actually, it's nice to be kind of blissfully unaware of what people are writing.

Do you ever worry about being misquoted?

No, I don't really care. This isn't like I'm trying to negotiate treaties between warring countries, where one missed phrase can doom thousands of people. If they quote me out of context, make me look stupid, that's fine. You look stupid for a week, and then the newspaper's in the trash and no one remembers it.

I try to quote people accurately, but I've had complaints on occasion. I like to point out that this isn't the Nuremburg War Trials we're talking about here. It's just music.

Yeah, it's just not that important. So, tell me about your projects with Sundazed [New York '60s reissue label].

Okay, right off the bat, we've got the first two Beau Brummels albums on Autumn coming out with extra tracks.

Yeah, that's great. No one's ever done much with the early Beau Brummels. It's funny because one of the guys in that band, I could never figure out who [Ron Meagher, the bass player], is a dead ringer for me when I was about twenty two—shaggy hair, big nose and kinda darker skin. When I first worked in a record store, the boss who hired me put that record up in the window and wrote under it, "Our clerk, Peter Buck, in his former incarnation" [laughs]. It looked enough like me, when I was young, that people really thought it was me, and I'd tell them, "Come on, now. How old do you think I am?"

You've done tons of interviews in your career. Do you ever get burned out on 'em?

Yeah, we've just done two weeks where I did ten interviews a day. That's like having a hundred job interviews in a row, and it's kinda tough. You're talking to, like, French journalists who maybe don't have the whole story, and you have to really fill 'em in on the basics. Something like the *Bob* is kinda cool because it's specialty-oriented. No one's going to read the article and not know who we are. They might not like us, but. . . . In France, or some of these countries where we've just had a couple of hit records, we're still kinda mysterious, and they'll ask things like "When did you get together? [laughs]. You do about a hundred of those and you're just going, "God." And, of course, this year, we—boy, this is really rockstar-ish—rather than travel to do interviews, we went to Ireland and rented a castle with forty foot ceilings. And they came to us. I'm sure everyone wrote about the castle and said, "What are these shmucks doin' here?"

So, how do you feel about the impending year-long tour with the twins only five months old?

It's gonna be wild. They're coming along for all the dates. I wouldn't have kids and then leave 'em home for that long. Last time we did a major tour we were all in our twenties, and we'd drink until dawn every night, and wake up, and the liver was pounding and heads were hurting, which was fun, but it's a little different now. This time, when we start, the kids will be crawling, and when we finish they'll be talking and walking. Not to say that they're going to see every single date. They might miss a week here and a week there, but I'm just not gonna be apart from them for more than five or six days at a time. They're going to see all of Australia, New Zealand, Asia and maybe come home a week early from Europe. And then all of America. It's especially good for Stephanie, because she's never seen the [U.S.] Midwest. And I'm not gonna go on the Midwest on vacation. I've seen it too many times already. I mean, really, am I going to Cincinnati for any reason except to play there? Probably not. Nothing wrong with Cincinnati, but, if I'm going on vacation, the beach at Cincinnati is probably a little chilly.

And you're going to South America too, right?

Yeah, at the end of the year. We've never really played down there. We went down to do some environmental stuff a couple of years ago, to Paraguay. And they stopped all the local TV soap operas and had these minute-by-minute press reports that R.E.M. was in the airport. It was a really big deal. They told us they hadn't had a news story there that big since their coup in 1989. I hate to brag, but we outsell Madonna ten to one in some of these countries, and now we're finally going down there to play, for just a couple of weeks—Brazil, Paraguay, maybe a Rain Forest benefit thing. When Stephanie and I were in Africa two years ago, we'd take these little planes and fly for four hundred miles and see maybe twenty or thirty really big fires, which was incredibly depressing.

How does fatherhood feel after half a year?

It's great. Although my sleep schedule is totally whacked out. Last night one of 'em was up on the hour for the entire night.

How did you pick the names, Zoe and Zelda?

Well, I didn't want to name them after anyone I'd ever met. So I just face-tiously suggested that we pick a letter of the alphabet and that would cut the selection down by twenty five times. So we said, "How about Z?" Zoe and Zelda are semi-literary names—Zelda Fitzgerald, and I forgot at the time that Zoe was the boy in [J. D. Salinger's] *Raise High the Roof Beam, Carpenters*, but it was spelled differently. "Z" is a letter that hasn't really been used up yet.

And I can tell you from personal experience that when someone in the vicinity calls out, "Hey, Jud, I know it's for me." I've never met another one.

Well, there's the guy who sang "I'll give you a daisy a day" [Jud Strunk] and Judd, with two D's Nelson. And there's also Judd Hirsch too, right? So there you go, commoner than you think. It is a cool name, kind of a manly adventurer type guy.

How are you going to do it logistically, take the kids along?

Well, it's not like I'm in the van anymore. We'll have a nanny. And I'll get to spend most of the days with them. We'll just have to have someone there to give us a hand during the shows and with waking up at eight A.M. if I've gone to sleep at three in the morning. We finish the sets by 11:30, but I won't get back to the hotel until 12:30 or 1:00, and no matter how tired I am, I can't go to sleep until 2:30 or 3:00. I'm not really worried about it. I think it should be a cool thing. They've traveled a lot. They've already had about eight or ten plane flights. They should have frequent flyer cards.

Have you ever thought about doing your own R.E.M. book?

Funnily enough, although I haven't signed any papers, on this tour I'm going to keep a diary. I keep them intermittently anyway, very wordy and verbose, maybe four or five pages a day. It wouldn't be like a tell-all because there's really nothing that exciting. As a fan though, I'd be kind of interested in what really goes on, the reality of it. I think it would be interesting to read about the people we meet and the places we go. Travel writing is always autobiography anyway. But I might chicken out and decide I don't want to go up against Graham Greene. I don't think any-body's ever done something from the inside that isn't about sex, drugs and rock 'n' roll. We're just not that kind of band anyway. If I wind up with a couple of hundred pages of something better than, "Got up. Had break-fast." and can keep it flowing, who knows?

How does Seattle feel after a couple of years there?

It's nice. One of the things about it is that it's not on the way to some-where else. Most other places I've lived, the freeway shoots right through it, but to get up here you have to really want to be here. I like that.

Do you try to maintain an anonymous profile there?

Well, we have lots of friends, but we [R.E.M.] aren't at that level of fame where it's really a problem.

I know people in Seattle who've told me, "I wouldn't dare go up and talk to the guy." Do you run into that kind of attitude?

Well, the people who don't dare come up and talk to me don't dare come and talk to me, so I never know who they are [laughs]. When I go out to see a band I always talk to people, but at the bookstore or the super mar-ket it doesn't happen quite as regularly.

You must, from time to time, pinch yourself and wonder how this all hap-pened to you.

None of us planned this. We were always good at what we did, but I never figured I'd be here now, living in a big house and having money and stuff. And, yeah, quite often I still feel, "I can't really believe I'm doing this." I always figured I'd be a guy living in an apartment, playing to two hundred people a night and maybe every now and then putting out a little record on an independent label. Which would be totally satisfying for me. I did that for years. It's a very weird thing to be sitting in a castle with people flying hundreds of miles to talk to you. I think, "God, I can't believe peo-ple are that interested in us."

Was there ever a turning point, when you realized this really was happen-ing, and the scuffling days were over?

Well, it was so long ago, but when we signed our first [I.R.S.] record contract in 1982, Mike and I were living next door to each other, both totally broke, and we were walking downtown to go to this restaurant where we knew someone who would slip us free slices of pizza and draft beer. I remember telling Mike, "You know, there are millions of people in this world playing music, and nobody gets a record deal. It doesn't matter if we're totally poor, we've got a record deal." And then it just kept getting weirder.

Everybody always says about the band, "They're such nice guys." Did you consciously cultivate that when you started out?

When we started out we were so poor, we had to depend on our friends, like Blanche DuBois [laughs]. A lot of my best friends now are people who would take me to their house for spaghetti when I was starving, and they'd let us sleep on their floor. In 1982 it was a different world. You didn't have MTV and even college radio was playing Journey and Styx. We'd find the seekers, who were looking for something different, and we had a lot in common with the people who became our friends. If you hang out in dingy bars five or six nights a week for five years, you're going to meet some people.

Have you ever wondered why R.E.M. made it rather than the other 1980 bands that were equally as good?

Actually I've thought about that a lot. You know, a lot of bands that were as good as us didn't work as hard as us. Black Flag—they had legal problems and broke up—but they worked really hard. And now Henry Rollins works really hard, and look at him. You wouldn't think of him as a big media figure, because his music is really out there as far as mom and dad are concerned. But all of our peer groups—the Dream Syndicate, Hüsker Dü, the Replacements—they all broke up, or for whatever reason, didn't persevere. We were a really good band, but there were a lot of good bands. When we started, Love Tractor was at the exact same level as us. They did great work, but they never toured and didn't work really hard at it and just kind of let it slip. We always tried to become better songwriters and be a better band. In a lot of ways it's just because we did beat our head against the wall for ten years. It does help—how should I put this, because this is the sound we wanted to make, and we weren't doing it to be commercial—that our sound wasn't offensive to some people, like

Black Flag was. Black Flag never bothered me. I loved Black Flag. But we were probably the weirdest record in a lot of people's record collections for a long time. We appealed equally to people who listened to a lot of stuff and people who would say, "All I really like is the Beatles, but you guys are really good. You're not like. . . ." And then they'd name whatever punk band was around at the time. But I did get the feeling that we were cheek by jowl in some record collections with people I've never listened to. I read something in *Billboard* once which said that ninety percent of record purchases are spur-of-the-moment, something the person hadn't intended to buy, and that it's by someone who only buys three to five records a year. People in the mall, just there to buy jeans, walk in and buy a record. That's who the big audience is.

My watershed experience for you making it was when I saw this eight-year-old kid in a mall record store dragging his dad to the counter to buy an R.E.M. album. Dad thought that R.E.M. was a rap artist, and at that moment, I said to myself, "Hmmm, this is getting really big." How much do you think an artist owes his audience? Do you feel you can always pretty much do what you want?

We've always done just what we want. What we owe the audience is to make the best record we possibly can. We spent years not selling records because we wanted to do it our own way. Now that we've sold a lot of records, I wouldn't know how to record someone else's idea of a hit. I'm not even sure what a hit is any more. If you ask people what they want, they're going to want just what they had last week. If people liked one record, they'll want the next one to sound just like it, and that's just not the way we go about it. We are at the point where we can do whatever we want, I think. But this record could stiff, although it looks like it's not. But if this record only sells half what the last one did, that's still a lot of records. And I'll make a record the year after that and the year after that too.

Well, do you ever get to the point where you wonder if this new material really works?

I think everyone in the band, in the back of their mind, feels that eventually we're gonna really fail. But as long as we like the record when we've finished with it, I'm not really worried if we fail commercially. We just don't want to reach the point where we don't know when we're putting out bad work. How many people, great artists, can you think of where all of a sudden they're putting out shit? I'm afraid that'll happen. One year we'll decide, ahh, that's what we want to do—the polka record. And it'll come out, and everybody will finally say, "What were those guys thinking of?"

Can you see yourself, year by year, convincing yourself—like the Stones, for example—that you should stay around maybe longer than good sense would dictate?

Well, I really like the Rolling Stones. I feel that whatever they want to do, they should do. Personally I wouldn't want to play to fifty thousand people when I'm fifty years old. But they do. They want to go for it. But then maybe when I'm forty-five I'll feel I still have something to say to eighteen-year-olds. I'm sure the band will reach a point where we won't tour or we won't do videos because we're not into that anymore. But look at Van Morrison. He sells his three hundred thousand records a year, and he doesn't care.

Or Neil Young. He seems to just get better and better.

Yeah, as long as whatever we do doesn't make us look stupid, there's a way to go about it. We'll just keep going, I guess.

Here's the way I see it: I'd say you're at the point where breaking up is irrelevant. You can either play a lot or not at all, but the band will always be there when or if you want it.

Yeah [laughing] and what's breaking up if you don't ever play together anyway? Except for the fact that we've made two records in the '90s, most people would consider us as having already broken up. We haven't toured and so forth. If we decide after this next tour that we don't want to do it for a while, we'll take some time off.

You told me recently that this will probably be the last mega tour.

You never say never, but I can't really imagine doing something like this five or ten years from now.

But isn't that maybe the same way Mick and Keith felt fifteen years ago?

Maybe. One thing though. We've never toured and been totally success-ful everywhere we've gone. This will be the first time for that. We quit touring in '89, when we were still kind of unknown in parts of Europe and Asia. We were playing to eight hundred people a night in some places back then. They were sold out shows, but they were clubs. This is a big step up for us, a massive, what I assume will be sold-out all over the world tour. We'll do that, and then we will have done it. There are ways to do it where you don't have to continually be on the road. I think it's more important to make records at this point for us.

Will you continue to do the occasional tiny venue, like that London show a couple of years ago at the Borderline, billed as Bingo Hand Job?

You know, I enjoyed doing that. It's a real pain in the ass because people yell at you for not getting them on the guest list. But who knows? There might be a time when we play those dates to pay the rent [laughs].

Climbing back down the ladder, like Blue Oyster Cult?

There's no guarantee we'll always be successful. And that's cool. So far we've seen the up side of everything. But when the down side comes, I'll be ready for it, I think. You've got to go through that. Just as long as we can keep doing good work.

The classic example of that would be the Beach Boys: from massive '60s success to slim pickings in the '70s, then back to stadium level and now sinking again.

They played a show in Atlanta last summer after a baseball game, and they had no Wilson brothers. It was just Mike Love and Al Jardine. Their contract states that whenever two original members show up, it's a Beach Boys show. Maybe that's why they're not as successful as they once were.

So, if one day Mike and Bill want to go out as R.E.M., they can do it?

Feel free. I had friends who saw the Mike Clarke tribute to the Byrds show. It was apparently him and some carpenter friends of his. They said it was like the Doobie Brothers. Ideally that won't happen with us.

Has the songwriting process changed much over the years?

It's the way we've always done it, but it seems to have gotten easier over the years. Maybe we're just getting better at it. We write more, and we throw more away. Sometimes we'll present Michael with some changes with no melody to it, and sometimes we'll give him a melody. Sometimes he'll use that melody, and sometimes he'll make up his own.

When you're doing interviews, do you find yourself tempering your opinions, not to step on any toes?

As much music as there is out there, I really despise a lot of it for ethical reasons. But I don't really need to be dissing people in newspapers. I could be pretty mean about other performers, but I don't really need to do that. Politically, I say what I want about that stuff. It's not like I hold really radical opinions. I don't believe in armed revolution in the streets.

Why hasn't there been a Peter Buck album? Have you guys agreed not to do that sort of thing?

No, anyone who wants to can. I just think my skills are better suited to being a sideman, to being an arranger, to being a songwriter. We all help lead and guide the band, and I don't really want to be in the spotlight. I don't like my singing voice. Live, I really have trouble pitching when I sing. I sing to my kids, and I sing to myself. Here's how little I like to sing: I've never sung a song from beginning to end. After the first two verses I'm tired of it. I wouldn't mind doing some things outside the band, but I already do those. I'm going to concentrate more on songwriting over the next three or four years and work with some other people.

What about this Kurt Cobain quote, that you guys "wore your fame like saints?"

We dealt with the position we were in pretty well, I think, but nobody in this band is a saint. For one thing I'm impatient [laughs]. I think having a four-person democracy helped us weather situations better than if we'd been focused on just one person. Generally, we all feel what we do, writing songs and making records, is a pretty great thing. And everything else is really silly—like award shows. It's just stupid. I got talked into going to the Grammies, but I'll never go again. All night, it was "Whitney Houston, Whitney Houston, Whitney Houston." And I don't have anything against her. But it's really these old guys who run the business. And they're still trying to close the drapes and pretend that this rock 'n' roll thing will go away if we ignore it long enough. They just thank god when they can find some middle-of-the-road balladeer, like Christopher Cross. You look over the years, when all these great records came out, and they always pick some non-entity to praise, because they're real safe and quiet and mellow.

Any major regrets over the last fifteen years?

I should never have gone to see *Rocky IV* [laughs].

Tell me about the selection of Scott McCaughey as your jack-of-all-trades on tour—certainly a very cool choice according to all my friends.

Well, first of all, we wanted someone we could get along with, and Scott's a friend of ours. And I know his tastes. The fear is always that halfway through the tour you'll find you've hired a guy who turns into Yngwie Malmsteen [laughs] and lays hot licks on us. We've been rehearsing, and it sounds great. I didn't know if he wanted to do something like that, because he's got a family. But I just said to him, "If I suggest you—and there's no guarantee you'd get it—would you do it?" And he said, "Yeah, sure I'll try it. Why not?" So we flew him down to LA for an audition, and he said, "Even if I don't get it, it's been great. I've never flown in the front part of an airplane before." So I called him up and told him, "You've got it." And he just says, "Well, cool."

The R.E.M. gig that sticks out most in my mind was in 1986 at the Pacific Amphitheatre, an outdoor place in LA. It was raining like a monsoon, and everybody assumed the show was canceled. But you guys played anyway with about a hundred and fifty people there, all hiding under trash bags.

Yeah, the real horrendous ones are the ones I remember. We had a great one in Detroit. We'd just signed to I.R.S. and every review said, "The best band in America." We drove to Detroit and four people showed up. They were all on mushrooms and laughing and dancing. So we did "Whole Lotta Love" for fifteen minutes, and they wanted an encore because they weren't done dancing. So afterwards we took all four of them to a Greek restaurant and got really bombed and went dancing with them. We were smashing plates, and we all ate and drank up our $200 guarantee.

Let's pay the bills and talk about Monster. *You said you consider it a garage album for the '90s.*

It was recorded in a warehouse. So much of what passes for heavy rock is influenced by heavy metal, which I've never listened to. For me it's like a white heavy rock record, but without the poodle haircuts.

What's the obsession with the tremolo sound from that Mission of Burma song?

Yeah, "Trem Two." And someone else mentioned the Lyres. Well, we found an amp that had tremolo in it and wrote two songs immediately. It was meant to be a loose, rough record, but when you get in the studio, things get tarted up a little bit. It's pretty amazing how much of it is live track with one or two little overdubs on it. On "Kenneth" all we did was add solos. Other than that it's a completely live track. We just got tired of being sitting-on-our-stools acoustic players. Knowing we were going to tour, certainly it helped having something a little bit noisier to play.

The plan is to play mostly Monster *on tour?*

The latest three records, and then we're already writing new songs. It may be overly ambitious, but I think what we want to do is write ten to fifteen new songs, do five of 'em a night, and at the end of the tour record a week's worth of shows and get a live record with all new material.

You've always had the reputation, kind of like the Grateful Dead, of being very tolerant of bootleggers. How does everybody else feel about that?

I know that it pisses Michael off, because he likes to be in control of his output. When he hears a demo with him singing flat, it drives him nuts. Personally I'm kind of flattered. As long as they do nice three-color covers and don't put an '85 show with a '91 picture. Just as long as they do a good job, I think it's kinda cool.

OK, a premature question, maybe one for a retired Hall of Famer. Do you ever think about R.E.M.'s place in the Big Rock Picture?

I don't know. Some days I'm really arrogant about it and I think we're a pretty great group, and some days I think we'll disappear, it'll be over and no one will even care. I can't make up my mind about the whole thing.

Twenty years from now we'll go have a beer, sit by the spitoons, and maybe it'll be perfectly clear to you.

[Laughing] And maybe it won't.

CHARLES AARON

R.E.M. COMES ALIVE (1995)

Spin, *August 1995*

In the ruins of Ancient Rome, tourists peer through the locked gates of the Coliseum as tomcats scurry and vendors hawk sidewalk sketches of Judy Garland and Shannen Doherty. An Italian boy whistles from a passing bus and points out the obscenity he's scrawled on a dusty window. To the north, near Villa Borghese (Rome's Central Park), a handful of forlorn girls linger in the drizzle for a glimpse of celebrity outside the Hotel Excelsior, where Kurt Cobain botched a suicide attempt over a year ago. To the south, a clump of teenage boys and girls huddle under a cloud of cigarette smoke beside a bootleg T-shirt stand in the parking lot of an intimidatingly bland sports arena. Across the numbing hum of the highway, a planned residential community waits for daylight to expire and the kids to come to bed.

But first, there's some rock 'n' roll business to be conducted. So the boys and girls are huddled in the Universal Exposition of Rome (or EUR, pronounced sort of like "Eeyore" from *Winnie-the-Pooh*), a mini-city outside the city originally intended to host the 1942 World Expo until construction was halted by World War II. Completed for the 1960 Olympics, this conglomeration of housing and stadiums, charitably described in travel guides as "sterile" and "ugly," is now home to a sizable chunk of Rome's upper middle class. And this gloomy February evening, its Palazzo dello Sport, or "Palaeur," is host to the first-ever local concert by R.E.M., genial guidance counselors of alternative rock and resident hipster uncles of pop music's upper middle class.

With the college-radio days of the early '80s a trace memory, and their albums now guaranteed million-sellers, the members of R.E.M. have devoted much of the '90s to figuring out how to finesse the bigness of success without grossing themselves out, emotionally or musically. After 1989's Green tour, the band retreated, not playing live to support the follow-up albums, 1991's *Out of Time* and 1992's *Automatic for the People*. They did virtually no press, pursuing other interests—singer Michael Stipe's film production companies, C-00 and Single Cell Pictures; drummer Bill Berry's gentleman farming; bassist Mike Mills's golf game; guitarist Peter Buck's divorce, remarriage, and parenthood. But with the release of *Monster,* and for R.E.M.'s first tour in five years, the band has apparently decided to reenvision itself as the R.E.M. Traveling All-Stars and Motor Kings, reentering arenas and entertaining enough press requests to run down Drew Barrymore's batteries.

But from where I'm loitering, it's a pity that anybody has to pay to hear the neatly situated glam-pop, garage punk, and trembly ballads from *Monster* in this gray, echoing dome, which is better suited for team gymnastics or the 400-meter freestyle. A fuzzed-up comment on arena-rock machismo, that album doesn't project so well in an actual arena. All the nuance and humor and coy sexiness fades into forced posturing. The tremolo loses its ironic twinge, and your focus wanders to Mills's hideously unironic, spangled cowboy costume. "Whenever we do 'hard' rock, or whatever this album is, it's always going to be just a little bit off," concedes Buck.

Admittedly, I'm in no position to be objective, after enduring a six-month, can't-get-there-from-here interview runaround: lame video shoot for "Bang and Blame" (where I dispiritedly watched Stipe, MTV journalist Tabitha Soren, and grunge plaything Stephen Dorff shoot squirt guns into each other's mouths); New York hotel conference-room how-don't-you-do; Italian hotel breakfast mess (don't ask). Of course, R.E.M. doesn't owe the press anything, and I appreciate the chance to fly over and check out St. Peter's Basilica, but if setting up an interview is going to be such a federal case, why is Warner Bros., the group's record company, even bothering? Is somebody worried that if R.E.M. doesn't bleed its publicity stone dry album sales will lag? (The triple-platinum *Monster* rests at No. 72 on the *Billboard* charts.) Is the band itself worried or feeling obligated? "These are all things we could say no to," says Mills. "But there's no point in being that difficult." The whole enterprise has the aroma of corporate responsibility, which is fine, if you cop to it. But R.E.M. also insists on pushing its integrity-dignity party line. Seems like every third person associated with the tour has to testify to what normal joes the guys still are compared to most big-shot rock stars.

So why are they putting on a big-shot rock tour? The stock answer is that the band members felt detached from each other (Buck now lives in Seattle) and longed for the closeness they once shared as a touring band. But taking a gander at the six equipment trucks and nine buses and 47-person road crew crowding the back of the lot at the Palaeur, not to mention the wives and kids and chefs along for the ride, I wonder if maybe the band wouldn't have been better off just getting together for a summer barbecue. Wasn't it Stipe, 35, who said after the Green tour that it took him a year to feel like a real person again? Mills, 36, strides around like a burnt-out Burrito Brother, shades on, guard up. Berry, 36, who first encouraged the tour, has dropped out of sight, suffering from fatigue. (A week later, Berry would collapse onstage in Lausanne, Switzerland, undergoing successful surgery for a double aneurysm, thus ending the European tour.) And sure, Buck has always wanted to live his own verson of one of those crinkled paperback rock bios he read as a college dropout working at used record stores in Atlanta and Athens, Georgia. But with two kids now in tow (year-old twin girls, Zoe and Zelda), he sounds more like a dad caught in the headlights.

"I used to think I worked hard a couple of years ago, but that was nothing," says the 38-year-old guitarist, sitting in a wicker chair in a converted Palaeur locker room. The twins' purple trunks, with their names stenciled on the sides, are rolled up against the far wall. "My day is filled from the second I get up to the second I go to sleep. There are pleasure things I'd like to do, like go sightseeing, but there's hardly 20 minutes when I can take a nap. It's not like our nanny can do everything. . . . But one of the things we have to remember is that this *is* our life, this is what we do. This is how I choose to live my life and I'm happy about it."

On the Palaeur's concrete concourse, crew members with panicked eyes and upbeat expressions whisper into walkie-talkies. I feel like I'm waiting for a blind date to a prom held in a bomb shelter. Finally, Stipe turns up, publicist and assistant alongside, looking surprisingly spry. He's wearing a knit ski cap with a question-mark logo pulled tight over his bald head, leather jacket over a floppy T-shirt, big pocket key chain clanking against black jeans, and stylishly clunky motorcycle boots. Very Warhol superstar, in a neatly pressed, approachable way. He extends a hand, fingernails painted blue and chipped, grins sheepishly and gamely remembers my name.

"You know," I venture after we've retired to the locker room, "I've begun to think that R.E.M. stands for 'Really Elusive Michael.' I didn't expect such a hit-and-miss interview ordeal."

"When was the last time we talked?" Stipe sits up, elbows on knees. "In New York, during the Grammys?"

I tell him it was at the MTV Video Music Awards.

"Well, you shouldn't take it personally."

I don't, really, and I guess I should thank the band for blowing me off in New York since I scammed a free trip to Italy out of it.

"We weren't blowing you off," Stipe says, slightly offended, his good cheer visibly dissipating.

"I know that, but for the past six months I've kind of felt like I was standing in a stag line with Old Man Schwump, like on *The Andy Griffith Show*."

"I never watched that show."

Awkward silence. I wonder again if this isn't kind of an overwhelming, counterproductive process.

"In spite of myself, in spite of my history," he begins, taking a deep breath, "I try to make these things into conversations, you know, which depends on who I'm talking to. But basically, everybody asks the same four questions anyway, particularly in Europe."

"Well, after reading all your interviews, it seemed like you gave the same four answers no matter what questions anybody asked."

"I don't know what you mean." He pauses. "I'm confused."

"Anyway, when we talked last year, you said that you were scared of repeating the Green tour experience. Have your fears been justified at all?"

"Oh, not really. I just eventually got tired of using that line." He laughs, breaking the tension. "Now I'm loving touring. The travel has been grueling, and we're only seven weeks into it, but we're taking as many precautions as possible so we don't fall apart again or whatever. . . . At the end of the last tour, I felt like somebody dumped my body out at the bottom of my driveway at home and I couldn't move. Right now, it's still kind of fresh and exciting."

I suggest that he finally seems to have the faith of his own pretensions, that he's no longer going out of his way to seem so self-effacing.

"No, I still think I'm pretty self-effacing." Deadpan pause. Then he grins. "You know, I like this idea of doing an interview about doing interviews, though. That's kind of wild."

"I thought about bringing in all the clips, spreading them out on the table and asking, 'So why did you say all this silly shit?'"

"Yeah, it's like I'm being reflected in the mirror which is reflecting the camera which is taking a photograph of the mirror." His voice trails off as he reconsiders the question of his so-called pretensions. "Well, of course, there's a point, at which it gets ridiculous, the whole self-effacing act, and truthfully, believe me, I do and don't take all this very seriously. But I can't possibly take it seriously all the time or I'd go batty. Then again, I've never thought I was as pretentious as everybody else thought. But maybe by saying that I'm being pretentious. I have no idea anymore."

Maybe people think you're pretentious, I offer, because of the games you play in the press with your sexual preference. It sometimes comes off like a put-on to get attention.

"Well, just in defense of myself, and not in a defensive way at all, I've always fucked around with gender. And I've never played the game of arriving at big media events with supermodels to try and prove that I fuck women. If I suck dick or suck pussy or if I alternate between the two, it's my business and nobody else's. People can make whatever assumptions they want, and they have. I think a lot of people just assume that I'm queer and that's fine. I've never been ashamed of anything and I've never denied anything."

"It's interesting that you've talked a lot about Patti Smith being your main inspiration for getting into rock 'n' roll. I can't think of any other male rock star who has ever said that about a female musician."

"Patti Smith was a woman, but she was also in that gray area that I feel like I embody as a public figure, the neither-nor. I've always responded to that in a big way. She was not a woman as women were generally defined in 1975 in the United States, she was something wholly other, and not just because she looked androgynous. And I kind of made myself, as much as I could, without it being some kind of theft, into my version of her. You know, I spoke to her for the first time on the telephone recently. I called her from this anarchist book store in San Sebastian, Spain, and it was really great just to talk, because I've, in the past, exalted her to some kind of heroic, unreasonable level. That first album [*Horses*] was the most important thing in the world. It was always like, 'God, she's sending some weird, secret message to me.'"

I mention that what struck me about *Horses* was the way Patti Smith sang about religion. She was so turned on *and* disgusted by it.

Stipe hesitates and sits back. "I never really got the religious thing. I mean, it's there, 'Jesus died for somebody's sins, but not mine.' But I didn't grow up in a strict religious situation, so. . . ."

"But wasn't one of your grandparents a minister?"

"My grandfather on my father's side was a Southern Methodist preacher. But it wasn't like a Fundamentalist, born-again Baptist thing. The Methodist church doesn't try to dictate every single aspect of your life."

"Yeah, I was raised Southern Baptist and I resented the Methodist kids because they got to wear turtlenecks to Sunday service and sing cool songs."

"Really? Oh, Jesus." He scoots forward, laughing. "Well, Methodism was started by John Wesley, who was, in his way, a really radical guy who believed in a lot of individual responsibility. It's not the kind of religion that's right around your throat. Actually, I was named after him, John Michael Stipe."

Since R.E.M. has always been thought of as a spiritual band in some undefined way, do you think your grandfather's preaching had an impact on you that surfaces in the band?

"Possibly. My grandfather wasn't generally a pulpit-pounder, although I do remember him doing that from time to time and it making a big impression on me. The excitement from that, for a kid, can be really overpowering. I don't know what the right word is, it was more than just a 'kick' or a 'thrill.' It was just like, 'Wow!' It's such great theater and can be so beautiful. I guess I wanted to be a part of that somehow, maybe not the religion, but just that feeling that my grandfather was giving off."

"You've got to remember one thing about R.E.M.," my friend Stephen advised in an eerily Stipean mimic. "This is bigger than you . . . and you are not me." Of course, he was simply adding to the "Losing My Religion" jokebook, but he was also making a crucial point. For many people—likely including Stipe's close friend Kurt Cobain—R.E.M. was never really about the music. It was an iconic, almost religious presence, a dues-paying symbol of how to survive as artists amid the exploitation of the music business. Good-hearted corporate aesthetes who lived the American bohemian dream—buying in without selling out—and wrote the business prospectus for alternative rock that Nirvana capitalized on. That *Automatic for the People* was one of the most wittily self-aware and exquisitely mournful albums ever recorded, or that *Monster* raised the stakes by roughing up the band's entire sound and persona, was secondary to R.E.M.'s rigorously respectable public image. The band members never pushed our buttons with self-serving feuds or drug-rehab journeys. But now everybody "respects" R.E.M. so damn much (e.g., magazines chronicling their importance by printing set lists like sacred texts) that compliments start to sound like backhanded insults, and you forget how fun *and* smart their music can be.

For instance, when I asked Courtney Love why R.E.M. was so important to her and her late husband, she rambled on about being Buck's neighbor in Seattle, how she gave him a prototype of a guitar Kurt invented for Fender, how she saw the band do "Let Me In" (the song on *Monster* about Kurt) live in Budokan and almost cried, and how she gets such a feeling of "well-being" from R.E.M. "Michael Stipe is the sexiest man in America by a fucking country mile," she crows, "and if he ever decides to breed, I would appreciate being in the top five. In fact, I demand it." Typical Courtney. But also typical R.E.M. fan. Always going on about all the stuff around the music.

Which is bizarre, since my idea of what rock'n' roll should sound like was explicitly shaped by R.E.M. while I was a student in the early '80s at the University of Georgia in Athens. At one point, the band played every three weeks for two dollars at Tyrone's, a run-of-the-mill bar that started a new wave night in 1980–81 because of Pylon's popularity and lucked out as R.E.M. packed the place. Instead of thrusting out at you from the stage, R.E.M.'s songs subtly swept you forward. The rhythm section's melodic swirl and Stipe's lulling vocals were immediately intriguing. As a result, everybody danced, but in this introverted, twitchy way I've never really experienced since, except maybe at raves. It was the spectacle of uptight white kids trying to feel good about their bodies, and succeeding.

What Athens brought to rock 'n' roll was this nonmacho, nonconfrontational, communal stance. It was not punk. Nothing sucked and hostility was in bad taste. Lead singers didn't beg you to fuck them or hate them. R.E.M.'s guitar-pop aesthetic was influenced by a scene enamored with European new wave, funk, '70s soul, and glam rock, plus the liberating groove of the New York gay club scene. Compared to most other American rock bands at the time, R.E.M. was practically disco—all bass lines, nifty beats, and superfluous, sensual lyrics. I figured the band was too specific to Athens's subculture for anybody else to get it.

Guess not. *Everybody* got it, or got something about it (the dance-culture twist straightened out as Buck's guitar playing improved). And R.E.M. became the most beloved band of the '80s, releasing *Murmur* (the doleful pop-rock debut album that was nothing like its live show) to great acclaim, touring endlessly when few had the nerve, helping create an underground where none existed. And as the years passed, the band remarkably reinvented its sound a number of times, leaving Stipe's vocals the primary signifier, possibly accounting for fans' inability to describe the band's lingering appeal.

R.E.M. has inspired legions of other bands, from goody-goodies such as Live to cut-ups such as Pavement. "When I was 15 years old in Richmond, Virginia, they were a *very important* part of my life," says Pavement's Bob Nastanovich, "as they were for all the members of our band. [Singer-guitarist Stephen] Malkmus was heavy into them when he went to school in Charlottesville [at the University of Virginia]. I bet [guitarist Scott] Kannberg bought *Monster* the day it came out and played it ten times. [Drummer Steven] West was even in an R.E.M. soundalike band. They were always this uniting force. People who liked Black Flag liked 'em, people who liked the Dead liked 'em. They were the first band that the frat guys looked at and didn't say, 'Oh, let's beat up some fags.' . . . It also turned people's attention to the South. People never thought about places like Georgia or South Carolina. Then they were taking vacations down to 'R.E.M. country,' just driving around listening to R.E.M. records. It was a weird fashion thing too, like in my high school, you had large cliques of people who would dress like Michael Stipe, you know, raiding thrift stores and wearing really neutral Army khaki stuff. . . . Now, I don't know what's up with those guys. It's almost like a college team trying to play in the NBA."

R.E.M.'s fans have often poked the band when its sincerity shtick got too thick or self-congratulatory. Last year, the Beastie Boys' Adam Yauch, disguised as an enraged sheep farmer, hijacked an MTV video award from Stipe. "I was just howling," says Buck, "but everybody around us, like Aerosmith, were all tensed up." Usually the digs have taken the form of song parodies, indirectly revealing a deep appreciation for the band's music. Like when the Butthole Surfers, who moved to Athens in the mid-'80s, covered "The One I Love" while burning dollar bills. "I have a bootleg of them doing that," says Buck proudly. "I thought it was great that the Buttholes took the time to learn one of our songs." Or when the Dead Milkmen came to Athens dressed in long-sleeved white shirts and black vests (à la Buck) and did an obscene version of "Driver 8." "It's cooler than a tribute album," Buck laughs.

One tribute, however, that the band has admittedly never made sense of, and in its own smirky-quirky way may be the most insightful assessment of R.E.M.'s meaning and appeal, is Pavement's "Unseen Power of the Picket Fence" from the *No Alternative* compilation. "Classic songs with a long history," declares Malkmus on the grinding buildup, and he's so quixotically passionate, his clipped voice listing all the songs on *Reckoning* so dutifully, right down to "Time after Time (Annelise)"—his least favorite song! Sing it, brotherman!—that you actually believe he believes in something (even if it's not R.E.M.). The inevitable invocation of General Sherman becomes a perverse vision of Stipe et al. as the chosen survivors of Southern culture's scorched earth. It's preposterous and touching. And proves that you can love and respect a band and still hear their career as a precious charade.

In the Spike Jonze–directed video for R.E.M.'s "Crush with Eyeliner," Japanese teenagers lip synch, pose dead-cool, and mug impetuously inside and outside a restaurant-bar, practically smooching the camera, as Michael Stipe purrs in the background, "We all invent ourselves / And you know me." He's getting off on a familiar paradox—watching someone you think you know remake themselves.

"I don't think the idea of slipping in out of different personalities is unique to performers or people who are part of the pop-culture pageant," says Stipe. "Everybody does it every day, no matter what their job or life is like. I love that commercial where this white, geeky guy stands on a corner and everybody who walks by him morphs into a white, geeky-guy version of themselves. It's for TDK or something. All this happens and they sell a product in the meantime. That could be 'Crush with Eyeliner.'"

Ostensibly, "Crush" is about a girl faking it so real that all her dreams come true. But even more, it's about being obsessed with *watching* that girl, gazing at the dizzying swoosh of youth culture and wondering where you fit in, when you should get out of the way and to what extent you're responsible for what's going on. R.E.M. has never been totally in with the in crowd and they know that's part of what makes them so sympathetic. They watch, like most of us, and pick up on things over time.

Jonze deletes the band members from the video until the closing frames, when Stipe briefly appears in a crew-neck sweater and white button-down shirt, sitting at a table in the shadows. He's not lurking, just observing. As Buck once said, "Michael's got this great ability. . . . If he doesn't know something, he'll latch on to people and learn from them."

There was a time when R.E.M. wouldn't even appear in its videos, let alone lip-synch, which was interpreted as a no-sell-out move. But the band just hadn't learned how to use the medium to its advantage. In retrospect, videos were a godsend for R.E.M., allowing it to regain some measure of mystery and intimacy. And control. The reticent pop artists could hide in the margins, or, when they were ready, show up as carefully considered images. With the poignantly studied "Losing My Religion" in 1991, and 1993's "Everybody Hurts," Stipe seriously stepped out in front of the camera, playing an almost preacherly role in the latter clip, leading a somber group of commuters away from their traffic-jammed lives.

"Michael is probably the best artist I've worked with in terms of understanding his performance, even though he's so insecure all the time," says the director Jake Scott. "In 'Everybody Hurts,' he felt exposed and agoraphobic and I think that worked for the video. It's rare that someone has the confidence and awareness to look awkward and quite afraid in front of the camera."

With Peter Care's video for "Man on the Moon," R.E.M. achieved a sense of pop community that was probably the most confidently sublime of its career. Shot in naturalist black-and-white, Stipe strides through a barren stretch of the southwest, a snake slithering around his boot, cow-boy hat cocked on his head, like a wide-eyed army brat duded up as James Dean in *Giant*. He's a figure, not yet tragic or comic, transfixed by the possibilities of America's expansive spaces. While projections of the come-dian Andy Kaufman flash overhead, Stipe reaches a highway, does a quick Elvis wiggle, and hitches a ride on an 18-wheeler driven by Berry. When he gets off at a truck stop (his "St. Peter's"), the other members of the band, as well as patrons of both sexes and various ages, are offhandedly singing the words of the song to each other, like a comforting conversa-tion. It's one of those potentially corny moments that transcends itself and demonstrates the power of pop music to connect people's lives.

And that's why the Monster tour, or at least what I saw of it, was so disheartening. R.E.M., after proving it could be an inspiring international pop icon on its own unconventional terms, was now attempting to prove it deserved that status, but on everybody else's conventional terms. While the album makes rock star life seem like an absurdly affecting holiday, the arena show clocks in, clocks out, and heads to the hotel bar. I was reminded of something Berry said in New York before the European tour and his near-fatal collapse. "It really is ironic. Something starts from your soul, and when it becomes a song, right at that moment, it stops and becomes a game. If you want it to be heard, and we do, then you enter the business world. You don't have to make certain decisions, but if you don't, somebody else will make them for you. It's frustrating sometimes. All of a sudden, you're in a room talking to somebody like you, which is fine, but I had to do it at 3:15 on a Sunday afternoon for exactly X number of minutes. Everything is so regimented. Like, I know on April 24, 1995, exactly where I'm going to be, what time I'm going onstage, and how many people are going to be in the audience."

But on April 24, 1995, Berry wasn't onstage. He was recovering from surgery and trying to get himself back in shape for the rapidly approaching American concert dates. A brutally challenging situation, at best. So, in mid-May, with the tour set to kick off, I wanted to ask either Berry or one of the other band members if they were having any second thoughts. After a number of unsuccessful tries to get Mike Mills on the phone, a Warner Bros. publicist called me one last time from the Shoreline Amphitheatre, an outdoor venue near San Francisco and the site of R.E.M.'s first U.S. show in five years. She said the band had just sound-checked, and Mills didn't feel up to talking. A thunderstorm was looming and the show had to go on "rain or shine" and well, what else could go wrong? I told her I understood.

Part Five

NEW ADVENTURES

ROBERT HILBURN
THE LOWDOWN ON *HI-FI* (1996)

Los Angeles Times, *September 8, 1996*

A song called "Electrolite" on R.E.M.'s new album, *New Adventures in Hi-Fi,* describes the exhilaration of riding along Mulholland Drive and gazing at the beauty of the stars above and, especially, the lights below.

The Los Angeles hillside setting makes the narrator feel so special that he identifies with actors who represent to him the essence of glamour and cool: "I'm Steve McQueen . . . I'm Jimmy Dean."

It's a telling moment because there is something tragic about both of those actors, and you sense that the character in the song is in some type of trouble—and that Mulholland is simply a momentary refuge from his real and complicated world.

In a way, R.E.M. experienced the emotional ups and downs hinted at in "Electrolite" during the year or so that the group spent recording the new collection, which arrives in stores Tuesday.

The band members' trials began with a series of illnesses during their 1995 world tour. First, and most seriously, drummer Bill Berry suffered a brain aneurysm in Switzerland. It was followed by bassist Mike Mills' abdominal surgery and singer Michael Stipe's hernia surgery.

The tension continued after the tour as the band went through what guitarist Peter Buck describes as the most "soul-destroying" period in the quartet's 16-year history. Buck, 39, said he is prohibited legally from talking about the matter, but he is apparently referring to the group's break in May with longtime manager Jefferson Holt.

Sources said Holt, who resigned, was asked to leave after the band investigated allegations that he sexually harassed a female employee at the band's Athens, Ga., office.

R.E.M.'s refuge during these periods was music—first the concerts and the sound checks, where the members recorded the bulk of the songs for the new album, and then the studio, where they put the final touches on *New Adventures*. The result is a stirring collection that mixes some of the pure rock fury of 1994's *Monster* with the lighter, more graceful elements of the band's earlier work.

On the eve of the album release, an upbeat Buck, the father of 2-year-old twin girls, spoke from his home in Seattle about the highs and lows of making *New Adventures* and the future of the band, which last month signed what is believed to be the largest record contract in history: a five-album deal with Warner Bros. Records worth an estimated $80 million.

Question: Weren't you originally planning to play all the new songs in the show and then record them for a live album?

Answer: That thought came up when Bill and I were doing interviews together for *Monster*. We said we might write a bunch of songs and then record them on the road, so that by the end of the tour we'd have a finished album. But it didn't quite work out. For one thing, some of the stuff we were writing was just too delicate to stand up to being played in front of 20,000 people who were screaming for "The One I Love" or whatever.

Q: How many songs did you end up recording during the show?

A: We played five new songs in the tour—four of which ended up on the album: "Undertow," "The Wake-Up Bomb," "Departure" and "Binky the Doormat." We also played a song called "Revolution" on almost the entire tour, but it didn't make the record because by the time we got into the studio the song seemed a little old and didn't fit in. But it will definitely show up in the long-form version of *Road Movie* (the concert video that will be released in conjunction with the album). We recorded another eight songs or so at the sound checks.

Q: How was it playing in an empty arena?

A: Usually sound checks are boring because you do like four songs that you play every night anyway. Instead, we were coming in with all this new stuff. Even the road crew, who usually never watch sound checks, ended up bringing their dinners and watching us play, and it was a nice feeling. We took this eight-track machine on the road and it proved to be much more relaxed than sitting in the studio where you always have the red light reminding you that the studio is costing you $2,000 a day or whatever, so you'd better get to work. It was a real liberating experience.

Q: When you are making a record, do you think about the large audience waiting to hear what you've done? You guys have sold more than 12 million albums in the U.S. alone since SoundScan *began in 1991. Does that inspire you or intimidate you?*

A: The writing is pretty much done before we think about what the audience is going to expect, but there is a point where you start thinking about all the people who are going to be hearing the record—and I like that feeling. I realize we are going to be held to a higher standard than someone on an indie label or something, and I think that's fair because we have a lot of advantages over someone who is making an $8,000 album on a tiny label. For one thing, we don't have any day jobs. We can do things twice if we need to in order to get just the right sound on the record.

Q: But isn't there a temptation at some point to take things easy and maybe lean on what has worked before for you?

A: I think the idea of certain formulas that lead to success are more a preoccupation with record companies than with bands. I just read somewhere an article that said only 7 percent of the records released in America sell more than 10,000 copies. When you hear that, you realize that most people don't know what it is that makes a record successful. I always felt the only test we apply to a record is to try to make it challenging and interesting and forward-looking.

Q: What about the song "Electrolite"? How did that come about?

A: A lot of the songs on the album speak about restlessness and other feelings that you get being on tour. A lot of them, in fact, are literally about going from place to place. The character in that song is driving through the hills of Mulholland, looking at the beauty of Los Angeles at night. Everyone really does feel like Steve McQueen or someone when they are on top of the hill. I don't know what really happens to the guy at the end of the song . . . when he comes down to reality.

Q: Do you see any parallel to being on stage and then coming back to reality?

A: I doubt very often or ever Michael writes specifically about being in the band, but I think it would be natural to include some of the feelings you get on tour in songs. On tour, you just get into such a weird mental state and I think a lot of the characters that are written about in the record are in that state . . . a dislocated kind of feeling. It's just they are placed in other situations.

Q: Do you ever have periods where you think the band seems to be getting stale?

A: Oh sure, I think every band goes through cycles. I think we felt a bit like we were at the end of our ropes around 1985. We were on the road 360 days a year . . . just home for the week around Christmas. We eventually decided we didn't have to be on the road like this all the time. We had other things we wanted to do in our lives. For instance, we won't tour with this record. Instead, we'll probably go back into the studio and make another record. Then we'll put it out in about a year and go on the road and play them.

Q: Did you have any fear when you had children that you'd lose some of your focus and drive in rock 'n' roll?

A: You mean the old idea of the tortured artist? I'm not going to deny that turmoil and unhappiness fuels a lot of creativity, but I think everyone growing up has enough of that to last them the rest of their lives. Everyone I know has enough bad times and struggles in their lives to draw upon for a lifetime.

Q: What happened following Bill's aneurysm? Was there a point where you feared that might be the end of R.E.M.?

A: First we just worried about Bill. But there was eventually a point where I assumed the tour was over and that we might never tour again. None of us had an interest in hiring a session drummer and going on the road. But, thankfully, it never got to that point.

Q: The new Warner Bros. contract calls for five more albums. How long do you see R.E.M. going?

A: That's something we've talked about since our second gig ever and we've always said we'll just play it by ear. When we did the *Monster* record, however, the last few weeks were really hard for some reason. If we had faced signing a new contract then, I might have doubted how long things would go. But this record and the traumatic experiences pulled us together in a way that makes me feel confident about the future again.

Q: What do you think about all the reunion tours going on these days? Can you ever picture R.E.M. going out and just doing the old favorites?

A: I've long been terrified of letting the past overtake us. I still don't want to be one of those bands that has to go on the road and play all old stuff and only one song from the new record. I am going to fight that as long as I can.

But you know what? There may be a time when I might go, "Let's go out and celebrate. Let's do some of the songs that we haven't done in 15 years."

I saw Neil Diamond the other night and it was great. He got out there and played some of the old songs with a lot of commitment. It looked like he was having a great time and the audience loved it. There are a lot of memories in our old songs and it might be good to share them again some day.

Peter Buck on tour, 1997. *Photo © David Atlas.*

TOM DOYLE

REMEMBER US (1996)

Q, *November 1996*

"This fame thing, I don't get it." At this precise moment, the irony of this key line from "E-Bow the Letter" is surely not lost on Michael Stipe.

Though supported by the comforting presence of his three band members and staring fixedly at the ever-present musical stand that props up the single's Dylanesque ramble of a lyric sheet, the scalped singer is suffering a slow, uncomfortable draining of the soul, as more camera lenses than you would witness even outside the Princess of Wales's Chelsea health club of a Saturday morning point in the direction of his slight frame.

In an effort to combine some of the promo duties for their 10th album, *New Adventures in Hi-Fi,* R.E.M. had decided to allow legions of photographers and TV crews from the furthest reaches of the Western world to converge on this tiny video set in North Hollywood for one (and strictly one only) half-mimed performance of the introspective track. By the ill-at-ease looks on their faces, they are regretting it, since the result—foul-tempered camera folk fighting one another in the hope of getting a better angle than their rivals (and worse, getting in the way of the video crew themselves)—resembles a multi-media motorway pile-up.

Peter Buck, a laid-back individual ungirthed with the steely constitution common to the more regularly paparazzi-pestered celeb, has been visibly rattled by this irksome evidence of his group's undoubted stardom. Beating a hasty retreat at the song's close, he turns to *Q* and with a certain weary wisdom notes, "Well, I think that was unique in the annals of publicity."

The video set for "E-Bow the Letter" is a white fairylight-festooned chamber of icy beauty and contrasts sharply with the baking 85 degree heat of the parking lot outside Shortino's, the small Burbank rehearsal facility that R.E.M. have commandeered for this two day shoot. Stipe stands shirtless in the studio's parking lot, picking bird-like at the catering company's "snacking table," this seemingly being his major source of daily sustenance—the odd M&M here, paper bowl of tortilla chips and guacamole there, along with one over-sized watermelon slushie that will last the day, the occasional cup of—as he obliquely describes it—"octagonal espresso," and regular doses of his favoured health drink, spirulina—basically a herbal juice swimming with algae ("It's my spirit animal," he says).

He is certainly on perkier form than he was yesterday, when, jet-lagged as the result of a flight from Europe—where he'd joined "E-Bow" co-vocalist Patti Smith on the Italian and Spanish legs of her European tour—he'd grown more fractious as the day unfolded.

The video is being directed by his old friend Jem Cohen (whom the band had previously commissioned for the haunting "Nightswimming" promo) with Stipe as unofficial co-director, and the claustrophobic nine-by-nine dimensions of the set and Cohen's apprehension surrounding his first major clip for the group had made for a stressed and frosty atmosphere.

Yesterday, when the time came for the frontman's solo close-up, Stipe had performed the song with a charisma-charged intensity as the camera swung ever closer towards his face. When the track ended, he'd appeared almost half-embarrassed by having to be so "on" ("E-Bow" being close in spirit to "Country Feedback," a song he performed nightly during the *Monster* tour with his back turned to the audience). Everyone bar the production crew were politely but firmly ordered out of the room. By the evening, his conversation had been reduced to a collection of tetchy grunts.

Today, though, he is in a charming and talkative mood, clearly energized by his European trip and, in particular, one strange coincidence. "I met this guy when I was at Heathrow Terminal Four, he says, "and he knew who I was and he asked me where I was going and I told him Los Angeles. He said he was going to Seattle for the first time and so I told him about this really great restaurant he should check out."

"So I'm sitting in this restaurant in Seattle," continues Buck, "and this guy comes up to me and says. You're Peter Buck from R.E.M., aren't you? You'll never guess who I met this morning at Heathrow . . . and it was this same guy Michael had met. It had only been, like, 12 hours earlier."

There is a buzz surrounding the R.E.M. camp at the moment which serves to confound the recent wild rumours that they were in fact on the verge of splitting: speculation stirred up by the sudden termination of their relationship with long-term manager Jefferson Holt (of which more later), and then neatly quashed by their swift, subsequent re-signing to Warner Brothers Records for another five albums and of course—that $80 million.

Propelled by the varying trials and glories of the 11-month *Monster* tour, they have worked almost constantly since the rehearsals for that album began back in January '94 (save for the weeks of Bill Berry's recuperation from his aneurysm and a 12-week cooling period that sandwiched the end of the tour and the band's decampment to Seattle to complete the new album) and there is a triumphant feeling that their ambitious idea of writing and recording songs during their transcontinental touring jaunts proved so successful. As their attorney-turned-manager Bertis Downs IV had announced to assembled journalists in London only a fortnight before, "We didn't think we'd have a new album ready as soon as this, but . . . here we are." As Stipe is today eager to inform *Q*, "I spoke to Bono the other day and he was *cursing* me for having a record finished."

By the end of the Monster tour, R.E.M. had the basic tracks for seven songs, recorded during soundchecks and stage performances. There were innumerable takes of each and so the daunting task of sifting through over 100 shows' worth of tapes was handed over to tour guitarist Nathan December. Regrouping at the Seattle studio Bad Animals in March, the band augmented these live takes and went on to record purely studio-based versions of the songs they hadn't managed to commit to tape while on the hoof. The result, it has already been said, combines the legs-akimbo rock of *Monster* (if anything, improving on it) and the dark, complex emotions of *Automatic for the People* and challenges the listener to spot the joins between the live and studio recordings while making great stylistic leaps between tracks. As Buck puts it, "It's kind of like a compilation of a bunch of different bands except we made all the music."

As is perhaps typical of the launch of any R.E.M. album campaign, and is perhaps necessary in the light of recent murmurings of *New Adventures in Hi-Fi* being the group's last LP, the band are making a show of their solidarity. Shrewdly, all photo sessions will involve the whole band (neatly scotching any magazine articles or covers featuring—gasp! Michael alone), and Stipe, though not exactly ducking around corners to *avoid* the press, is making sure that Mills and Buck conduct the interviews early in the album's life.

While on set, Stipe breaks up the between-take monotony by toying around with bad waltzing alone to a private tune or sitting around constructing an endless stream of roll-ups, while Mills and Buck, ever the compositional workaholics, trade ideas for new songs (both reckoning that they've come up with the bare bones of a pair of new tunes in just the past two days). Even though director Cohen's fairylight set is starkly simple, there are teetering piles of props littered around the limited workspace, and these stacks of CDs and vinyl albums (*In Utero, The Clash on Broadway, Exile on Main Street,* even *Automatic for the People*) and books (Patti Smith's *Early Work,* Elias Canetti's *Auto-da-Fé,* Hemingway's *The Sun Also Rises*) provide flick-through distraction for the band between performances, as a powerful fan is switched on to replenish the oxygen level of the tiny room.

During the supposedly *au naturel* nonperformance shots, Mills and Buck chat, Berry sits behind his kit reading a Lenny Bruce biography and Stipe, his famed posturing always evident (even in the way he baroquely rolls a fag or throws snake-hipped shapes when he's only standing around drinking coffee) uses the opportunity to carefully, even artfully, tear up strips of gaffer tape and apply them to the left-hand side of his lyric sheet, for no apparent or logical reason whatsoever. On these occasions, it's important to remember that Michael Stipe is very much a *rock star.*

Outside sit two comfortably large, soothingly air-conditioned Winnebagos. One trailer has been given over to "production" and this is where you're most likely to find Stipe during lengthier breaks in the day's proceedings. The other is where the rest of the band hang out—a mess of magazines and bread sticks and bottles of water (there is even a button badge pinned to the roof in support of O. J. Simpson's dearly departed that reads "remember Nicole 1959—1994")—and this is where Peter Buck is enjoying his burrito-based lunch break.

Relaxed and affable as ever, he is on fine form. Buck's relocation to Seattle was the main reason for the band basing themselves there for the recording of *New Adventures in Hi-Fi,* the tongue-in-cheek title of which still amuses the guitarist ("It's inspired by the titles of all those '50s records. The alternative titles we were coming up with were things like *R.E.M.'s Own Thing* and *Revolution of Our Minds* and *In Stereo*"). While here in LA for the video shoot, he is staying at the plush Four Seasons hotel (since, being something of a book-devouring night owl, he can order a pizza at 4 A.M.), while Stipe is located at the distinctly grungier Chateau Marmont (where, apparently, 4 A.M. pizza is difficult) and Berry is bedding down in the spare room of Mike Mills's new house in the hills.

Despite operating on limited sleep due to his erratic resting habits, he is alert, enthusiastic about almost any subject, and talks at a breakneck, sometimes barely comprehensible speed, in lilting tones that, even when he doesn't entirely agree with a point, still give the impression that, y'know, sure, he's cool with that.

Most groups would take at least a year off after a tour of *Monster's* enormity, and R.E.M. have only had three months. One imagines them fuelled entirely by some insane strain of workaholic adrenaline.

"Well yeah," he begins, "once you get in the groove, you want to keep going. There wasn't a lot of sense in staying home. If we'd taken a year off, I don't know what would have happened. I mean, we probably would've hated the songs. And nobody expected us to do it. Even our lawyer was like, Oh you'll take a year off starting November, and I said, Well, I think we're going to make a record, y'know. By the end of the tour, everyone was excited and we were talking about when to book the studio. Still, we made sure there was enough time for us to take a little vacation and, you know, listen to tapes and figure things out."

Even though the plan was always to release a new album after the tour, were you surprised that it actually worked out?

"Since it's the very first thing that we've ever done that worked out the way we planned it, yeah. It was kinda odd. The original idea was that by the last month of the tour we would have 12 songs finished and then we'd just play five or six of them live every night. Then we'd record for a week and we'd have a live album with all new songs. But we didn't finish that many, and we just kinda thought, Well let's take all we've got, then put it together and make a studio record that starts out in that kind of chaotic live fashion."

On the *Monster* tour, Buck explains, the normally dull rigmarole of soundchecking actually became a high point of the day. For the band, it helped break up the grind of the touring experience by giving them time to work on and record new material; for the road crew, it became a morale-lifting private performance of R.E.M.'s new songs. (The guitarist is delighted to note that the roadies would sit and watch the band while having their lunch instead of making a swift exit as soon as their work was done.)

Although many of the songs on *New Adventures in Hi-Fi* were worked into the live set as the tour progressed ("Undertow," "The Wake-Up Bomb," "Binky the Doormat" and "Revolution"—left off the album "because we had so many other things"—all becoming cemented into the nightly repertoire), others were still in skeletal form by their finale in Atlanta in November. "New Test Leper" had been tried out only once in a soundcheck; "E-Bow the Letter" was completed, though Buck admits that only half of the band had felt confident enough to add it to the set and so, to avoid arguments at the close of the tour, the notion to perform it was ditched at the last moment.

When you were adding the new songs to the set; was it real flying-by-the-seat-of-your-pants stuff?

"If you're asking if we fucked them up, yeah, we fucked them up [laughs]. One night with "Revolution" in—I think Dearborn in Michigan, for some reason I got really confused where I was and just kinda stopped and everyone just kept going and then everyone got confused just as I figured it out, and they stopped and I kept going. You know, we ended together, which is probably all that you can hope for in that situation. There were shows that were just one disaster after another. Like the third day at Madison Square Garden when all my equipment broke. Every single thing I own for some reason broke in the one day—my amp was smoking, my guitar started crackling, the works."

Though the circumstances surrounding the recording of *New Adventures* appear fairly unique, there are parallels with other albums. U2's *Zooropa*, for instance, was recorded amid a particularly hairy tour schedule ("You know, we didn't think of that one consciously"), while David Bowie's *Aladdin Sane* similarly bears the names of different cities after the title of each song . . . and there is even a reference to that album's title track in Mills's unhinged piano solo in "How the West Was Won and Where It Got Us."

"Well we were actually thinking Thelonius Monk, but I listened to *Aladdin Sane* about a month ago, and that piano solo came in and I went, Oh my God! I bet that was kind of in the back of my head too, that whole deconstruct-the-song-for-16-bars thing. You know, I think the most current inspiration was someone like Pearl Jam with "Vitalogy." When they were touring, they would do a week of shows and then they would stay three extra days in the last city and go in a studio and they'd just jam and Eddie would sing to it. I really liked the fact that it was that spontaneous. Personally I wanted to get a little bit more song-orientated. But that to me was kind of inspirational—it's like, Yeah we can just do this, it doesn't matter what anyone says."

When you listen to the album now, does it remind you of the places where the songs were written? Is it like snapshots of the tour?

"Yeah, to a certain degree. 'Departure' was written entirely in one sitting in San Sebastian, Spain, when we were rehearsing to start the American leg of the tour. It's a little Basque town and they had a riot every night. Honestly, every night at about seven o'clock, they would turn a car over, set it on fire and kick in a window—and you knew, you'd sit in a bar and they'd go by, and you were able to time it.

"I remember writing 'Bitter Sweet Me' in San Francisco at a soundcheck at the first show when Bill came back from his aneurysm. 'Undertow' was written in Athens when we were rehearsing to make sure Bill could play. I mean, he wanted to, and he said, I've been playing, I'm great. He was like, Let's just start the tour tomorrow. And we were like, let's just do a week's rehearsal in San Francisco and hang out and not rush back into it. Just see how it goes."

Were you nervous when he picked the sticks back up again? As horrible a thought as it may be, was it like, Will he suddenly be slowing down and speeding up and we can't say anything?

"[Twisted laugh] Yeah, well, y'know, awful as that sounds. . . ."

One of your closest friends in a life-threatening situation must bring everything else sharply back into focus.

"Well it certainly does. We spent that month in Switzerland just hanging around with Bill and seeing what was going to happen. We were more concerned about Bill than anything else of course, but after about a week I suppose we were all kind of thinking, Well maybe the band's over, but as long as Bill's going to be OK or get pretty close to OK, then that's fine. I really was willing to trade everything for Bill's health: I could always work. I've got money, I don't care. As it turned out, apparently the doctor said that he'd had an almost unprecedentedly quick recovery. But yeah, once you get back to it, you really do think every day, this was almost gone, and it could happen easily. We call it the Meteorite Scenario, that one of us gets hit by a meteorite. Because what are the odds of anything? But people die."

If that hadn't happened, do you think you'd have grown pig sick of the sight of each other? Living in one another's pockets for 11 months at a time can't be comfortable.

"I don't know. Maybe. [Smiles] Well, we always used to. . . ."

Halfway through this work-intensive week for R.E.M., there is a late afternoon video press conference for South East Asia scheduled with Buck and Mills. This is to take place at a satellite broadcast facility in a particularly grimy downtown location. En route, Buck stares out through the darkened limo window and, as the car glides smoothly through the graffiti-stained streets, he spots a sidewalk hamburger stand surrounded by heavy-looking Hispanic dudes and says, not without a hint of irony, "I bet you can get the best chili dog in town right there." Still, neither he nor Q seem keen to actually stop and test out this theory.

"You know, today was one of those days that I always imagined every day would be like when you're a rock star," he muses. "You get up, go out and buy a couple of cool shirts, do a couple of photo sessions, sit around in a limo with a journalist. . . . It's very easy to get used to this life, particularly on tour. But it's kinda fun. I enjoy the travelling around in limousines and private jets sometimes, and y'know, What do you want to eat? We'll fly and get it for you. I kind of enjoy all that, but the second it's over I just go home and sleep for a week and I'm fine."

The satellite facility turns out to be an area no bigger than an average living room, with a sofa positioned in front of two large TV monitors, one showing Mills and Buck as they will appear on the screens on the other side of the planet, the other displaying rows of jittery, nervous Orientals from, in turn, Taipei, Singapore, Hong Kong and Bangkok. Despite perhaps unsurprising difficulties with sound and language, the conference soon becomes a jocular affair, even though the sometimes cruel tittering of those Warner Brothers and R.E.M. management people present—but not in camera shot—can be clearly heard echoing around the globe.

Strangely, one of the first questions concerns the band's "possible cooperation with Morrissey."

Buck: "We haven't actually talked to him about working together. I think he and Michael at one point were friends, and wrote to one another occasionally. But, um, he seems to be doing pretty well by himself." [Ripple of laughter around room.]

Another writer asks what they would have in mind were they to write a song for Hong Kong.

Buck: "Probably 1997 would be the topic on everyone's mind over there, so I'm sure there's something to be said about that."

Mills: "[Hopefully] Or maybe we could write a song about the new airport. . . ."

One brusque and instantly dislikable U.S. journalist says, "Peter, I have a question. We heard about half of the album the other day, and this is not meant to be uncomplimentary because I love R.E.M. and I always have, but it sounds a lot like R.E.M. has in the past. Do you guys ever feel like, What new is there left to write?"

Buck remains tactfully mute. Mike Mills chooses a diplomatic course: "We do actually throw a lot of songs away because we feel they sound too much like an old R.E.M. song. Y'know, we're always trying to be better songwriters and *I* think we're doing OK."

One asks if Stipe's quote in *Q*112 about "audiences that we could have chopped up and sold as hamburgers" was referring to Asia, and is rather sweetly told no. Another asks if "The Wake-Up Bomb" was written about the Oklahoma bombing and is told no, it's about a glam rock club in New York that Michael visited. One says: "Hootie and the Blowfish say that you are the best band they have ever heard of, so what do you think about it?"

Mike Mills props himself up in his seat, attempting to suppress a wry smile—with only partial success—and says, "Well, they're right." The resounding chorus of hearty laughter that follows can literally be heard in two continents.

As soon as the press conference is over, Mills heads off to his new home to prepare for a small party he is throwing tonight for the band and their management. Buck meanwhile has promised to drop by the studio where his friend Lindsey Buckingham is continuing work on his next solo album.

Back in the limo, he talks about the lyrical slant of some of the tracks on *New Adventures in Hi-Fi*, at least the way *he* sees them. "Quite literally," the guitarist baldly admits, "unless there's some thing that specifically confuses me, I don't ask Michael what the songs are about."

For the record, Stipe will reveal that the verses of "E-Bow the Letter" were constructed from an actual unmailed missive that he wrote on the road ("He sometimes writes letters like that, believe it or not," marvels Buck. "His postcards especially are like scripts to some weird movie that you're only getting the middle part of . . ."). What Stipe won't say is who the letter was *to*. "New Test Leper," though seemingly designed to court controversy, isn't Stipe declaring that he's an atheist, and furthermore, isn't about him appearing on a TV show ("It's written from the perspective of a character that Michael *saw* on TV on a talk show. But are people going to think Michael's talking about himself not liking Jesus? I don't think that people just take us that seriously. It's not like we're tearing up a picture of the Pope on television"). The achingly beautiful ballad "Be Mine" was purposefully roughened up musically and given a Zen lyrical touch after producer Scott Litt enthused about the likelihood of it being Number 1 in the U.S. for months ("That way we don't have to worry about landing in Whitney Houston territory. Michael could have taken three lines out of that song and it would be a huge hit").

We arrive at Ocean Way Studios in East Hollywood, which became unarguably the most legendary studio in Los Angeles when Phil Spector's favoured recording haunt, Gold Star, was torn down in the '70s to make way for a car park. Buck, infectiously enthusiastic when it comes to matters of musical history, guides Q through the corridors linking the different recording rooms and points out grainy black and white pictures of some of the regular clients of the complex in its '60s and '70s heydays: Sinatra with Mia Farrow, Brian Wilson, Lenny Waronker (famed producer of Randy Newman and Van Dyke Parks, and MD of Warner Brothers Records when R.E.M. first signed to the company).

In Studio C, he is welcomed by Lindsey Buckingham and Mick

Fleetwood, who have been holed up in this room for over a year trying to complete Buckingham's album. Buck has been called upon to add some guitar (his Rickenbackers have already been delivered, though he decides to wait until the weekend to return and play) and to lend fresh ears to the project. Buckingham instructs the engineer to reel up the first of nearly two dozen tracks, all of which the pair listen to intently, with Buck providing suggestions at the end of each, which Buckingham—wired and slightly apprehensive about letting his famous friend hear his new songs—quickly scribbles down. The odd bit of guitar feedback here? A cello there perhaps? Most, offers Buck, sound like they're already finished.

It is close to midnight by the time the guitarist and Q step back into the car. Buck knows the wood-for-trees obfuscation that Buckingham is experiencing, since R.E.M. suffered the same problems in the latter stages of *Monster*. "Some of those songs have only three instruments on them," he laughs, "and yet we just couldn't mix them." He can also empathise with Buckingham's eagerness to involve his former Fleetwood Mac bandmates (Fleetwood, both McVies, even Stevie Nicks) in his project. "I know that with R.E.M.," he says, "sure, we can all make music individually. But I think we're smart enough to know that the music we make together is far better."

And with that, he drops Q off at the hotel and asks the driver to point the car in the direction of the house in the hills where his bandmates—quite probably "hammered" on the sparkling white by now—are waiting for him to return. The following day, the group gather together at noon to begin shooting footage for the "Bitter Sweet Me" video on a large West Hollywood soundstage formerly owned by Charlie Chaplin. The site also has its own place in R.E.M.'s history, since the office above was formerly the headquarters of I.R.S. Records, 15 years before they would eventually sign the biggest recording deal in music history, it was here the band inked their first contract. "It was a big day for us," Bill Berry remembers, "but Miles Copeland walked straight past us because The Lords of the New Church had just arrived."

Mike Mills, having just enjoyed a hangover-shaking rubdown provided by the on-set masseuse, is slightly evasive about the previous night's social activities at his house. How was the party, wonders Q?

"Appropriate," he says.

Appropriate to what?

"Whatever, . . ." he retorts, blankly.

To your current state?

"Um yeah."

According to those around him, the bass player and keyboardist has walked noticeably taller since the Monster tour. In the band's recent *Road Movie* concert film, there is even a moment during "Losing My Religion" where he actually "works the crowd."

"Well, yeah," he begins, a touch sheepishly. "Well, it was fun. It's not something that you normally associate with me or R.E.M., but I never wore my glasses on stage until this tour, and for the first time I could actually see the faces of the people I'm playing to. We were selling 360 degree seating at a lot of the shows, so I could go back and actually communicate with people. That's mostly what it was. I'm not trying to pump the crowd for more applause, as much as I'm just trying to catch people's eye and wave and say, Isn't this fun?"

Do you think that level of touring does good things or bad things to your ego?

"It all depends on how you handle it," he decides after a lengthy pause. "If we were 22 and had done that tour, it would probably have done horrible, horrible things to our egos. But having come up gradually like we did, you realize that you have to have a good handle on yourself, or your head will explode like a balloon. When I come off tour, my friends have told me I'm very different. It takes me a week or two to go back into being normal Mike Mills."

What are you like? Just cockier?

"Yeah. Extremely cocky. And you have to get used to not having things done for you, you know. When you come down and you're back, you sort of have to *decompress* back into normalcy."

Like finding yourself walking across the room to get a beer from the fridge and expecting applause?

"Yeah . . . it's like [laughs], that was *me*. Didn't you see *me* there?"

Mills will readily admit that the making of the new album was a breeze in comparison to *Monster* ("With this one, everybody basically said, 'Look we almost broke up the band on the last record. Let's not get so caught up in what we're doing that we lose sight of the big picture'"), and doesn't seem to have been particularly marked by the split rumours that preceded the arrival of *New Adventures in Hi-Fi*. After all, there have been dark clouds of rumour or doubt over the past two R.E.M. albums—there were the rumblings about Stipe's health before the release of *Automatic for the People;* with *Monster,* there was a critical wave of disappointment filtering out before the record had reached the public.

"I'm proud of *Monster*, I think it's a really good record," Mills states firmly. "Is it our best record? No, I don't think so, but there's nothing on there I'm ashamed of. Sure, I think there are better songs on this album, but you know, not *hugely*. As far as personal rumours, well, everybody being happy and healthy is great, but it isn't news. There's no real rush of adrenaline in discovering that someone is happy and healthy. It's like, the band's fine and doing great, Well, gee, that's nothing exciting. People always want to hear that a band is in some sort of trouble."

Though no one in or around R.E.M. will comment on Jefferson Holt's departure (citing legal constraints), Mills can accept that both the media and public were bound to perceive it as the first crack in the band's armour.

"Right," he says. "But you know, people have always respected us over the years and they generally respect the decisions we've made."

Buck, for his part, acknowledges that their break-up with Holt wasn't in any sense seen as being an amicable split. . . .

"There are plenty of rumours that I've heard going around," he admits, "and they're all pretty interesting. But y'know, I may not be a gentleman or whatever, but I know how a gentleman would act, and I'm not going to say anything about it. It *wasn't* amicable on either of our parts, but y'know, big deal. Jefferson has said the only thing that's been quoted in public and he said that sometimes people change and go on to do different things, and that's true and maybe that's what it's all about. Maybe not. Who knows. *I* know, but I'm not gonna tell you."

Have you had any contact with each other apart from through lawyers?

"No. Not me, no."

Do you think you're likely ever to speak again?

"No."

It must have been pretty bad then.

"I can guarantee I'll never be in the same room with him again. But you know, whatever . . . I mean he would say the same thing to you, I'm sure."

Is there a certain amount of sadness in that?

"Um. Yeah. That's not the only thing that shook down in the last year either. Things change, people change, situations change. Things change in our lives just like everyone else you know. There are people who jump off the boat, there are some people that get left behind, and there are people who, y'know, we write out of the books or whatever."

During the day's shooting, there is a wide-grinning camaraderie evident between the four members of R.E.M. Earlier, Michael Stipe had sat down with the on-set sound technician for half an hour and repeatedly asked him to replay certain sections of the song that he sheepishly admitted to having already forgotten. Pen in hand, he re-pieced together what he referred to as his "picture puzzle" lyric for Bitter Sweet Me.

Despite countless R.E.M. shoots, he reveals he still feels uncomfortable miming ("Don't worry, you look really natural," Buck reassures him). When he begins performing, he hits upon the idea of lip-synching only some of the lines and silently wandering off in the middle of others while scratching his head or pulling idiot faces. As the shoot progresses, this becomes the source of much hilarity within the band, who attempt—with diminishing success—to perform the song straight-facedly.

There are light-spirited touches like this throughout the day. After the fourth take, Buck launches into a rendition of the Split Enz classic "I Got You" with much throaty, strong-lunged harmonizing from Stipe and Mills. At one point, Buck tells the director Dominic De Joseph that as long as he doesn't make him look "bald, fat and old, that's good. Even if the rest of them look like shit, that'll be fine."

Later he makes several attempts to mime the guitar-picking intro to the song, and on the first take where he is successful the camera zooms in onto Berry in time for him to fluff his simple drum intro. This results in a round of cheerfully sarcastic applause from the crew, of the sort that follows someone dropping a glass in a pub.

The day's work is completed by six in the afternoon, and perhaps as a result of this being R.E.M.'s last official day of work for some time (they will regroup later in the autumn to film another two promos for tracks from the album), crew and band alike are suddenly keen to retreat to the car lot outside the Chaplin sound stage to simply stand around, socialize and catch what's left of the day's sun.

Stipe plays with the toddling child of some recently arrived friends, keeping the perma-crawling kid amused by attempting to block his way and enlisting the help of Mills and Berry to form a human "leg cage" around him while the infant takes delight in wriggling free. He walks over to Q. "Safe flight home," he offers thoughtfully, before suddenly adding, "I'm sorry, I shouldn't say that," and forcing a superstitious wood-touching ritual by the sound stage's back door.

"I'm a very nervous flier these days," continues the singer by way of explanation. "I never used to drink on planes, but now I really do knock it back. Beer and Scotch is good. Go for beer and Scotch."

Buck lingers, ruminating upon the group's future plans which, encouragingly at this stage, are to begin rehearsals for the next album in April of next year and begin recording by the summer. "Personally I would like to have a record out in '97 and tour in '98," he says. "I've been playing with a lot of people in an acoustic setting using kind of ethnic instruments and stuff and maybe it would be interesting to write and kind of push the band in that direction for a record."

You get the vague feeling that Buck has been secretly flattered by the exaggerated reports of his group's demise, it being a mark of their current gravitas in the rock world after all. "I remember when Led Zeppelin or the Stones left a year between records," he recalls, the fan within (as ever) barely inches from the surface. "Certain magazines would always go, Is it over for the Stones? I read one of those like a month before *Exile on Main Street* came out—The Stones' Last Days? And that was 1972."

R.E.M. haven't always been nice to one another—the early days are littered with evidence of snidey Stipe/Mills friction—but, talking in purely hypothetical terms, if they were all to have a fist fight, who would come off worst?

"Oooh," Buck wonders, with an indulgent smile. "Michael is really strong in a wiry kind of way. Michael and I would sometimes roll around the floor together, but that was, like, 15 years ago. If you could knock Mike's glasses off, you'd be alright. The thing is that Mike probably wouldn't be paying attention. Mike is the kind of guy who in a bar room brawl would get hit on the side of the head when he's looking the other way."

Hardly the fight of the century then. And for the time being, it would appear to have been postponed until further notice.

Mike Mills on tour, 1997.
Photo © David Atlas.

TIM ABBOTT

R.E.M.: LIVE ADVENTURES IN HI-FI (1997)

Record Collector, *August 1997*

In the last ten years, R.E.M. have toured precisely twice. The press calls them lazy, but maybe they're just being sensible. Despite their virtual retirement from the road in recent times, this bunch of slackers have still played something like 800 shows in the last 17 years.

There's never been an official R.E.M. live album, something which the bootleg industry has been quick to capitalize on. Not even their legendary performance on MTV's *Unplugged* tempted them to rush a cash-in album into the shops. But since the mid-'80s, many of their singles have featured concert recordings as bonus tracks. In the absence of a definitive, Bruce Springsteen–style live retrospective, though, R.E.M. collectors have been forced to delve into the murky waters of the music business underworld.

From the beginning, R.E.M. shows have been like nothing else in rock. The band's eclectic taste in covers has always ensured that a surprise (often an unrehearsed one) is just around the corner. They've often responded to requests for songs that, no, they can't quite remember—but hey, we'll play 'em anyway! Unlike their major league contemporaries, they've never fallen into the trap of pounding an absolutely unchanging set-list round the stadiums of the world, repeating the same "ad libs" night after night. In fact, their unwillingness to play live in the '90s has probably increased as they've watched their fellow supergroups indulging in more and more grandiose (and less spontaneous) concert experiences.

None of that was on the agenda in early 1980, when Bill Berry, Peter Buck, Mike Mills and Michael Stipe were all attending the University of Georgia in Athens. Rehearsal sessions led up to their first ever show on Saturday, 5th April 1980, at a birthday party for their friend Kathleen O'Brien, in the converted Episcopal church where Michael and Peter were then living. Their performance was good enough to get bookings for another party and then a handful of gigs. As the local paper *The Red and Black* put it, "the group is the best in Athens, and they just keep getting better."

Gardening

Throughout 1980, the band played at favourite clubs like Tyrone's and the 688, venturing as far afield as North Carolina on a couple of occasions. New material emerged, like "Gardening at Night" and ("Don't Go Back to) Rockville," which would remain in their live set for many years to come. On the 6th December, R.E.M. played their most important show to date, when they opened for the Police at the Fox Theatre in Atlanta.

In 1981, the band stuck to many of the same local clubs, but also began venturing further afield to other Georgia and North Carolina venues. Their first (albeit short) jaunt important enough to receive a specific name was the "Rapid.Eye.Movement.Tour.1981," which covered just seven shows in two weeks. Then in June, they opened several shows for one of their favourite British bands, the Gang of Four. Meanwhile, the style of their new material was changing, as new songs like "Stumble," "Wolves, Lower," and "Shaking Through" displayed a stranger, darker side to their music.

The following year, the band were signed to I.R.S. Records, soon delivering their debut EP, *Chronic Town*. As it was released, they visited California for a mini-tour of San Francisco and Los Angeles clubs. By September, they were visiting Arizona and Illinois during another short tour with the Gang of Four, although by now the band could draw a big enough audience to be headliners themselves—which finally happened when dB's member and future "fifth R.E.M.er" Peter Holsapple became opening act for a tour through October and November. But the band kept in touch with their local fan base with frequent shows at the I & I Club and Mad Hatters, the uninsured Tyrone's having burned down in January 1982.

The release of their first LP, *Murmur*, in 1983, proved to longtime fans how much their repertoire had changed since 1980. Few of their live favourites made the track listing, and newly-written songs like "7 Chinese Brothers" and "Harborcoat" were already in place for their next LP, *Reckoning*.

In August 1983, the band reluctantly received what looked like their biggest break, but turned into something of a disaster (and a sore point in subsequent interviews)—opening several stadium gigs for the Police. The experience was enough to persuade them that this wasn't the route they wanted to follow.

They were more at home in October and November, when their producer Mitch Easter's band, Let's Active, were their opening act in New York and California. Later in November, the band visited Europe for the first time, for just two nights in London (Dingwalls and the Marquee) and then two more in France. But their cult following in Britain was big enough to justify a larger tour five months later, which took in seven shows around the country.

Little America

Returning to the U.S., R.E.M. embarked on the Little America tour in June and July 1984. Supported by Dream Syndicate, they covered eleven states and Canada before preparing for a break in Georgia with a final show at the Fox Theatre in Atlanta. Little America then continued through September and October, this time with the dB's tagging along as the support act. Then, only after a two-week break, they were off to Japan for five shows, returning via the U.K. for their second tour of the year. This time their 13 shows embraced England, Scotland, Wales and Ireland. The band then celebrated the end of the busy year on New Year's Eve at the Fox Theatre, which was fast taking on the mantle of a hometown haunt.

The early months of 1985 were set aside so that the band could prepare for their third album. Songs like "Driver 8" and "Auctioneer (Another Engine)" had already been tried and tested the previous year, but the rest of the material for *Fables of the Reconstruction* was brand new. In February, they warmed up for the recording sessions with two local shows—one a benefit for the L.E.A.F. charity, and the other a "surprise" show for which they were billed as Hornets Attack Victor Mature.

After spending March in London recording the new album with producer Joe Boyd, they were ready for the Preconstruction tour of American colleges and universities in April, selling out virtually every venue with ease. In fact, a standard part of their show was now the moment when the band would threaten to stop playing until everyone moved back, to alleviate the crush. "Now we're gonna play a game," Michael would announce, "and its called Simon Says. Everyone take three steps back . . . 1–2–3."

Still the relentless touring schedule continued. June saw the band back in Europe for dates throughout the U.K., plus the Torhout and Werchter festivals in Belgium. Their next U.S. leg, Reconstruction I, featured Robyn Hitchcock and later the Three O'Clock as supports. Then they were back in Europe for Reconstruction II, covering Holland, Germany, France and Switzerland. But their main fanbase on this side of the Atlantic was still in the U.K., where another eight-night stand began, with the Faith Brothers as their opening act.

The final part of the tour, Reconstruction III, was drawn out over two months and a procession of U.S. auditoriums and universities. Throughout all the '85 shows, Michael's pre-song stories (or "Fables") were a recurrent theme, as he talked about local characters like Howard Finster or old man Kensey (as immortalized in the song of that name).

It took the making of another album, this time *Life's Rich Pageant,* to interrupt the touring commitments. But in January 1986, R.E.M. did take part in a benefit show at the 40 Watt Club in Athens, the proceeds of which went towards funeral costs for Dennes Boon, the guitarist with the Minutemen, who had supported R.E.M. during "Reconstruction III" last year. Dennes had been killed in a car accident whilst driving through Arizona during the holiday season.

With work on the album complete, normal rock service was resumed. The three-month Pageantry tour kicked off in September, crawling across 34 U.S. states for 62 shows. Among their support acts were 10,000 Maniacs, whose singer, Natalie Merchant, often joined Michael on stage for some duets.

Memorable

One of R.E.M.'s most memorable performances came on 24th May 1987, when they played another benefit, this time for Texas Records. The venue was McCabe's Guitar Shop in Santa Monica. Their new *Document* material was louder and harder than anything they'd written to date, but it translated surprisingly well for this one-off acoustic show. Some new songs were also aired during two shows at the 40 Watt in Athens, where R.E.M. performances were becoming very rare indeed.

The aptly titled Work tour was set up for the end of the year, but during September, which should have been their vacation, the band took time out to visit London, Utrecht, Paris and Düsseldorf for press interviews and a handful of live shows. October and November saw them back in America, once again supported by 10,000 Maniacs, plus their old friends, the dB's. As usual, the tour ended at the Fox Theatre for four consecutive nights. During soundchecks and travelling, the band still managed to come up with some new material, and two incomplete songs performed during the tour, "Pop Song '89" and "Orange Crush," were completed for the following year's *Green* album.

In 1988, the group's recording contract with I.R.S. expired, leaving them free to negotiate a new deal with Warner Brothers. The band members went their separate ways for a while Peter Buck touring as extra guitarist with Robyn Hitchcock & the Egyptians, Michael spent some time writing and performing with the Indigo Girls in September. By November, R.E.M.'s first Warner Bros. release, *Green*, was completed. The band reconvened and readied themselves for their biggest tour to date.

Part one of the Green World Tour (subtitled The East) comprised shows in Japan, Australia and New Zealand. The presentation was much the same throughout the year as Michael wore a baggy white suit and blacked out his eyes like a raccoon. Chat with the audience was restricted to set parts of the show, while the spontaneity of being able to choose off-the-cuff cover versions was also beginning to disappear. Not that their sets were entirely predictable: they sometimes include Gershwin's "Summertime," while the band put a tune to Syd Barrett's "Dark Globe."

During March and April 1989, part two of the tour returned to North America, Robyn Hitchcock, the Indigo Girls and Drivin' N' Cryin' all taking supporting roles. Part three took them to Germany, but after just one show Bill Berry fell ill. He made a rapid recovery though, and within a week the tour was to continue in Holland and then, without further hitches, through a sold-out series of shows in Britain with the Blue

Aeroplanes as support. Two extra dates in June were quickly arranged to satisfy the overwhelming demand for tickets. After more dates on the continent, this time mostly at summer festivals, part four of the Green World Tour whizzed all over the northern states of the U.S.A. with a bunch of old friends from Athens—Pylon, who had recently reformed several years after splitting up.

A decade of virtually nonstop touring had obviously exhausted R.E.M. Other bands might have chosen this moment to split, but instead they took a whole year out to write and record their next album, *Out of Time*, with no immediate pressure from Warner Brothers. During 1990, Peter Buck—always the most restless member—took part in a long and meandering tour of the States with Kevin Kinney, front man of Drivin' N' Cryin'. The band also found time for a handful of surprise one-off shows at the 40 Watt, one of which, on 5th April celebrated their tenth anniversary.

Previously, R.E.M. had managed an album a year (not including the *Dead Letter Office* or *Eponymous* compilations), so it was with great anticipation that the world waited for their next release. Beginning in March 1991, the band set out on a promotional tour for *Out of Time*, stopping off mostly for interviews but also some surprise live shows—notably those at London's Borderline club, where they were billed as Bingo Hand Job. A week later, they played in Italy at the Shocking Club to a rather less perceptive audience. They also fitted in various television and radio shows across Europe and America, with their *Unplugged* performance in April showing off their new acoustic approach.

Eighteen months later, another new album took the world by storm. But *Automatic for the People* was released with a "no tour" announcement that disappointed their fans. Instead, R.E.M. played a solitary show at their old haunt, the 40 Watt club, in November. The one-off gig mainly showcased *Automatic* material, along with favourites from *Out of Time*.

Over the next year, rumours started to accumulate that Michael Stipe was seriously ill. Though the evidence was skimpy, to say the least, the band did nothing to dispel them, and their only performance of 1993 was at the MTV Video Music Awards. They chose to play a salubrious "Everybody Hurts," flowing into a new, funkier version of "Drive," with the band—especially Michael, who jumped all over the stage, and Mike with his new look of long hair, beard and sparkly Nudie suit—looking decidedly healthy!

Much of 1994 was devoted to writing and recording *Monster*, and when it was released in September, the question on everyone's lips was,

"Will R.E.M. tour?" The request was finally answered and tickets went on sale immediately for the 1995 Monster World Tour, which the band threatened might just be their last.

The first night, ironically on Friday 13th January at the Perth Entertainment Centre in Australia, was marred by technical problems. The media response was harsh, and the five-year lay-off between tours had obviously taken its toll. But they quickly picked themselves up, and before long Michael Stipe was saying things like, "I want to do this again next year." Then disaster struck. Onstage in Lausanne, Switzerland, Bill Berry collapsed halfway through the performance. The band brought on Joey Peters, drummer with support act Grant Lee Buffalo, so they could finish the set. First reports claimed that Bill had suffered nothing worse than a bad headache, but further investigation revealed a potentially life-threatening ruptured aneurysm on the right-hand-side of his brain. The complete tour, and the band's career, was put on hold until an emergency operation was performed. Luckily no lasting physical or mental damage occurred, and Bill's faster-than-expected recovery allowed R.E.M. to resume the Monster tour two months later.

Not that their troubles ended there. In July, Mike Mills had to undergo stomach surgery, which forced the cancellation of another six dates. Then in August it was Michael Stipe's turn, when he suffered a hernia, although this time the tour continued without cancellations. When the last leg of the tour concluded with three nights at the Fox Theatre, the band had survived and triumphed through 132 Monster shows.

Is that the end of R.E.M.'s live career? Not if Warner Brothers have anything to do with it, as they have recently allowed the band one of the most lucrative record deals in history, and won't be delighted if Stipe, Buck, Berry and Mills refuse to promote future albums.

As for R.E.M. themselves, they've usually deflected that kind of question with humour. Asked in a 1992 interview, "How long do you think you'll last?" Bill Berry quipped: "We'll play one last show at midnight on New Year's Eve 1999, and then break up!" This quote was taken literally by many people, so Peter Buck decided to keep the joke rolling: . . . "then we'll come on and do an encore. We'll be the first band to span two Millenniums!"

R.E.M.ember Every Moment

In 1985, when asked the age-old question of what the letters R.E.M. stood for, Michael Stipe replied: "My Grandmother says it means Remember

Every Moment." Thankfully, many of the best moments from R.E.M. shows, from their beginnings in 1980 through to the last world tour in 1995, have been preserved on vinyl and CD—most of it by the bootleggers.

The first R.E.M. bootleg surfaced in 1983—a single LP titled simply *L.I.V.E.* (on the Bandido label), containing a show from earlier that year. Since then, more than 200 illegal LPs and CDs have appeared, many later ones containing the same concerts duplicated over and over again. But every now and then, recordings of an early or unknown show turn up. Here are fifteen of the more memorable nights that have been preserved on bootleg.

1 Tyrone's, Athens, Georgia (10/4/80)

Taped six months after the band's formation, this performance shows off the band's earlier, more energetic song style—with a young-sounding Michael Stipe chuckling and giving requests to friends in the audience, throughout the show. The set mostly comprises newly-written songs, like "Mystery to Me" and "Smalltown Girl." Highlights include an almost double-speed thrash of "(Don't Go Back to) Rockville" and a very harmonious "I'm Not Your Stepping Stone," sounding every bit as '60s as the Monkees' original.

Bootleg: It's available on the LP Body Count At Tyrone's *(Brigand) and the second part of a 2-CD set,* 20th Century Boys. *The source is a soundboard tape, so quality is excellent throughout. A slightly longer audio tape is in circulation.*

2 Tyrone's, Athens, Georgia (5/12/81)

By this time, R.E.M. had recorded the tracks for their first single, "Radio Free Europe" on the Hib-Tone label. Many of their early songs remained in the set but much new material that was later included on the *Chronic Town* EP and *Murmur* LP was also being tested out. Indeed, some of the new songs, like "Skank" and "That Beat," were never actually released. There was a definite change in style, though, with the advent of songs like "Stumble" (which lasted for a full seven minutes) making the subject matter seem somewhat darker and more oblique. Michael's famous early mumble was prevalent, as he missed syllables out of words and words from sentences. The rapidly increasing local R.E.M. following can be heard shouting requests.

Bootleg: Available on the CD That Beat In Time *(O.M.K.), which was later reissued with a different sleeve inlay. It was taken from an excellent* soundboard recording, although the order was slightly adjusted. A 90-minute audio tape is in circulation, containing more tracks but in poorer quality.

3 Merlyn's, Madison, Wisconsin (4/24/82)

"We're R.E.M., have a nice evening," Michael announced politely. During 1982, R.E.M.'s live set stabilised, usually beginning with the new "West of the Fields" or (as in this case) "Gardening at Night," and featuring mainly the same group of songs. One newish song at this show was "Catapult," which they had been reworking for a while. Peter's guitar technique had obviously improved, while Michael now spent less time chatting to the audience.

Bootleg: The single CD Carnival of Sorts (Great Dane Records) captures this soundboard recording in its entirety and gives, for once, an accurate track listing.

4 Atlanta Arts Festival, Piedmont Park, Atlanta, Georgia (5/14/82)

This was the band's first show to be broadcast live on radio. It began in unusual style, when the opening number, "West of the Fields," stopped abruptly after just 25 seconds. "That was our longest song," joked Bill. "Here's our dramatic beginning," continued Michael, as they attempted, with more success, to begin again. Much laughter came from the band and audience as a pith helmet was continually passed between (and worn by) Michael and Peter whilst they were playing! Despite some sound problems, they stormed through an entertaining set which included the brand-new "Pilgrimage" and the by-now-popular "Radio Free Europe."

Bootleg: A low-quality audio tape of this FM radio broadcast had been circulating for years, but recently a far better copy emerged on the CD Radio Free Georgia (Red Robin Records) no doubt taken from the original recording of this show.

5 Larry's Hideaway, Toronto, Ontario, Canada (7/9/83)

This show during the band's first trip to Canada was recorded for radio broadcast. Three months after the release of Murmur, R.E.M.'s audiences were growing in size and appreciation, and the band—together now for three years—were very tight. The first request on this glorious night, the Velvets' "There She Goes Again," followed an impromptu intro of "Moon River." A real warmth came across from this show, with the band seeming genuinely pleased to be there.

Bootleg: By far the best quality version of this show can be found on the single U.S. CD Rising *(Red Robin), issued later in Europe with a different cover (on the SPQR label) and sourced directly from the soundboard recording. Tapes of that night's incomplete radio broadcast have been available for years on boots like* Mada Mada *(double LP, Toasted) and the CD* Streets of Millionaires *(Raid Masters).*

6 Stithcraft, Athens, Georgia (9/30/83)

After surviving their opening slot for the Police in August, the band played two local shows, one of them here on the basement floor of a warehouse. Athens clubs were now becoming too small for R.E.M. to play in—especially when, as on this occasion, admission for the show was free.

"This song is not out of pure respect," was how Michael introduced a dubious rendition of "I Got You Babe," taking time to change many of the original lyrics. A lot of newly-written material turned up, mostly songs targeted for the next album, *Reckoning.* The band were in a real party mood, bashing out classics like "Route 66," "Rave On" and even Johnny Cash's "Folsom Prison Blues." A new song, "Six Stock Answers," written for the yet to be seen film *Just Like a Movie* by the band's friend and photographer, Laura Levine, was performed at this show—and has never been heard since.

Bootleg: A double CD set titled 20th Century Boys Vol 1 + 2 *(released on an anonymous label) contains about 90 minutes of this show, although the performance may have considerably longer. The running order of the boot also seems to have been altered slightly. Some cover versions from this show, including a wonderfully raucous "Sweet Jane" (by the Velvet Underground), turned up on an early bootleg LP,* Do You Remember— Dead Giveaway Office *(no label).*

7 Music Hall, Seattle, Washington (6/27/84)

This show for radio was originally captured on NBC's *The Source* transcription double LP, which in the States has sold for anything up to $1,000! The week before, Michael had been on crutches after he stepped on a poisonous fish whilst swimming in San Diego, but he had returned in high spirits. The show ended on a high note with the Byrds' "So You Want to Be a Rock 'n' Roll Star" and the ska-like rhythms of "Skank," R.E.M.'s most peculiar song to date, which was once demoed but is unlikely to ever see the light of day.

Bootleg: Two tracks, "Catapult" and "Driver 8," were officially released by I.R.S. as B-sides. The whole show, excluding these two tracks, is available on the CD Rock and Roll Stars *(Howdy! Records). Many other unofficial versions of this show have been released, including the double LPs* Blue *(Spliff) and* We're Blinking Just as Fast as We Can *(Great Live Records) and single CD* Boston 1984 *(sic!, Mistral Music). Most of the bootlegs seem to be direct copies from* The Source *Lp set, although the song "Sitting Still" is not available on any bootleg release.*

8 Hammersmith Palais, London (10/29/85)

During the band's second U.K. tour of '85, they stopped off in London for two consecutive nights at the Hammersmith Palais. The second night was recorded by Capital Radio, but for unknown reasons was never broadcast. The band appeared to be tiring after their busy Reconstruction Tour schedule, having already played nonstop through October. But they managed to stay on their feet long enough to rattle out an entertaining show, and Michael still had the energy to spin around the stage whilst yelping and growling his way through the funky "Can't Get There from Here." The new song in this year's set was "Fall on Me," though its acid rain lyrics changed considerably before it was recorded for the *Life's Rich Pageant* LP. As a final delight, Michael showed off his way with cheerleading chants before an uplifting "We Walk," which in the chorus had the rest of the band counting "one-two-three-four" in as many different languages as they could remember.

Bootleg: The bulk of this show is available on the CD These Days *(Why Not), having been edited to leave out seven songs. The quality is excellent and almost certainly comes straight from the original Capital Radio recording. An audio tape is also in circulation with the full 90-minute set.*

9 McCabe's Guitar Shop, Santa Monica, California (5/24/87)

New *Document* material, some of which had been written and recorded in a Nashville studio just a month earlier, was showcased at this benefit performance for Texas Records. The show featured various different lineups, other guests that night, including Steve Wynn (who played some songs with Peter Buck), Natalie Merchant and Kendra Smith (with Michael Stipe on some numbers) and Peter Case (with Peter Buck).

The new songs adapted surprisingly well to the show's acoustic format, with just Peter on guitar and Michael supplying vocals for the first R.E.M. set. Band friend and I.R.S. employee Geoff Gans played acoustic guitar on "The One I Love" instead of Peter, who admitted that "he could do it better than me." Geoff also recorded the show on fairly basic audio equipment, from which three tracks were later released by I.R.S. as B-sides. Mike Mills entered the stage for the second set, adding a beautiful, haunting piano on "South Central Rain (I'm Sorry)" coupled with Peter Gabriel's "Red Rain." But Bill Berry was unable to attend the show, the highlight of which had to be Michael and Natalie's duet—Natalie singing John Denver's "Leaving on a Jet Plane" as Michael performed the Velvets' "Sunday Morning," before moving on to another Denver song, "Sunshine on My Shoulders." His performance collapsed into laughter, so perhaps to distract Natalie he amended the chorus to "I Got the Music in Me" (Kiki Dee), whilst Steve Wynn filled in any gaps left with yet another cover, the Velvets' "I'll Be Your Mirror." This amazing medley had the audience in hysterics.

Bootleg: Slightly different selections from the two R.E.M. sets can be found on the single CDs Acoustic '87 *(Nu Noize) and* Maps and Legends *(Mongoose Records), both listenable but taken from a mediocre audience recording. Some years later, another CD surfaced containing an excellent quality recording.* TMOQ *(which simply represents the label name, Trade Mark of Quality) was issued in a limited run in a black and white slip-case—though another bootlegger soon stepped in with an imitation.* Live at McCabe's Guitar Shop *(SPQR) features more tracks by Steve Wynn and contains only one of R.E.M.'s sets. Also omitted is the encore that spawned "South Central Rain" and Peggy Lee's "Fever," made up of the few original words that Michael could remember.*

10 Muziekcentrum, Utrecht, Holland (9/14/87)

Fans were deeply disappointed that R.E.M.'s 1986 tour was restricted to America, especially when the following year's Work tour was also due to stay in the U.S.A. But during September the band did eventually find time to visit Europe. They played one night each in London, Paris, Dusseldorf and on the 14th in Utrecht, Holland. To celebrate the occasion, this show was recorded for airing on Dutch radio.

The band kicked off with "Finest Worksong," while other *Document* material followed, like "Lightnin' Hopkins" featuring Mike Mills' dual chorus vocals, and "It's the End of the World as We Know It (and I Feel Fine)" which, as being R.E.M.'s longest ever song title, must surely have the fastest vocal of any song pulled off to perfection by Michael. And older songs also turned up, much to delight of the enthusiastic audience, of these, "Wolves, Lower," hadn't been played for a number of years, and the band forgot that the chorus line of "house order" should be sung four times, not three! The show ended with an acoustic medley of the rarely heard "Time after Time (Annelise)" from *Reckoning,* followed by "Red Rain" and "South Central Rain (I'm Sorry)." This trilogy was released as the B-side to "Finest Worksong" in 1988.

Bootleg: The first-ever R.E.M. bootleg release was Standing Room Only *(Swinging Pig Records) which featured this show as it had been broadcast on Dutch radio. But a double CD,* Red Rain *(Silver Rarities), contains the whole 100-minute performance in glorious stereo.*

11 Pink Pop Festival, Landgraaf, Holland (5/15/89)

Just days after Bill Berry's recovery from his mysterious illness, R.E.M.'s Green World Tour was back on schedule. The first stop was this festival in Holland, where the band jumped head first into a powerful "Exhuming McCarthy." Next came "Turn You Inside Out," the chorus screamed out through a megaphone. Many of the songs on this tour had standard introductions—for instance, "World Leader Pretend" regularly began with Michael banging in time with a stick on a metal chair whilst singing the Gang of Four's "We Live As We Dream Alone." Likewise, "Orange Crush" began with the U.S. Army anthem "Be All That You Can Be in the Army." With the help of ex-dB Peter Holsapple, the band were able to enhance many songs with extra instrumentation, usually keyboards.

Bootleg: This festival gig was broadcast live on Dutch radio, as preserved on The Dream CD *(Red Phantom). This set boasts excellent sound quality and a sleeve that opens out to reveal exclusive photographs and a complete tour itinerary.*

12 The Borderline, London (3/15/91)

This legendary performance was one of two mostly acoustic club shows where R.E.M. were billed as Bingo Hand Job. The band members had pseudonyms too: Stinky (Michael), Raoul (Peter), The Doc (Bill) and Ophelia (Mike). Other guests included Spanish Charlie (Peter Holsapple), Violet (Robyn Hitchcock) with the Melonballs (the Egyptians), Conrad (Billy Bragg) and Stump Monkey (Chickasaw Mudd Puppies).

The *Out of Time* album had only just been released that week, but that didn't stop the audience singing along to most of the new material and shouting out requests. Michael was in a jovial mood, cracking gags between songs as the other guys swapped instruments. Billy Bragg was allowed his own set, where he was joined by Michael, their quite diverse styles merging suprisingly well on John Prine's "Hello in There."

Robyn Hitchcock also performed several numbers with the Egyptians, and Peter Holsapple played his own set. In fact, the show seemed to go on forever, as the musicians kept the songs and the different combinations coming. During the encore, the stage was packed with nearly all of the performers for Bob Dylan's "You Ain't Going Nowhere," accompanied by a barely visible Michael on organ. The Bingo Hand Job shows were definitely one of the band's finest moments, although at the time the U.K. music press couldn't have agreed less.

Bootleg: Easily the best recording is the double CD From the Borderline *(Red Phantom), housed in an attractive slimline case, with great sleeve-notes and many colourful pictures proving how cramped the stage really was. Though it's only an audience recording, the quality is near perfect. The double LP* As Bingo Hand Job *(Religious Records) captures fewer songs but is still worth a mention. Separate sets by Robyn Hitchcock, Peter Holsapple and Billy Bragg are in circulation on audio tapes only.*

13 Unplugged, Chelsea Studios, New York City (4/10/91)

Not too many major bands have missed a chance to issue their performance on *Unplugged* as an official album. But R.E.M. has always been concerned about the risk of "conning" their fans, and as bassist Mike Mills put it, "I'm sure there'll be a bootleg of it soon, so there's no need for us to release it." Their acoustic performance at this show can only be described as superb. It was dominated by tracks from fresh *Out of Time*, and "Half a World" and "Losing My Religion" more than equal impact of the original album tracks. "It's the End of the World . . ." was introduced by Michael as "the request of MTV. We had to get the words on a computer and I'm not sure they're right." In any case, the new acoustic structure almost twisted it into a different song.

Bootleg: Many CDs feature the complete 45-minute television broadcast, although some couldn't even manage that. Among the available titles are Animal's Attractions *(Speedball Company),* Blue—The Acoustic Concert *(Great Live Records),* American Acoustic Tour 1991 *(no label),* Hitting the Note *(Back Stage) and* Half a World Away—Part Two *(Mongoose Records), the last of these also containing "Endgame," which was used during the show's ending credits.*

Audience tapes are also in circulation, capturing 95 minutes of music including retakes and tracks not chosen for the broadcast, like the Classic IV's "Spooky" and the Motown classic "Smiling Faces Sometimes." A misleading bootleg titled The Complete Unplugged Session (no label) seems to contain this rare recording, but turns out to feature the broadcast show plus some official B-sides from the Green era, edited together with audience noise.

14 Watt Club, Athens, Georgia (11/19/92)

After the release of Automatic for the People in October 1992, R.E.M. played just one live show, in their hometown. The power needed to record the show was generated by a Greenpeace solar-power truck unit. R.E.M. weren't alone in this, as thirteen other bands (Sonic Youth, James, U2 and Soundgarden, to name but a few) also taped gigs via the Greenpeace truck. Selections from all these performances were compiled on the 1994 CD Alternative NRG (Hollywood Records), opening with R.E.M.'s "Drive."

This was the first time any of the Automatic songs had been performed in front of a live audience, before the oldie "Radio Free Europe" made a welcome return to finish the night on a high.

Bootleg: There are around twenty unofficial CDs featuring this performance. Their (very good) sound quality doesn't actually vary too much, so the most obvious differences are in the editing of the tape. Some bootleggers felt it necessary to leave out the spoken introductions by Michael and Mike. Overall, perhaps the best versions available are Automatically Live (Kiss The Stone) or This Is It! (Red Phantom).

15 Waldbuhne, Berlin, Germany (8/1/95)

Shows during the Monster tour changed from night to night, but were built around the same main group of songs. This performance included a few less familiar numbers, including "Near Wild Heaven," which proved how well Bill, Mike and Michael can harmonize together. Mike's lead vocals were a fresh addition to the band's normal repertoire, although at one point it did sound as if someone had fallen on the piano! During the encore, the band merged Fleetwood Mac's "Tusk" in and out of "Ghost Rider" by Suicide, before steaming into "It's the End of the World . . ." for a finale that just didn't want to end. Bill kept drumming while Michael called out "happy birthday Scott McCaughey" (one of R.E.M.'s extra guitarists for the tour) and tossed his mike into the air.

Bootleg: The whole 125-minute performance is contained within the double CD, Monster Radio (Moonraker), with some neat packaging that includes a complete rundown of the Monster World Tour.

Benefit for Tibet, Washington, D.C., 1998. *Photo © David Atlas.*

MIRIAM LONGINO

R.E.M.: TO A DIFFERENT BEAT THE FAMED ATHENS BAND BECOMES A THREESOME AS DRUMMER BILL BERRY LEAVES TO "SIT BACK AND REFLECT" (1997)

Atlanta Journal-Constitution, *October 31, 1997*

Athens—"It's sad. It's incredibly sad."

Michael Stipe, lead singer for the rock group R.E.M., voiced the words that were echoed by his bandmates and record label executives all day Thursday after original drummer Bill Berry announced that he is leaving the group.

Berry, 39, made his goodbye official to a handful of friends and reporters in informal meetings at the R.E.M. office in Athens, where reaction was a combination of shock and positive hope for the future of the band. He was joined by his longtime partners—Stipe, vocalist Peter Buck and bass player Mike Mills—as he explained, "I'm just not as enthusiastic as I have been in the past about doing this anymore. I've been doing this for 17 years, and it's been great. I have the best job in the world. But I'm kind of ready to sit back and reflect and maybe not be a pop star anymore."

Berry said he broke the news to his colleagues three weeks ago, as the band met in Athens to go over material for a new album set for production in February. "We got back together to rehearse those songs, and the first day (Berry) said, 'There's something I've got to tell you,'" said Stipe, 37. "And he told us. And it's still quite a shock."

The remaining members still plan to record the album, set for release by early 1998. "And there's a very good chance we will tour," Buck said. There are no plans to replace Berry. Buck's response to that query was short and to the point: "Bill is not replaceable. We'll hire people on a song-by-song basis."

The band had kept the news quiet since learning of Berry's decision. Mills said he and his bandmates wanted to contact the press officially, in small numbers, to "let people know what you see is exactly what is happening. There is no undercurrent or behind-the-scenes maneuvering."

Berry has been with R.E.M. since the band's inception in Athens in

1980. He has been a pivotal part of its sound, collaborating on songwriting and providing the strong underpinnings to its music. He traces the beginnings of his dissatisfaction with life as a rock star to the life-threatening brain aneurysm he suffered during R.E.M.'s 1995 European tour.

"It may have something to do with the fact I went through surgery," Berry said. "Physically, I'm in great shape. But there was a kind of spiritual ordeal I went through, and I don't know if that caused this; it may have. I used to be so excited about going into the studio I couldn't sleep the night before. But I was getting to the point where I couldn't sleep because I was worried about why I wasn't happy."

The news came as a shock to executives at Warner Bros. Records, which signed R.E.M. to an $80 million, five-record deal last year. President Steve Baker, in Athens from California on a trip to hear demos of the new R.E.M. songs, said he learned of Berry's decision Tuesday and that it in no way will affect the record deal.

"No, I'm not worried," Baker said, dashing off to the airport to return to Los Angeles. "Three amazing musicians remain, and we will continue to support them."

The remaining R.E.M. members say they are optimistic about the group's future. "We've got 40 songs, and it's good work," said Buck, 40. "We're really excited about it. It's going well for us. This appears to be a negative situation, but we can make it positive by seeing it as a change in life. Creatively we're in a good place."

Stipe described his reaction when Berry told the group of his plans. "Initially, very honestly, I thought, 'Is he clear in the head for making this decision?' For mercenary reasons, there aren't many people in this world who would walk away from the job Bill is walking away from," Stipe said. "I think it's really courageous and honest. I know it's genuine because I know Bill."

Mills, 38, says Berry's departure may be the impetus for yet another period of change and growth for R.E.M. "We were looking to go in a different direction for this record even before we knew this, in terms of using not a drum kit per se, but percussion and making our own drum loops," Mills said.

Stipe was more emotional. "Frankly, this has knocked the wind out of us creatively," he said. "We can't replace this guy. It's going to be really weird for us to be a three-piece. But I'd much rather be a three-piece and deal with the change than have Bill stay in the band and be unhappy. I applaud Bill for not wanting to fake it."

Berry, who is divorced and has no children, spoke softly and glanced at his bandmates often as he continued to explain his reasons for leaving.

"The idea of doing yet one more tour and spending three months in a studio . . . there's not a window in any studio I've ever been in. You spend 14 hours in there, and come out and it's dark. I'm unable to keep up the enthusiasm. Making music has always been a pleasure; I've done it all my life. I'm not sure if I'm capable of doing anything else. Maybe I'll play drums for my cat. Maybe three years from now I'll form a Bachman Turner Overdrive tribute band or something. I don't know. I want to find out. I'm not going to know until I stop. Water will find its level if you let it go, and I feel like I'm opening the floodgates."

In the years when R.E.M. has risen to national prominence, Berry has stayed close to home. He owns a farm in Watkinsville, where neighbors often see him on his bush hog. "I'd like to be on it right now," Berry quipped, adding, "The good thing is, I'll be able to see an R.E.M. show for a change."

———

R.E.M. members Michael Stipe, Peter Buck, Mike Mills and Bill Berry spoke Thursday afternoon with the *Journal-Constitution*. The following is an edited transcript of that interview:

Bill: Three weeks ago, after long and careful deliberation, it was evident I needed to go ahead and be honest with these guys, 'cause we always have been in the past about everything. . . . I think [things are] going to change real fast, starting today. Going to have to fight for good tables in restaurants. . . . The good thing is I'll be able to see an R. E.M. show for a change.

Michael: We were all together in April in Hawaii in a living room with a four-track, and we put down ideas for the new record. And then we got back together three weeks ago to rehearse those songs, and the first day he said, "There's something I've got to tell you." And he told us, and it's still quite a shock. Never said with such conviction.

Peter: There was definitely a feeling that sometime in the future Bill may not want to be involved. But, you know, what does that mean? Maybe he won't want to tour, whatever. To just quit it, it's kind of sad, but he said, "I just don't want to fake it." Most people would. There are a lot of good things about being in a band, not the least of which is being treated well and making money. A lot of people would fake it, you know, take the big check.

Michael: For mercenary reasons, there aren't many people in this world who would walk away from the job Bill is walking away from. I think it's really courageous and honest. I know it's genuine, 'cause I know Bill.

Michael: I think it's not uncommon for people who have come as close to death as Bill [to] reflect, and maybe there's a pivotal moment where you look at your life. You think you only get one go 'round, and I think it took Bill a couple of years to figure out that he really wants to explore, he wants to take a year off from everything and figure out what direction his life should go in.

Mike: Do not send tapes. We were looking to go in a different direction for this record—even before we knew this—in terms of using not a drum kit per se, but percussion and making our own drum loops. We're being pushed in that direction, but were thinking of doing it anyway.

Michael: In Hawaii we had a four-track and really didn't have room to set up a kit, and we just set up drum machines. Having lived with those tapes for the last 8 months, I really like the way they sound. They're demos and obviously we're going to work on them. But it's a very organic progression for us to go in. We can't emphasize enough [that the] one rule we've had for the 17 years we've been together is never say never amongst ourselves. I'm fine going project by project, album by album, tour by tour, working with other people. Tour plans are pretty embryonic at this point anyway. [But] the record comes out at the end of next year and there's a very good chance we'll tour.

Mike: We addressed all possible situations when we made the deal. [I think the people at Warner Brothers are more bummed out on a personal level. They are all glad we're continuing but legally we've got it taken care of.]

Michael: It's not a problem. They had no idea when we dropped this on them two days ago. They're OK with it. They know Bill well enough and understand his motives.

Peter: This appears to be a negative situation, but we can make it into a positive by seeing it as a change in life. We're going to go with that. Creatively we're in a good place. In a way it's going to be positive for everybody cause if Bill's happy, I'm happy. Who's to say three years down the line Bill's going to say, "You know what, I want to play drums again," and that's cool.

Bill: As weird as this is, people at Warner Bros. have dealt with situations that are a lot weirder than this. I'm not going to name names. You can look at their roster and figure out the train wrecks.

Mike: We don't want to make it maudlin; this is a serious adult [decision] someone is making, and we don't want to turn it into a sentimental event.

Bill: It really hasn't hit me, won't hit me till I walk out this door today. That's going to take some adjustment. I don't know what it's going to be like not to be in R.E.M. anymore. Meanwhile I'm going to buy a computer.

Peter: You can't talk someone in or out of making real serious decisions like this. Took weeks to work through it. Felt five different emotions when I heard it. I'm not mad at Bill. He's not doing a bad thing. He's doing something for himself and that's cool. I've come to the decision that this is exactly what he wants to do. To me, that's incomprehensible because I love music and can't imagine doing anything else. I understand what he wants and I respect that.

Michael: Initially, very honestly, I thought, "Is he clear in the head for making this decision? Is this something he really wants?" We've talked a lot in the past few weeks, and it's something he really wants. We have to support that. It's incredibly sad; I won't pretend that it's not. It's going to be really weird for us to be a three-piece. But I'd much rather be a three-piece and deal with the change than have Bill stay in the band and be unhappy.

Peter: We wanted to confront this the way we have everything in our lives. You can tell, no one is lying, no one is stressed out, there's no subterfuge. It's all coming out today. We've made phone calls. Then I never want to have to do this again. I'm going to dinner with Bill tonight; we're really good friends. He's just not going to be sitting behind me. That will be weird and distressing to some of our fans.

Michael: We wanted to present this for what it is. . . . [T]he three of us are excited cause we think what we've written in the last months is really good.

Bill: I had songs I had written and prepared before Hawaii, but basically I just sat out and watched waves.

Peter: In a way it was almost a relief because the last record we worked on, there was a lot of tense stuff going on around the band; I could tell Bill was really unhappy. I kind of felt guilty about it, because of all this ambition of mine. I felt like, "Am I making this friend of mine unhappy?" You have to worry about that. There are a lot of ramifications, doing what we do. We have to talk about what we're going to be doing two years from now. That can be tough.

Bill: Making music has always been a pleasure, I've done it all my life. I see myself continuing even if it's a harmonica in the basement. The idea of doing yet one more tour and spending three months in a studio—there's not a window in a studio I've ever been in. You spend 14 hours in there, and come out and it's dark. I'm unable to keep up the enthusiasm.

Mike: We wanted to move away from drum kit and use percussion things or [start] making our own drum loops. Going to dehumanize the drums anyway for this record. We know enough people who play drums—we can find them.

Michael: We have a desire to present this as it is. Hopefully fans will be able to come around to what we've come around to—that this is the best thing that could possibly happen.

Selected Discography

Albums and EPs

Note: Catalogue numbers refer to original releases only. Although the early albums were issued before the CD era, all are now available on CD.

TITLE	CATALOGUE NUMBER	RELEASE DATE
Chronic Town (EP)	IRS SP70502	8/82 (U.S.)

Tracks: Wolves Lower; Gardening at Night; Carnival of Sorts (Box Cars); 1,000,000

Murmur	IRS SP70014	4/83 (U.S.)
	IRS SP70604	8/83 (U.K.)

Tracks: Radio Free Europe; Pilgrimage; Laughing; Talk About the Passion; Moral Kiosk; Perfect Circle; Catapult; Sitting Still; 9–9; Shaking Through; We Walk; West of the Fields

  Note: 1992 U.K. expanded CD edition also includes "There She Goes Again"; "9–9" (live); "Gardening at Night" (live); "Catapult" (live)

Reckoning	IRS SP70044	4/84 (U.S.)
	IRSA 7045	4/84 (U.K.)

Tracks: Harborcoat; Seven Chinese Brothers; So. Central Rain (I'm Sorry); Pretty Persuasion; Time after Time (Annelise); Second Guessing; Letter Never Sent; Camera; (Don't Go Back to) Rockville; Little America

  Note: 1992 U.K. expanded CD edition also includes "Windout" (with Friends); "Pretty Persuasion" (live in studio); "White Tornado" (live in studio); "Tighten Up"; "Moon River"

Fables of the Reconstruction	IRS IRS5592	6/85 (U.S.)
	IRS MIRF1003	6/85 (U.K.)

Tracks: Feeling Gravity's Pull; Maps and Legends; Driver 8; Life and How to Live It; Old Man Kensey; Can't Get There from Here; Green

Grow the Rushes; Kohoutek; Auctioneer (Another Engine); Good Advices; Wendell Gee

Note: 1992 U.K. expanded CD edition also includes "Crazy"; "Burning Hell"; "Bandwagon"; "Driver 8" (live); "Maps and Legends" (live)

Life's Rich Pageant

IRS 5783	7/86 (U.S.)
IRS MIRG1014	8/86 (U.K.)

Tracks: Begin the Begin; These Days; Fall on Me; Cuyahoga; Hyena; Underneath the Bunker; The Flowers of Guatemala; I Believe; What If We Give It Away?; Just a Touch; Swan Swan H; Superman

Note: 1993 U.K. expanded CD edition also includes "Tired of Singing Trouble"; "Rotary Ten"; "Toys in the Attic"; "Just a Touch" (live in the studio); "Dream (All I Have to Do)"; "Swan Swan H" (acoustic)

Dead Letter Office
(compilation)

IRS SP70054	4/87 (U.S.)
IRS SP70054	5/87 (U.K.)

Tracks: Crazy; There She Goes Again; Burning Down; Voice of Harold; Burning Hell; White Tornado; Toys in the Attic; Windout; Ages of You; Pale Blue Eyes; Rotary Ten; Bandwagon; Femme Fatale; Walter's Theme; King of the Road

Document

IRS IRS42059	9/87 (U.S.)
IRS MIRG1025	10/87 (U.K.)

Tracks: Finest Worksong; Welcome to the Occupation; Exhuming McCarthy; Disturbance at the Heron House; Strange; It's the End of the World as We Know It (and I Feel Fine); The One I Love; Fireplace; Lightnin' Hopkins; King of Birds; Oddfellows Local 151

Note: 1993 U.K. expanded CD edition also includes "Finest Worksong" (other mix); "Last Date"; "The One I Love" (live); "Time after Time Etc." (live); "Disturbance at the Heron House" (live); "Finest Worksong" (lengthy club mix)

Eponymous (compilation)

IRS IRS6262	10/88 (U.S.)
IRS MIRG1038	10/88 (U.K.)

Tracks: Radio Free Europe (original Hib-Tone single); Gardening at Night (different vocal mix); Talk about the Passion; So. Central Rain (I'm Sorry); (Don't Go Back to) Rockville; Can't Get There from

Here; Driver 8; Romance; Fall on Me; The One I Love; Finest Worksong (mutual drum horn mix); It's the End of the World as We Know It (and I Feel Fine)

Green   Warners 25795   11/88 (U.S.)
                                 Warners WX-234   11/88 (U.K.)
Tracks: Pop Song 89; Get Up; You Are the Everything; Stand; World Leader Pretend; The Wrong Child; Orange Crush; Turn You Inside-Out; Hair Shirt; I Remember California; (Untitled)

Out of Time   Warners 26496   3/91 (U.S. and
                                                        U.K.)
Tracks: Radio Song; Losing My Religion; Low; Near Wild Heaven; Endgame; Shiny Happy People; Belong; Half a World Away; Texarkana; Country Feedback; Me in Honey

Automatic for the People   Warners 45138   10/92 (U.S.)
                                 Warners 45055   9/92 (U.K.)
Tracks: Drive; Try Not to Breathe; The Sidewinder Sleeps Tonite; Everybody Hurts; New Orleans Instrumental No. 1; Sweetness Follows; Monty Got a Raw Deal; Ignoreland; Star Me Kitten; Man on the Moon; Nightswimming; Find the River

Monster   Warners 46320   9/94 (U.S.)
                                 Warners 9362-45740-2   9/94 (U.K.)
Tracks: What's the Frequency, Kenneth?; Crush with Eyeliner; King of Comedy; I Don't Sleep, I Dream; Star 69; Strange Currencies; Tongue; Bang and Blame; I Took Your Name; Let Me In; Circus Envy; You

New Adventures in Hi-Fi   Warners 48320   9/96 (U.S.)
                                 Warners 9362-46320-2   9/96 (U.K.)
Tracks: How the West Was Won and Where It Got Us; The Wake-Up Bomb; New Test Leper; Undertow; E-Bow the Letter; Leave; Departure; Bittersweet Me; Be Mine; Binky the Doormat; Zither; So Fast, So Numb; Low Desert; Electrolite

R.E.M. in the Attic
(compilation)   EMI-Capitol/IRS 72438-21321-2-7
                                                        1/98 (U.S.)

Tracks: Finest Worksong (other mix); Driver 8 (live); Gardening at Night (different vocal mix); Swan Swan H (from the *Athens, Ga.—Inside Out* soundtrack); Disturbance at the Heron House (live); Maps and Legends (live); Tired of Singing Trouble; Just a Touch (live in studio); Toys in the Attic; Dream (All I Have to Do) (from the *Athens, Ga.—Inside Out* soundtrack); The One I Love (live); Crazy; Can't Get There from Here (radio edit); Last Date; Time after Time Etc. (medley)

Singles

Note: This listing is primarily of U.S. pressings, which were generally duplicated in the U.K. U.K. singles are only listed if they included different tracks. While the majority of the IRS tracks that were originally non-album have been reissued on compilation albums or the U.K. expanded CDs, there are, to date, no equivalent releases for the extraneous Warners tracks in either the U.S. or the U.K. The 1993 4-CD German box set, *The Automatic Box,* however, does contain most of the Warners nonalbum singles released up to that time.

TITLE	CATALOGUE NUMBER	RELEASE DATE
Radio Free Europe (original version) *Other tracks:* Sitting Still	Hib-Tone HT 1001	7/81 (U.S.)
Radio Free Europe *Other tracks:* There She Goes Again	IRS IR9916	5/83 (U.S.)
Talk about the Passion *Other tracks:* Shaking Through; Carnival of Sorts (Box Cars); 1,000,000	IRS PFSX1026	11/83 (U.K.)
So. Central Rain *Other tracks:* Voice of Harold; Pale Blue Eyes	IRS IRSX105	3/84 (U.K.)
So. Central Rain *Other tracks:* King of the Road	IRS IR9927	5/84 (U.S.)
(Don't Go Back to) Rockville *Other tracks:* Wolves; 9–9(live); Gardening at Night (live)	IRS IRX107	6/84 (U.K.)

(Don't Go Back to) Rockville   IRS IR9931   8/84 (U.S.)
    Other tracks: Catapult (live)

Can't Get There from Here   IRS 52642   6/85 (U.S.)
    Other tracks: Bandwagon

Can't Get There from Here   IRS IRT102   7/85 (U.K.)
    Other tracks: Bandwagon; Burning Hell

Driver 8   IRS 52678   9/85 (U.S.)
    Other tracks: Crazy

Wendell Gee   IRS IRMD105   10/85 (U.K.)
    Other tracks: Crazy; Ages of You; Burning Down

Wendell Gee   IRS IRT105   10/85 (U.S.)
    Other tracks: Crazy; Driver 8 (live)

Fall on Me   IRS 52882   8/86 (U.S.)
    Other tracks: Rotary Ten

Fall on Me   IRS IRMT121   9/86 (U.K.)
    Other tracks: Rotary Ten; Toys in the Attic

Superman   IRS 52971   11/86 (U.S.)
    Other tracks: White Tornado

Superman   IRS IRMT128   3/87 (U.K.)
    Other tracks: White Tornado; Femme Fatale

The One I Love   IRS 23792   8/87 (U.S.)
    Other tracks: The One I Love (live); Maps and Legends (live)

It's the End of the World as
We Know It (and I Feel Fine)   IRS IRM145   8/87 (U.K.)
    Other tracks: This One Goes Out (live); Maps and Legends (live)

The One I Love   IRS IRMT146   11/87 (U.K.)
    Other tracks: Last Date; Disturbance at the Heron House (live)

It's the End of the World as We Know It (and I Feel Fine)   IRS 53220   1/88 (U.S.)
   Other tracks: Last Date

Finest Worksong
(Lengthy club mix)   IRS 23850   3/88 (U.S.)
   Other tracks: Finest Worksong (Other Mix); Time after Time Etc. (live)

Stand   Warners W7577   1/89 (U.K.)
   Other tracks: Memphis Train Blues; Untitled

Orange Crush   Warners W2690   5/89 (U.K.)
   Other tracks: Ghost Riders; Dark Globe

Stand   Warners W2833   8/89 (U.K.)
   Other tracks: Pop Song '89 (acoustic version); Skin Tight

Pop Song '89   Warners W27640   6/89 (U.S.)
   Other tracks: Pop Song '89 (acoustic version)

Get Up   Warners W22791   10/89 (U.S.)
   Other tracks: Funtime

Losing My Religion   Warners W0015   2/91 (U.S.)
   Other tracks: Rotary Eleven; After Hours (live); Stand (live); Turn You Inside-Out (live); World Leader Pretend (live)

Shiny Happy People   Warners W0027   5/91 (U.S.)
   Other tracks: Forty Second Song; Losing My Religion (live acoustic); I Remember California (live); Get Up (live); Pop Song '89 (live)

Near Wild Heaven   Warners W0055   8/91 (U.S.)
   Other tracks: Pop Song '89 (live acoustic); Half a World Away (live); Tom's Diner (live); Low (live); Endgame (live)

Radio Song   Warners W0072   11/91 (U.S.)
   Other tracks: Love is All Around (live); Shiny Happy People (Music Mix); You Are the Everything (live); Orange Crush (live); Belong (live)

Drive   Warners W0136   9/92 (U.S.)
Other tracks: It's a Free World, Baby; Winged Mammal Theme; First We Take Manhattan

Man on the Moon   Warners WW0143   11/92 (U.S.)
Other tracks: Turn You Inside-Out; Arms of Love; Fruity Organ; New Orleans Instrumental No. 2

The Sidewinder Sleeps Tonite Warners W0152   2/93 (U.S.)
Other Tracks: The Lion Sleeps Tonight; Fretless; Organ Song; Star Me Kitten

Everybody Hurts   Warners W0169   3/93 (U.S.)
Other tracks: New Orleans Instrumental No. 1 (long version); Mandolin Strum; Chance (dub); Dark Globe

Everybody Hurts   Warners 40442   ca. 6/93 (U.S.)
Other tracks: Mandolin Strum; Belong (live); Orange Crush (live); Star Me Kitten (demo); Losing My Religion (live); Fruity Organ

Nightswimming   Warners W 0184   6/93 (U.K.)
Other tracks: Losing My Religion (live); World Leader Pretend (live); Belong (live); Low (live)

Find the River   Warners W 0211   11/93 (U.S.)
Other tracks: Everybody Hurts (live); World Leader Pretend (live), Orange Crush (instrumental)

What's the Frequency,
Kenneth?   Warners 41760   9/94 (U.S.)
Other tracks: Monty Got a Raw Deal (live); Everybody Hurts (live); Man on the Moon (live)

Bang and Blame   Warners W0275   10/94 (U.S.)
Other tracks: Losing My Religion (live); Country Feedback (live); Begin the Begin (live)

Crush with Eyeliner   Warners W0281   1/95 (U.S.)
Other tracks: Fall on Me (live); Me In Honey (live); Finest Worksong (live)

Strange Currencies Warners W0290 4/95 (U.S.)
  Other tracks: Drive (live); Funtime (live); Radio Free Europe (live)

Tongue Warners W0308 7/95 (U.K.)
  Other tracks: What's the Frequency, Kenneth? (live); Bang and Blame (live); I Don't Sleep, I Dream (live)

E-Bow the Letter Warners 43763 8/96 (U.S.)
  Other tracks: Tricycle; Departure (live); Wall of Death

Bittersweet Me Warner's W0377 11/96 (U.S.)
  Other tracks: Undertow (live); Wichita Lineman (live); New Test Leper (acoustic)

Electrolite Warner's W0383 12/96 (U.S.)
  Other tracks: The Wake-Up Bomb (live); Binky the Doormat (live); King of Comedy (808 State remix)

Selected Bibliography

Bowler, Dave and Bryan Dray. *R.E.M.: From* Chronic Town *to* Monster. 1995. (U.K. title: *R.E.M. Documental*).

Fletcher, Tony. *Remarks: The Story of R.E.M.* 1989 (revised 1993).

Gray, Marcus. *It Crawled from the South: An R.E.M. Companion.* 1992 (revised 1996).

Greer, Jim. *R.E.M.: Behind the Mask.* 1992.

Hogan, Peter, ed. *R.E.M.: In Their Own Words.* 1997.

Rolling Stone (the editors of). *R.E.M.: The Rolling Stone Files.* 1995.

Rosen, Craig. *R.E.M. Inside Out: The Stories Behind Every Song.* 1997.

Sullivan, Denise. *Talk about the Passion: R.E.M., An Oral History.* 1994.

Film- and Videography

Promo Videos

Almost from their inception R.E.M. have made promotional videos, and at various points most, if not quite all of them, have been compiled into long form and made available to the public. Apart from the videos themselves, these compilations have also included extra material including interviews and other extraneous material. To date they have released four films, as follows:

Succumbs (released 1987, covers 1983–87). Includes the promos for "Radio Free Europe"; "So. Central Rain"; "Can't Get There from Here"; "Driver 8"; "Life and How to Live It"/"Feeling Gravity's Pull"; and others.

Pop Screen (released 1990, covers 1987–90). Includes the promos for "It's the End of the World as We Know It"; "Finest Worksong"; "Orange Crush"; "Stand"; "Turn You Inside-Out"; "Pop Song '89"; and others.

This Film Is On (released 1991, covers 1990–91). Includes the promos for "Losing My Religion"; "Shiny Happy People"; "Near Wild Heaven"; and "Radio Song." *This Film Is On* also includes four films made by Stipe's C-00 company designed to "accompany" four of the tracks on *Out of Time* and barely feature the band members and were not designed as promos. Also included are two TV clips, featuring the band performing acoustic versions of "Losing My Religion" and the Troggs' "Love Is All Around."

Parallel (released 1995, covers 1992–95). A 72-minute film that includes all eleven videos made to promote the singles from *Automatic for the People* and *Monster,* plus a plethora of other footage including the band rehearsing.

Tourfilm (released 1990). An 85-minute film documenting, in R.E.M.'s typically idiosyncratic style, the last week of the mammoth 1989 Green World Tour. Different editors worked on each song, resulting in a myriad of different cinematic styles—some songs are completely out of synch, some look like examples of normal concert footage, and others are distinctly arty.

Rough Cut (released 1995). More documentary than concert film (although it does contain performances), the film follows the band through November 1994 and eavesdrops on a seemingly endless series of interviews and rehearsals. If nothing else it demonstrates how much stress and tedium there can be for members of a band of R.E.M.'s stature.

Athens, Ga.—Inside Out (released 1986). A documentary about R.E.M.'s home town, which features a whole raft of local bands, artists, poets and eccentrics. R.E.M. perform two songs (acoustic versions of "Swan, Swan H" and the Everly Brothers' "All I Have to Do Is Dream" and give individual interviews.

Permissions

Jim Sullivan, "Music Dreamtime with R.E.M.," *Boston Globe* (April 26, 1983), reprinted by permission of the publisher.

Joe Sasfy, "Reckoning with R.E.M.," *Washington Post* (May 10, 1984) , reprinted by permission of the publisher.

John Platt, "R.E.M.," *Bucketfull of Brains* (December 1984), reprinted by permission of the author and the publisher.

J. D. Considine, "R.E.M.: Subverting Small Town Boredom," *Musician* (August 1983), reprinted by permission of the author.

Adam Sweeting, "Hot Nights in Georgia," *Melody Maker* (May 5, 1984), reprinted by permission of the publisher.

Helen FitzGerald, "Tales from the Black Mountain," *Melody Maker* (April 27, 1985), reprinted by permission of the publisher.

John Platt, "R.E.M: 'Fables of the Reconstruction,'" *Bucketfull of Brains* (June 1985), reprinted by permission of the author and the publisher.

Fred Mills and Todd Goss, "R.E.M.—'86: Dogged Perseverance," *The Bob* (June 1986), reprinted by permission of the authors.

Tom Morton, "Southern Accents," *Melody Maker* (September 6, 1986), reprinted by permission of the publisher.

Daniel Brogan, "R.E.M. Has Little to Say and Says It Obtusely," *Chicago Tribune* (October 20, 1986), reprinted by permission of the publisher.

Mat Smith, "Welcome to the Occupation," *Melody Maker* (September 12, 1987), reprinted by permission of the publisher.

The Notorious Stuart Brothers, "A Date with Peter Buck," *Bucketfull of Brains* (December 1987), reprinted by permission of the publisher.

Elianne Halbersberg, "Peter Buck of R.E.M.," *East Coast Rocker* (November 30, 1988), reprinted by permission of the publisher.

Sean O'Hagan, "Another Green World," *New Musical Express* (December 24, 1988), reprinted by permission of the publisher.

Bo Emerson, "R.E.M.," *Atlanta Constitution* (April 1, 1989), reprinted by permission of the publisher.

Jim Washburn, "Spontaneity Missing in R.E.M.'s Concert at Pacific Amphitheatre," *Los Angeles Times* (October 20, 1989), reprinted by permission of the publisher.

David Fricke, "Moments in Love: 'Out of Time,'" *Melody Maker* (March 23, 1991), reprinted by permission of the author.

David Fricke, "Living Up to *Out of Time*/Remote Control," Parts I and II, *Melody Maker* (September 26, October 3, 1992), reprinted by permission of the author.

Steve Morse, "Surprise! New LP Takes Up Acoustic Challenge," *Boston Globe* (October 2, 1992), reprinted by permission of the publisher.

Allan Jones, "From Hearse to Eternity: 'Automatic for the People,'" *Melody Maker* (October 3, 1992), reprinted by permission of the publisher.

Greg Kot, "R.E.M.'s Best Album Side? Band Members Say It's Not 'Automatic,'" *Chicago Tribune* (November 27, 1994), reprinted by permission of the publisher.

Jim Sullivan, "New Snarling Frequency 'Monster' Marks Band's Next Stage," *Boston Globe* (September 25, 1994), reprinted by permission of the publisher.

David Cavanagh, "Tune In, Cheer Up, Rock Out," *Q* (October 1994), reprinted by permission of the author.

Jud Cost, "R.E.M. Interview: Breakfast with Buck," *The Bob* (1995), reprinted by permission of the author.

Charles Aaron, "R.E.M. Comes Alive," *Spin* (August 1995), reprinted by permission of the publisher.

Robert Hilburn, "The Lowdown on 'Hi-Fi,'" *Los Angeles Times* (September 8, 1996), reprinted by permission of the publisher.

Tom Doyle, "Remember Us," *Q* (November 1996), reprinted by permission of the author.

Tim Abbott, "R.E.M.: Live Adventures in Hi-Fi," *Record Collector* (originally published in slightly different form) (August 1997), reprinted by permission of the author.

Miriam Longino, "R.E.M.: To a Different Beat the Famed Athens Band Becomes a Threesome as Drummer Bill Berry Leaves to 'Sit Back and Reflect,'" *Atlanta Journal-Constitution* (October 31, 1997), used by permission.

Index

Page numbers in *italics* refer to illustrations.